What people say about The Virtues Project™...

"There are lots of band-aids out there. The Virtues Project is the cure. It's penicillin!" Lucinda Fess, Mayor, Piqua, Ohio

"The Virtues Project is the best thing to come along for children and adults in a long time." Janet Luhrs, author, *The Simple Living Guide*

"As a teacher, I felt that in one hand I had a box of tools that I could give to my students — academic skills, trade skills — but my other hand was empty. When I found The Virtues Project, I thought 'This is what goes in the other hand.'" Ray Tufts, teacher, Renton Alternative School, Renton, Washington

"We looked at all sorts of programs. The Virtues Project stands out because it is so simple. It cuts across cultural and religious barriers and has had such positive results world-wide." Peter Blanks, Healthy Communities Inititiative, New Zealand

"We have significantly reduced suspensions and have fantastic parental support for our discipline approach. The Virtues Project is a key ingredient in the formula." Michael Seltz, Vice Principal, Robert Frost Middle School, Livonia, Michigan

Other books by Linda Kavelin Popov

The Family Virtues Guide:
Simple Ways to Bring Out the Best in Our Children and Ourselves

Sacred Moments:
Daily Meditations on the Virtues

D1736754

THE VIRTUES PROJECT™

Simple Ways to Create a Culture of Character

Educator's Guide

LINDA KAVELIN POPOV

J

JALMAR PRESS
Torrance, California

Write to: Jalmar Press
P. O. Box 1185
Torrance, CA 90505 USA
Email: blwjalmar@att.net
Tel: (310) 816-3085 Fax: (310) 816-3092

Reproducible pages:

The first page of each Virtue, Student Activity Sheets, Virtues Vouchers and Hug Notes in this book are intended for reproduction in quantities sufficient for each classroom. Permission is hereby granted to the purchaser to reproduce these pages in quantities suitable for non-commercial classroom use only.

ISBN: 1-880396-84-X

Illustrators include Joan Badke and Matthew Ngongoragi.

Vector Images Copyright 1998 by Corel Corporation and Corel Corporation Limited taken from Corel GALLERY™ 1,000,000.

Printing: 10 9 8 7 6 5 4 3 2 1

Manufactured in the U.S.A.

The following terms have been trademarked:

> The Virtues Project
> The Art of Spiritual Companioning
> Spiritual Companioning

DEDICATION

This book is affectionately dedicated to the memory of Alexina Keeling, a Virtues Project mentor, who restored hope to so many children and youth, and always saw the light of virtues within them. Alexina, you are my guiding light.

SPECIAL THANKS

To "Girlfriend", Margery Clive, who nurtured the development of this book with years of patience and service to the goal of shaping character.

To my amazing husband, Dan, for his generous labor of love in preparing this book for publication.

To my colleagues and friends at Innnerchoice Publishing and Jalmar Press: Editor Susanna Palomares, for her encouragement, wisdom and friendship and Bradley Winch, whose enthusiasm and integrity brought this book to fruition.

To the principals, teachers and youth workers from the United States, Canada, South America, Australia, New Zealand, and other countries for their enthusiasm for The Virtues Project and their generosity in sharing their success stories.

To Jeanne Iler and my brother, John Kavelin, for their excellence and perseverance in helping to "make it beautiful".

Table of Contents

Section 1: Simple Ways to Create a Culture of Character

Strategy 5 - Offer the Art of Spiritual Companioning™

Section 2: Virtues: The Gifts of Character

Section 3: Resources

 **Preface**

When I was a young mother, raising my two boys in rural South Carolina, I was shocked and saddened to find my children coming home with values which did not fit our family's beliefs. I remember when my younger son Craig, in first grade, came home using racist words and making sweeping generalizations about people of color. When I questioned him, trying to get to the root of the logic, he spoke about "catching cooties" and other phrases he had heard. When I asked, "But Craig, what about John?" naming his closest friend whose skin was a deep chocolate, he said, in six-year-old logic, "Well, not him." When I asked why, he said "Cuz he's my best friend." We had long talks about seeing with your own eyes and thinking with your own mind, and I didn't hear anything more about the dangers of associating with others whose skin is a different color. My job of teaching respect, tolerance and unity was made harder because these virtues were not addressed at school.

I was also distressed by the fact that my older son was constantly overwhelmed by the noise and confusion of the "open classroom" experiment, a methodology which was launched without much understanding of the changes it required. There were no boundaries in the classroom. When I observed his "teaching area", children were running and shouting, my son among them. The noise was deafening. My heart went out to him and the other children who were ill equipped to cope with the chaos. My heart went out to the teachers too. I decided to do something about it.

The next day, I made an appointment with the principal. "I know this open classroom thing isn't working, but what can I do?" he said, looking dejected. I said, "Would you let me help in a small way?" "How?" he asked. "What is your hardestclass, the one with the most disciplinary problems?" He named the first grade class. He knew that I was a psychotherapist, working with children and families and he said "I don't know what you're going to do but please do it." I went to the first grade teacher, who had already raised a sweat by 11 AM. The children were restless. One little girl kept flinging herself at the teacher who kept saying, "Kimmy, stop it." I said, "I'd like to help you out a couple of times a week. Give me your five 'most challenging' kids, the ones who are hardest to handle. I'll take them out for a couple of hours twice a week." I will never forget the look on her face. She almost cried. She pointed them out, including Kimmy. A couple of days later, I arrived with drawing paper and crayons, a box of raisins, and an idea.

Mrs. Johnson yelled out the names of the five children and they gathered apprehensively around me. I knelt down and said, "I'm going to take you to a very special place. You have been chosen by your teacher to come with me." They looked only slightly less worried. They walked, hopped and meandered behind me to a tiny supply room in which I had created a circle of child-sized chairs. "Please sit down." As I looked at them, I did a quick scan of their characteristics. Leroy, whose eyes whirled involuntarily appeared to have some neurological impairment; Johnny was so hyperactive, he was literally attempting to climb the wall behind his chair; Kimmy's clothes were shabby, her hair unkempt, and her body movements agitated. I wondered about possible abuse or neglect; Raymond was slow and obese; Timmy looked very angry. Kimmy and Johnny were Caucasian, Leroy, Raymond and Timmy African-American.

I sat on the floor before their little circle and said, "We're going to learn together about three very special things, which everyone has inside. They are respect, patience, and self-discipline." I looked only at the four who were paying attention. I ignored Johnny, still standing in his chair but beginning to tire from his wall climbing attempts. He suddenly turned around and stopped, perhaps to see if I was watching him. I took advantage of the moment. "See how Johnny is looking at me right now and paying attention? That's the kind of respect I'm talking about." Johnny looked absolutely dumbfounded and plopped down into a sitting position. I had his attention. "This class will be a secret just between us, and when you learn these things – respect, patience, and self-discipline – then you can teach them to the rest of your class."

Each week, I made words of raisins and popcorn, and when the children were able to master the words themselves, the reward was to "eat my words." They laughed and munched. The main focus of our time together was some simple life skills to help them practice the three virtues. They learned that when the teacher asked for quiet, they were to "stop like a statue." They loved playing statues and they understood that it was a way to show respect in following directions. They learned that if they wanted to respond in class, instead of jumping on the teacher, or shouting, they were to put one hand over their mouth and the other in the air. This was a way of showing self-discipline. While the others drew, Kimmy practiced "the magic circle of respect". Having no sense of physical boundaries, she would literally jump on people like a monkey. I showed her the invisible circle of personal space which was a way of showing respect for herself and others. When she was able to go for an entire session without jumping on me or the other children, I would hold her in my arms for a long hug at the end of the class. Johnny received special acknowledgments for his self-discipline when he made the effort to pay attention. Raymond showed enthusiasm and excellence in recognizing words. They all began to read within a few weeks. I received reports from Mrs. Brown that these children were showing "miraculous" changes.

At the end of the term, with their drawings on respect, patience and self-discipline, the children paraded proudly into class. "We are your teachers for today," Raymond announced confidently. "We will teach you respect," said Johnny, grinning from ear to ear. "We will teach you patience," said Kimmy, smiling peacefully. Leroy and Timmy went on to demonstrate the left hand up and right hand over mouth technique. We played Respect Statues with the whole class. My kids beamed with pride as the other children applauded wildly. Based on that simple program of virtues development, the school instituted an ongoing program called "ABC: Aiding Behavioral Change". Other volunteers came forward to keep it going.

This early experience brought me hope and was the seed for The Virtues Project, which my husband, my brother and I founded 16 years later in 1991. It has become a grass roots movement spanning the globe, spreading the philosophy that by focusing on the virtues – the best qualities within our children – we can encourage them to be at their best.

We need ways to transform our schools into safe, happy learning environments. The purpose of The Virtues Project is to help develop a culture of character where respect, patience, self-discipline, tolerance and joy for learning are among the virtues our children master. The character education of our children has become our first priority. It's time to make our schools caring communities where all students are encouraged to live by the virtues – the best within them.

Linda Kavelin Popov

How to Use this Book

The Virtues Project Educator's Guide is designed to give educators tools and strategies to help them shape character by creating a positive, empowering culture or environment in which children are learning and growing. These strategies can be easily integrated into the curriculum, the disciplinary system and social atmosphere of any school or organization. The Virtues Project is a positive, holistic program which has been used in many cultures and countries throughout the world to bring out the best in children and adults.

This Guide highlights Examples of Excellence from schools around the globe to give you concrete examples of how to apply The Virtues Project strategies in your own school or program.

The activities at the back of each chapter and each virtue are designed for a wide range of age and grade levels, from K to 12. Many of them apply to all ages. However, we leave it to you to decide which activities are appropriate for the age, social and cultural group with whom you are working and how to adjust the activities to fit your students.

Counselors will find Chapter 5 on the Art of Spiritual Companioning particularly useful in their work with students. It presents a method which helps students to "get to the heart of the matter" and call on the virtues of their character to solve their own problems. It is a useful tool in grief work and suicide prevention as well.

This Guide is divided into three sections and contains:

Section 1: Simple Ways to Create a Culture of Character

• A chapter on each of the Five Strategies of The Virtues Project.

• Methods for applying each strategy.

• Examples of Excellence from schools and programs throughout the world.

• Classroom activities, student activity sheets, and school-wide activities at the end of each chapter.

• A Chapter Summary, with a list of key points.

Section 2: Virtues: The Gifts of Character

- 52 Virtues, from Assertiveness to Unity.

- How to use the virtues for classroom and school-wide activities.

- A definition of each virtue, why practice it, role-playing scenarios, signs of success and an affirmation on the first page of each virtue.

- Suggested activities, reflection questions, art projects, and "quotable quotes" which can be posted, on the second page of each virtue.

- A poster: "Virtues: The Gifts of Character" at the end of the section.

Section 3: Resources

- Information on The Virtues Project website.

- Books and music about the virtues.

- Information on how to order Virtues Project materials.

- How to arrange for Virtues Project presentations and workshops.

Introduction

Our Schools Are In Trouble

Too many schools have become war zones. The incidence of violence is alarming. The leading cause of death of youth in North America is murder. Many youth in North American cities go to school with weapons. Metal detectors and armed guards are needed at the doors. Too many of our children are technical wizards and moral incompetents. Students are dropping out of school at an alarming rate. Teachers are increasingly stressed by the threat of violence and are already overburdened by the demands of academic requirements. We know that unless we get to the root causes of these problems, they will persist and worsen.

The Loss of Meaning

A study out of the Harvard Center for Moral Education asked the question "Why did you do it?' of youth jailed for committing random acts of violence. Ninety per cent of these youth said "Because I was bored." Boredom is a spiritual disease – the disease of meaninglessness.

If loss of meaning is the disease, the cure must incorporate a way for young people to connect with meaning and purpose. There is a longing deep within adolescents to make a difference, to have impact. It comes from the developmental urge to fulfill their innate virtues of idealism, purposefulness, and creativity. It is the call of early adulthood saying "Make your mark." When that fierce idealism is not given a positive focus through opportunities for young people to explore and experience what is meaningful in their lives, it seeks another channel.

A Renaissance of Values and Virtues

Thankfully, there is a renaissance of values and virtues to address the heart of the matter. The purpose of life as described in all the world's wisdom traditions is the cultivation of the virtues. There is nothing new about justice. There is nothing original about love. Virtues are the oldest ideas in the world.

Yet, we are spiritually and morally parched for these simple, timeless practices. Many teachers and administrators are finding that applying the strategies of The Virtues Project is transforming the culture in their schools by helping them to create a **total environment** of caring and respect. They have replaced discouragement with empowerment, having discovered that words such as "lazy", "stupid", "no good", "hopeless", and "unacceptable" were literally de-moralizing and dis-courage-ing their students. When they fill their classrooms with encouraging words, such as "helpful", "excellent", "compassionate", "self-disciplined", and "kind", they find that these behaviors flourish.

Why Virtues? Why Not Values?

Values are what we value and care about. They could be anything. We may value getting rich and famous, we may value being the best criminal the world has ever seen, we may value power over others, but that doesn't mean we will have good character. Also, values are culture-specific. What some families or cultures value, others don't. Virtues are much more elemental than values. While values are culture-specific, virtues are universally valued by all cultures.

"Virtues are what's good about us."
Sharon, Age 6

An Inclusive Approach

Sometimes educators get bogged down in their pursuit of character education by the dilemma of how to introduce values without offending people of diverse belief systems, including the religious and the non-religious children. How do we introduce character education in a pluralistic society? How do we safeguard against imposing the values of any one belief system? A simple way to address this issue is by focusing on the development of virtues.

We cannot afford to wait until the values debate is resolved. Too many of our children are dying. And so this program side-steps the debate and gets on with the business of how to inspire the courage, honor, justice, and compassion in our kids. All parents, of whatever faith or of no faith, support having their children develop the integrity of their character.

The strategies of The Virtues Project are a simple, proven methodology which helps children to remember who they really are, and to know that the purpose of life is to have a life of purpose. Virtues are the content of our character, the elements of the human spirit. They exist within each child in potential. What is needed is a method to help children act on the best within them. The purpose of a true educator – which literally means "one who leads forth" – is to awaken the virtues which **already exist** within a child. This book is about simple ways to do that.

The best time to awaken a child's qualities of character is in the early years. Early childhood education is the ideal time to introduce an awareness of virtues as the core of life's meaning, yet we have found it is never too late to help them discover it.

Virtue is alive and well within our children — it merely needs to be awakened. As this practice spreads, "virtue will triumph everywhere".

"Cultivate Virtue in your self, and Virtue will be real.

Cultivate Virtue in the family, and Virtue will flourish.

Cultivate Virtue in the village, and Virtue will spread.

Cultivate Virtue in the nation, and Virtue will be abundant.

Cultivate Virtue in the world and Virtue will triumph everywhere."

Lao Tsu

Five Strategies for Creating a Culture of Character

*"Character is a
perfectly educated
will."*
Norvallis

Background

The Virtues Project was honored as a model global program for families of all cultures by the United Nations Secretariat during the International Year of the Family. The Virtues Project is not about the practices or beliefs of any particular religion. It is based on the simple wisdom of the world's diverse cultures and religions about living by the best within us – courage, honor, justice, kindness and all of our innate virtues. Schools, businesses, diverse faith communities, prisons, counselors, drug and alcohol recovery programs, and families throughout the world are using the Five Strategies of The Virtues Project with transformational effect.

- Teachers in alternative schools for drop-outs and gang members found that they were able to get through to students for the first time by naming the virtues they saw in them.

- A young mother of four in Washington State went to a school after a tragic shooting by a student, to offer healing. The whole community rallied behind her "Virtuous Reality" campaign to put up posters of virtues in storefronts, on buses, in school hallways and in homes.

- Sixth grade students in Western Australia formed an "elders' council" of students which met weekly to solve problems posted in the "Virtues Post Box" by other students, guiding them to the virtues they felt would empower them to change their lives.

- Schools in Russia, Eastern Europe, and Asia have adopted the strategies as the basis of their moral development curricula.

- Boys & Girls Clubs in the U.S. and Canada are using it to address the spiritual component of their mandate to help the whole child.

A Holistic Approach to Character Education

The Five Strategies of The Virtues Project are a means to transform the culture of our schools and provide simple tools to use every day to make character education a natural part of the child's experience.

To create a **culture** of character, a school does not need to change the curriculum or introduce a special curriculum. It is far more powerful to **integrate** the cultivation of virtues into the existing curriculum, the discipline system, the counseling experience, and daily classroom life. Children learn within the **context** of what they experience in daily interactions.

It is also important that character education appeal to the **diverse learning styles** which children have – visual, auditory, kinesthetic, etc. Throughout this guide there are Teaching Tips and multi-sensory activities that help to bring out the best in students.

Building a Community Safety Net

Through the power of networking, it is possible to create a true safety net for our kids. Schools which have high levels of parental involvement are shown by research to have the greatest success in transforming schools that have been battle zones into peace zones. The unity of teachers and parents, particularly when it is focused on positive virtues in the behavior of students, gives students the greatest opportunity for success. When parents and teachers are singing the same song, and speaking the same language – the virtues-based language of positivity – the self-esteem, idealism, respect, and safety of students increase dramatically.

"Parents can be the greatest asset to student assistance. The involved parent, even if unsophisticated in parenting, if willing to work together with the school, can turn around a failing student."
Michael C. Seltz, Vice-Principal, Frost Middle School, Livonia, Michigan

Community volunteers who come in to offer assistance to teachers and mentorship to students are one of the most powerful resources any school has. More and more corporations are giving something back. Colleges and universities can provide student intern mentors from their education faculties. With a little training in the Five Strategies of The Virtues Project, a corps of dedicated mentors made up of parents, elders, business people and others in the community can make a world of difference to our children.

> ## Example of Excellence
> ### "Virtue of the Week":
> ### A Tool for Parent/Teacher Partnerships
>
> **Nancy Portillo, mother of five boys, in San Jose, California,** initiated The Virtues Project in their elementary school when she sent notes to her son's teachers naming the "Virtue of the Week", which they were working on at home and asking for teachers to give her feedback about how the boys were doing. The teachers sent home notes about ways they saw the Portillo boys practicing the virtue of the week. At the end of the year, the boys made gifts for their teachers and cards acknowledging the special virtues which they appreciated in them. Nancy and Carlos Portillo came to school with a cake for each teacher inscribed with the virtues the boys saw in them. This simple acknowledgment process built self-esteem in the boys and their teachers, too!

Community Mentors can:

- assist during recess and help keep it a Peace Zone

- be on call to help students resolve conflict or just have someone to talk to about their problems

- be a companion and guide for students in suspension

- provide job coaching

- serve as special presenters at job fairs

- offer summer employment for students.

The Five Strategies of The Virtues Project

1. Speak the Language of the Virtues

Language has great influence to empower or discourage. Self-esteem is built when shaming or blaming language is replaced by naming the Virtues, our innate qualities of character. Virtues are used to acknowledge, guide and correct. The Language of Virtues helps us remember what kind of people we want to be.

2. Recognize Teachable Moments

This strategy is a way of viewing life as an opportunity for learning, recognizing our mistakes, our tests and challenges as opportunities to hone our virtues. It is an approach to bringing out the best in each other by asking, "What can I learn from this situation? ", "What do I need to do differently next time?", and "How can I make it right?"

3. Set Clear Boundaries

Clear boundaries, connected to a Shared Vision of the virtues with which we want to treat one another, help to prevent violence and create a safe learning environment. Clear ground rules based on virtues build an atmosphere of order and unity. This strategy offers a positive approach to discipline, emphasizing both assertiveness and restorative justice. It helps us to identify what bottom line behaviors will not be tolerated as well as how amends can be made.

4. Honor the Spirit

School spirit grows through simple practices that illumine our sense of values, such as creating Shared Vision Statements. A school-wide moment of silence each morning can bring a sense of peace to the day. Virtues Sharing Circles allow us to reflect on what matters to us. Participation in the arts honors meaning and creativity. Celebrations make special events meaningful. This strategy helps us to address the spiritual dimension in a way that respects our diversity.

5. Offer the Art of Spiritual Companioning™

This is an art and skill which supports healing, encourages moral choice, and allows the safe expression of feelings. It helps in counseling, conflict resolution, and disciplinary situations. Companioning helps us to get to the heart of the matter when individuals are in grief or crisis. It involves true presence and listening, asking clarifying questions, which allow individuals to empty their cup, and then to solve their own problems with the help of the virtues.

Summary of Ideas

- ✓ Use an inclusive, virtues-based approach to bring out the best in students.

- ✓ Integrate The Virtues Project into your current curriculum and discipline system. It doesn't have to be an additional program.

- ✓ Students learn in the context of every day interactions.

- ✓ Use the 5 Strategies of The Virtues Project as a framework for positive change.

- ✓ Use multi-sensory approaches which appeal to all learning styles when focusing on virtues.

- ✓ Tap the power of partnership between parents and teachers.

- ✓ Tap the resource of potential mentors among the citizens and businesses in your community.

Section 1

Simple Ways to Create a Culture of Character

1 Speak the Language of the Virtues

"The mind is not a vessel to be filled but a fire to be ignited."
Plutarch

 ## Language Shapes Character

The way we speak and the words we use have great power. Language is the vehicle for meaning, and above all else awakens the character and shapes the self-esteem of our children. It shapes the very culture of our homes, schools and workplaces. Words have the power to break a heart or inspire a dream. The Language of the Virtues empowers children to act on the best within them. It is the main ingredient in creating a culture of character.

There is an expression among the Maori of New Zealand: "I see you." To see a child in light of his or her virtues is to nurture the moral champion within that child. To see a child as a bundle of problems and misbehavior is to reinforce an already negative sense of self. Children tend to act according to the way adults in their world see them. An old blues song says "My name is trouble." Many children come from environments where they are seen as "trouble". Virtues are innate gifts within every child. Therefore, an educator does not have to impose the virtues from without, but rather awaken and strengthen the virtues that are already there.

Teachers have enormous power in children's lives. Their power comes primarily from the value they see in a child's being, and whether they see a child in a negative light or in light of their positive possibilities. The old expression went, "Sticks and stones may break my bones, but names can never hurt me." The power that teachers and other caregivers have to shape a child's sense of self, merely by the words they use about that child, defies the validity of the old saying. In truth, it should be revised to say "Sticks and stones may break my bones, but names can break my spirit." We can choose to call children names which deepen the rut of their negative behavior patterns, using words like "lazy", "stupid", "shy", "mean", or "quitter", or we can call them by the names of their inner strengths, calling them to the virtues of determination, respect, friendliness, confidence, kindness and gentleness. A television talk-show host once said to me after hearing me speak about the strategy of Speaking the Language of the Virtues, "How can they turn away when you call them by their true names?"

First Nations people of North America speak of the "Four Medicines" or personal powers we have:

The Power to SEE

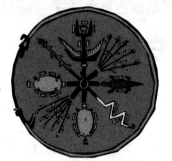

The Power to HEAR   **The Power to SPEAK**

The Power to ACT

Using the Language of the Virtues as a framework for shaping character involves more than speech. It is a way of thinking, a frame of reference, and a "frame of reverence" for relating to our students in light of their innate nobility. It includes:

- SEEING the virtues in each student, whether in a small glimmer of possibility or a brilliant gem.

- HEARING our students, using listening skills which call on our own Kindness, Compassion and Justice.

- SPEAKING with the power of virtues such as Enthusiasm, Tact, Honesty, Love, and Gentleness.

- ACTING with virtue, to model the virtues we are helping our students to cultivate, including the Humility to recognize, accept and learn from our own mistakes. We don't need to be "paragons" of perfection, but paragons of virtue – modeling day by day the will to cultivate, or perfect, our own virtues. We can even ask for help from our students. If we are having a bad day we can say "I'm going to really need your Helpfulness and Cooperation today because I'm not feeling very Patient."

Awaken the Virtues in Every Child

It is really important to find SOMETHING about each student which you can legitimately appreciate and enjoy. Every child needs to see someone's eyes light up in recognition, with a look which says "I see you, and you matter to me." At some point, almost every child, youth and adult feels parched for meaningful recognition. By identifying a virtue and naming it, you will see their eyes light up in recognition – of their own value.

How to Speak The Language of the Virtues

There are three fundamental ways to use the power of language to awaken the innate virtues in students, and thereby to bring out the best in them:

 to ACKNOWLEDGE or praise them for a virtue they have practiced

to GUIDE or prepare them to practice a virtue

to CORRECT or remind them when they have "forgotten" themselves and failed to practice a virtue, when they have done something wrong or made a mistake.

Speak the Language of the Virtues to Acknowledge

The objective of ACKNOWLEDGING virtues is to help build authentic self-esteem and to ENCOURAGE virtues when you see them.

Acknowledge Excellence and Effort

The first and perhaps most important way to speak the Language of the Virtues is to acknowledge a virtue when you see a student practicing it. Say it when you see it! When a student hears one of his or her virtues acknowledged, it awakens their awareness that they actually have this virtue, that acting on it is a choice, and that they can choose to practice this virtue in other situations. **"I have this virtue. I can choose it, and I can use it."** The latin root of the word "virtue" is "virtus" meaning strength, power, capacity, and energy. Naming a virtue encourages its mastery and communicates the message "You have this power. I see it in you." Don't dilute the power of the acknowledgment by adding a lecturette about how the child should try harder. Just let the acknowledgment stand.

Teaching Tip

What? Give a Virtues Acknowledgment
Why? To encourage and reinforce emerging virtues.
When? When you see a student "doing the right thing" by exhibiting or practicing a virtue, especially when it is a new or challenging virtue for them.

Example: "James, you are being very Peaceful today in the Gentle way you have been playing."

Say it when you see it!

Example of Excellence

Virtues Circle Time

Erola Whitcombe, a relieving (substitute) teacher in the Kapiti region of New Zealand, thinks carefully about the classrooms she revisits frequently and decides which virtue she wants to use with the group the next time she will be working in the class. One virtue she uses regularly is peacefulness. She begins the morning Circle Time with a discussion about what peacefulness is. She writes the virtue up on the whiteboard and tells the children that she will be paying careful attention to peacefulness that day. When she sees someone being peaceful she gives a virtues acknowledgement and writes that child's name on the board. Soon everyone's name is on the board, often with two or three ticks beside their names to show how they have practiced peacefulness during the day.

Give a Virtues
Acknowledgment to
a typically aggressive
student who is now
being peaceful.

Example: "John, you
showed excellent Self-
Discipline today. You
were Peaceful all day."
or
"John, you had half the
fights today you had
yesterday. I see real
improvement in your
Self-Discipline to be
Peaceful.

Catch them in the Act of Committing a Virtue

Teachers, counselors and administrators, with sufficient discernment, can spot virtues in even the most troubled child. It is like putting on a helmet and miner's light and entering a mine in which you know there are hidden gems. When you see a glimmer, shine your light on that gem of virtue. The most powerful virtues acknowledgments – those which have the greatest impact – are directed at virtues that a student is showing in an area which is a challenge for the student, namely a "growth" virtue. Acknowledge them for any improvements in their growth virtues when you see even small progress! By naming the virtue, you are encouraging the student to bring it to light, to let it shine.

See the Glass Half Full

At a conference where I was the keynote speaker, a harried youth coordinator came up and asked me to do a workshop for the youth who had accompanied their parents to the conference. When I walked into the room, four young women of about twelve to fourteen were on the floor in a parody of meditation, making the "OM" sound and laughing. I immediately said. "Please be respectful. This is an honored practice by people of some religions." The young woman who appeared to be leading the others looked disgruntled, but she and the others went back to their seats. I began the virtues workshop. Several times in the first 20 minutes, Martha, the same girl, attempted to gain attention from the other youth with humor, to distract them from small group exercises. Each time I would go over to her and whisper "This is a reverent activity" or "Please be respectful" and she would straighten up. Finally, she became engaged in the process and went along with the rest of the workshop without incident.

At the end of the 90 minute workshop, I brought out a beautifully decorated box containing sand and "gems" – beads of colored glass. I said "I want to acknowledge you all for your enthusiasm and honesty in sharing in this workshop on 'Virtues, the Gifts Within.' I will now choose four people for special acknowledgments for virtues I noticed today." The first one I called up was Martha. She looked stunned, and paled instantly. She walked up to me at the front of the room. I noticed she was shaking. I looked into her eyes and said, "Martha, please choose a gem. I want to honor you for the virtue of obedience. Whenever I spoke to you today, you immediately responded obediently. So take this gem to remind you that you are a gem." She began to cry and smile at the same time. I also honored the best behaved child in the room who continually raised her hand in response to questions, but often put it back down, seeming to want to give others a chance. I said to her, "I honor you for your consideration and humility. You had lots of ideas and yet you gave others a chance to speak." She was also moved, but Martha needed the acknowledgment more. A bit manipulative? Perhaps. But my intent was to reinforce the positives I saw in her rather than focus on the negatives.

The next day one of the boys found me in the conference hall in the midst of two thousand people. "I've been looking for you. I was up all night. I'm really upset." "What's upsetting you?" I asked. "I felt that I was disrespectful yesterday. I laughed at Martha sometimes and I wasn't respectful of what you were teaching us. It was really important." "I forgive you. Thank you for the humility to apologize." He continued to look distraught. "What would help you to forgive yourself?" "First of all, I will never do it again to any teacher and also...I'm going to practice the virtue of respect." We smiled into each other's eyes.

Example of Excellence
Catch Them in the Act

A Montessori School principal in Victoria, British Columbia, Canada had a seven year old with Attention Deficit Hyperactivity Disorder sitting in her office for a disciplinary "Time Out". The child was reading. The principal looked up and said "Annie, you are being really Purposeful. You have been reading for quite a few minutes, really concentrating." The child's face lit up in amazement and delight. She was so used to having her misbehavior commented on but rarely heard what she was doing right.

Later in the week, the child's teacher came to the principal and said "What did you do to Annie? She has been extending her attention span every day, working hard at everything, behaving Peacefully. She changed dramatically. What did you do?" The principal explained the power of seeing and acknowledging the virtues in a child, particularly one who rarely hears positives. "We need to let her know she isn't a 'disabled' child. She IS able – able to practice her virtues every day. We need to acknowledge her when she does."

Use The Language of Virtues to be Specific

The language of virtues is specific, clear, and most important of all, easily internalized. It builds authentic self-esteem without over-dependence on approval. General terms, even when they are positive, do not hit the mark. Terms such as "Good girl", "That's a boy", "Good on you", "Great job", are too general for students to internalize. These terms promote people-pleasing as they only indicate that you are pleased with the student, without giving them any specific information about what they did that was "excellent", "helpful" or "creative". Giving a specific virtues acknowledgment is different than making general statements of praise which can create guilt. It is not helpful to label a child in any way, positive or negative. We don't say: "You're such a kind boy". We say "It was kind of you to show our new student where to sit. I'm sure it made him feel welcome."

Naming a specific virtue is a call to the child's character that resonates with her deepest self. The use of the virtue word "Purposefulness" was much more powerful than "Good girl. You're reading longer." The child can then say, "I AM purposeful. I can be that way. I have it in me." It's in every one of us to be wise, to be purposeful, to be kind, to be self-disciplined, and verbal acknowledgment is one of the ways to bring it to our awareness.

Example of Excellence
Peace in the Classroom

At Paekakariki Primary School in New Zealand the teachers of the Bilingual Unit work together with 40 children ages five to twelve, delivering a comprehensive program which includes instruction in Maori as well as English. Mika Tawhara-Tamihana, the teacher of the younger classroom, often gives Virtues Acknowledgements to her children. "I use the strategies of The Virtues Project most effectively in my classroom. They help me in my efforts at creating a peaceful, harmonious environment for my children. Perhaps the most important benefit that the Virtues have brought to me is my own sense of peacefulness. It's easier to understand what the children's real needs are and how I need to respond. This has relieved a lot of tension."

Speak the Language of the Virtues to Guide

The objective of GUIDING is to PREPARE students for a virtue they need to practice. It is often used in setting a boundary.

Use the Virtues to Invite Positive Behavior: Focus on Do's instead of Don'ts

We often tell children what we DON'T want them to do, thereby focusing them on the very behavior we intend for them to avoid. "Don't run" suggests running. "Don't fight" focuses on fighting. "Stop that whispering" doesn't give them a positive focus for what you want from them. Focusing on what we DO want them to do is far more likely to obtain positive results. "Be considerate. Walk in the hallways" encourages them to walk. "You need to work that out peacefully" encourages them to call up their peacefulness. "Please look at me and listen respectfully" goes beyond an order to stop whispering and gives them a clearer, more positive idea of what is called for. "On our field trip today, what will help you to be patient on that long bus ride?" "John, let's see how peaceful you can be today. What would help you to be self-disciplined about staying peaceful?"

When a positive statement of what we do want from them is linked to a virtue, it has the greatest impact. It engages their moral and spiritual awareness. At times ask for a commitment to practice a virtue: "Please raise your hand to show you are ready to be considerate."

Speak the Language of the Virtues to Correct

The objective of CORRECTING is to remind students of the virtues when they are misbehaving, when they have failed to choose a virtue or have simply forgotten themselves.

Use the Virtues to Build Conscience

Virtues as guidance occurs BEFORE an action. Virtues as correction occurs AFTER an action has happened that needs correcting. The purpose is not to shame a student into changing behavior. Shaming only undermines virtues and hardens the heart. A virtues correction touches the child's conscience and awakens the moral purpose of the change that is called for.

When you correct behavior by focusing on a virtue you are practicing Assertiveness rather than aggression. You are modeling Justice. To say to a student who is bullying others "You're such a bully. I'm calling your parents. You just can't treat people that way." is name-calling, labeling, shaming and non-specific. It fails to educate. To say to a child who is bullying "Jim, you need to be peaceful. How can you be a friend to other children even when you're angry? How would a friend act? What kind of a person do you really want to be with others?" This way you are calling the student to the virtues of peacefulness and friendliness and holding out hope that he will indeed respond because he HAS the virtues within him.

> ### Teaching Tip
>
> **What?** Give Virtues GUIDANCE
> **Why?** To focus and guide behavior.
> **When?** When a child needs guidance, <u>before</u> the situation in which a particular virtue is called for.
>
> **Example:** "During the test today, please remember to be Considerate of each other and remain very, very quiet. Even one pencil rattling can distract someone."

> ### Teaching Tip
>
> **What?** Give a Virtues CORRECTION
> **Why?** To stop misbehavior, restore justice and build conscience.
> **When?** When behavior is out of line with the virtues, when improvement is needed.
>
> **Example:** "How could the two of you have worked this out Peacefully instead of fighting?"

Replace Shaming with Naming Virtues

At the core of every meaningful action is the intent, and that intent is always reflective of one of the virtues.

When we fill a classroom with discouraging words, such as "lazy", "stupid", "hopeless", "unacceptable", we are literally de-moralizing and discouraging our students. When we fill a classroom with encouraging words, such as helpful, excellent, compassionate, self-disciplined, kind, cooperative, we are inviting and reinforcing those behaviors. Above all, when we focus on virtues rather than judgmental statements of good or bad, we are creating a context for character, a climate of meaning. At the core of every meaningful action is the intent, and that intent is always reflective of one of the virtues.

From Shaming to Naming

A young primary school teacher in New Zealand shared her story of how shaming affected her as a child: "When I was six years old, I had trouble learning to read. Perhaps I was a bit dyslexic. My teacher was irritated with me and other students who were slower and having more difficulty. Regularly she would make one or the other of us stand on a chair in front of the classroom and say 'I am stupid. I can't read.' It was then, when I was only six, that I resolved to become a teacher someday and that I would never do this to children." She has now gone even further with her dream of influencing education. She now trains other teachers in the strategies of The Virtues Project.

Name the Act, Not the Actor

How many of us had experiences of being shamed in school, which discouraged us and became a self-fulfilling prophecy of failure, leading to a lifelong battle with self-esteem? Humiliation discourages our students, while the practice of naming virtues builds authentic self-esteem and real conscience. Holding a student accountable for their actions in a firm, respectful way, and in the context of their ability to choose virtues, is an open invitation to do the right thing.

It does not serve children in the cultivation of their character to be "shamed, blamed, or framed" for a misdemeanor. It serves them to be held accountable, to be held responsible, and enabled to make amends and to focus on the virtue they were forgetting to practice. When one child is aggressive toward another, after the virtue is named – usually peacefulness or respect – justice needs to be restored with an act of reparation.

How to Give a Virtues Acknowledgement

I see your	kindness	in helping our new student, John.
I honor you for your	kindness	in the way you helped John.
I acknowledge your	kindness	in the way you helped John.
That showed a lot of	kindness	when you helped our new student.
It was	kind of you	to help our new student.
You were being	kind	when you helped John today.
Thank you for	being kind	when you picked up my papers.

How to Give Virtues Guidance

We need to be	kind	to our new student.
You need to be	patient	while you wait for recess.
I need someone to be	helpful.	I dropped my papers.

How to Give a Virtues Correction

Please be	kind	to John, not teasing but friendly.
What would help you to be	peaceful	with each other?
What would be a	kind	way to say that?
Be	cooperative	now.

ACT with Tact: Virtues in Student Evaluations and Feedback

When giving feedback such as report cards, it is encouraging for children to receive a "Positivity Sandwich." ACT stands for Acknowledge, Correct, and Thank. Sandwich suggestions for change or improvement between two positives. Ending feedback with a positive helps to sustain self-esteem and gives encouragement rather than discouragement. In this way, you can be extremely honest while also being tactful about changes that are needed.

Example:

We APPRECIATE in Amy:
Consideration, Kindness, Excellence
Amy shows kindness to new students. She is considerate of others and extends herself to be helpful. She is showing excellence in math lessons and in spelling, receiving high scores in all tests.

Amy's CHALLENGES are:
Assertiveness and Creativity
Amy needs to learn to set clearer boundaries with more aggressive students and ask for help from our Peacekeepers Patrol when she needs it. She also needs to trust that she has the freedom to be creative in some of her assignments. She does them reliably yet also needs to have a bit of fun with her story writing and drawing.

We are THANKFUL for Amy's:
Helpfulness and Purposefulness
Amy is helpful both to students and to teachers, has a strong sense of purposefulness, stays on track and takes on every task with a clear focus on the goals of the lesson.

"A Paragon of Virtues"

You don't need to be a paragon of perfection, but you do need to be a paragon or model of virtue. Model the virtue you are asking students to practice. For example, courtesy. If you want to bring a room of noisy students to order, you will have more success by focusing on those who are sitting respectfully and quietly, rather than shouting at the ones who are making noise. "Thank you, Andy, Mark, and Mary for the way you are sitting peacefully." When you want to move from a small group activity and have the students return their attention back to you, give a pre-arranged hand signal to the class that it is time to bring their attention to you. Some teachers find it more peaceful to ring a small bell, play music, or raise their arm, with the children raising their arms, as a signal for silence. After giving the signal, you can say "Jim, Tamara, Jacob, thank you for being so courteous and respectful. You brought your attention back to me right away." Focusing on those practicing the virtue and the behavior you DO want is far more instructive and courteous than focusing on those who are showing behavior you do NOT want.

"What you are speaks so loudly I can't hear what you are saying."
Henry David Thoreau

Cultural Change Begins with Leadership

The impact of a teacher's integrity in living by and sincerely modeling the virtues has even more effect than the words a teacher uses. If a teacher is having an "off" day, for example, asking for patience and kindness in a humorous way is a great model of humility and invites students to show some generosity of spirit.

"Men do not attract that which they want, but that which they are."
Anonymous

Schools with successful climates of character are those whose leaders model the five strategies, speak the language of virtues, appreciate staff, use ACT with Tact in performance appraisals and model the virtues of enthusiasm, compassion, and justice themselves. When school administrators conduct themselves in this way, it has a powerful effect on staff, students, parents, and the community.

For Administrators: Include Appreciation in Your Staff Appraisals

The ACT with Tact approach is for adults too! Teachers need a positivity sandwich as much as students, in receiving performance feedback. It is said you can tell anyone anything if you do it with tact. People tend to welcome information about their challenges when accompanied by an accurate description of their strengths in the language of virtues. The same format recommended for student reports is also needed in giving periodic performance appraisals, appreciations and suggestions for improvement to staff.

Activities

As you are learning to "talk the talk and walk the walk" of virtues, you will find your students following your example. Students tend to learn language very quickly, particularly in their younger years. It is their "critical period" for linguistic development. The Language of Virtues is no exception. To teach virtues language skills directly, you can have specific lessons on it as well as weave it into lessons you are already giving.

These activities work for a wide age range, so use your own judgment as to which activities are appropriate for the age group with whom you are working.

Virtues Diagram

Create a diagram of the "Virtue of the Week", using Signs of Success as the elements.

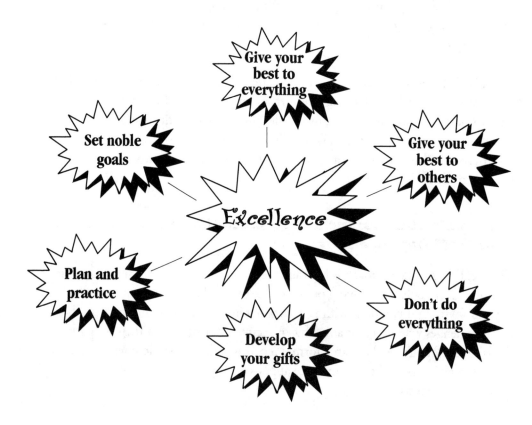

Virtues Role Play

Invite students to describe a typical interaction, for example, a fight on the playground, before the students involved know about the Language of the Virtues. Then role play what the same situation would look like using the virtues rather than aggression. Ask the class to think of other phrases which each student could have used to be assertive, or courteous, or honest, or peaceful, in solving the problem.

Scenario Description: One child shoves another one off the rings he has been using. Teacher to class: "What virtues could the child who was on the rings call on to solve this problem?" "What could the child say when he is being peaceful and assertive?" Be prepared with suggestions such as "I want to ask you to be fair. I had the swing first, and in one minute, if you're patient, I'll give you a turn."

Name That Virtue

At times, point out to the class how two students have just used one or more virtues to solve an actual problem. "Tanya and Juan just decided to use their virtues instead of arguing with each other when they both wanted the same book. What virtues are Tanya and Juan practicing?"

Secret Pal Program

In each group or class, place the names of all members, including teachers and volunteers into a decorated box. Include everyone. Each person draws a name at the beginning of the week, and keeps track of virtues noticed in that individual. At the end of the week, these lists are read aloud.

My Secret Pal
(Name)_____ practiced these virtues in the week of (date)_____.

VIRTUES	ACTIONS
Kindness	She helped a student get up when she fell.
Helpfulness	She erased the board.
Friendliness	She said "Hi" to lots of people.

Integrate Virtues Into Songs

Younger: The Virtue in Our Class (sung to "The Farmer in the Dell").

Younger: "Old MacDonald" had a virtues farm...and on this farm he had some kindness, ei-ei-o. (See Resources Section for suggested music resource).

Younger and *Older:* "I Think You're Wonderful" (Substitute a virtue for "wonderful" and sing a number of verses); Red Grammer, "Teaching Peace" album and "Hello World" (See Resources Section).

Younger and *Older:* "Love is Like a Magic Penny." Keep adding new virtues in place of Love, singing it several times with a different virtue each time.

Older: "Oh, When We Act with Love and Tact" to tune of "When the Saints Come Marching In".

Older: Teach them to sing "Hero", accompanied by a tape of Mariah Carey.

Virtues Games

Virtues Fruit Salad

Objective: To teach the language of virtues using whole body movement and connecting with students' life experiences. This game can be used by one class or as a whole school activity.

Key Point: This game has been used with young children, older children and adult groups as well. It is very energizing and enjoyable. It is most fun with a large group, with everyone racing for a seat, but can work with small groups too.

Materials needed: Poster with list of virtues (See Section 3) or individual virtues posters around the room.

Room Arrangement: Arrange one chair for each student except leader, placed in a circle. You can also do this game standing close together in a circle.

1. Designate a leader who stands in the center of a circle in which students are standing close together or each has a chair. You can do this in a large circle (more energy that way) or circles of six or seven.

2. Give the boundaries: Instruct students that the boundaries for this game are to practice integrity and honesty. "When the leader says a virtue you have practiced today you MUST leave your chair (spot) and you cannot go back to the same chair (spot). If you have not practiced this virtue today, be honest and stay in your place. If you do not find another empty place (or chair), you become the next leader. Tell the group in a loud voice:

    1) How you practiced the virtue today
    2) Think of a new virtue and say,
        "Who has practiced the virtue of _____ today?"

Then quickly find a new place for yourself.

3.

The first designated leader says: "Today I practiced the virtue of helpfulness when I helped my Mom make lunches for my brothers and sisters. Today, who practiced the virtue of _____?" Whoever is left standing after the scramble to find new seats, says how s/he has practiced this virtue. Then that person says "Today who practiced the virtue of (names a different virtue)."

Wheel of Virtues (Version of Wheel of Fortune)

Materials Needed: Overhead projector, overheads for assemblies, flip chart or blackboard for classroom use.

Instructions: Supplying the letters, r s t l n e, put up a virtue word with the rest of its letters blank, just as they do in the television show, "The Wheel of Fortune".
        _ _ _ _ _ SS _ _N (For COMPASSION)

Then, invite a student to come up with four other letters. Write them onto your overhead or board if they fit into your pre-selected virtue, e.g. C, A, R, D

        C _ _ _ A S S _ _ N.

Give extra points to the student if he or she can give a definition or example of the virtue.

Key Point: You may wish to call on a student as a reward for showing improvement in a particular virtue, even a slight improvement in gentleness, for example, by a student who has challenges in that virtue. These students need the most self-esteem building. Vary rewarding challenged students by also acknowledging excellent students who are very confident, so that there is balance in your acknowledgment system.

Virtues Jeopardy

Instructions: Create "answers" based on information found in the Virtues Section of this Guide.
Answer: "Showing you care about anyone or anything that crosses your path." Have students compete to ask the right question, for example: "What is kindness?"

Key Point: You can mix academic questions with virtues questions. For example: Category: Little Women
Answer: "The sister who showed courage and assertiveness to follow her career."
Question: "Who was Beth?"

Virtues Charades

Invite one person to pantomime a virtue s/he finds on a list you have placed on the board or you may use a Virtues Poster.

From Shaming to Naming

Objective: to create awareness of the power of our language to hurt or help one another, to put each other down or lift each other up.

Time Needed: 20 minutes to 1/2 hour

Materials Needed: A board and chalk or flip chart and markers.

Instructions: Create the climate by introducing this exercise by speaking of the power of words and writing "From Shaming to Naming" on the board. You may want to write a quote on the board as well, such as, "Sticks and stones may break my bones, but words can break my spirit." Invite students to express their own thoughts about what words can do, and how we feel when various words are used about us.

Establish the Boundaries: "We are going to show respect by listening without comment to each other, and showing respect for what each person says. We will also use our honesty and courage to tell our own experience."

Procedure: Draw five columns on the board or flip chart. Write the headings as shown below above each column. Share with the class a negative label or

"Put down" you were called by your peers when you were in school, to set an example and get the ball rolling. As you share how you felt, you are creating safety for students to disclose their experiences. Write your label in the first column and how you felt in the second. Ask the students what virtue the person could have used with you instead and how that word might have felt to you.

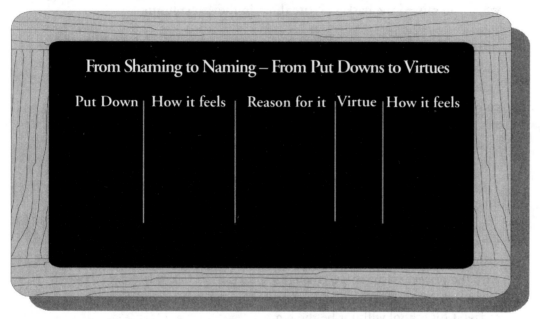

OPTION: You can invite students to go into pairs or sharing circles of three to share with one another a label or "Put Down" they have been called and how it felt, or you can do this with the class as a whole. Put the above columns on the board.

1) Share with a partner or group a disrespectful label or put down you have been called by others.
2) How did you feel when you were called that?
3) Describe the reason why others may have called you this name. (e.g. were annoyed by you, felt you were moving too slow, just trying to get your attention, felt you did something mean, or no reason, just abuse)

We don't put each other down. We lift each other up.

Ask five people to call out labels. (They will be things like "stupid", "useless", "jerk", etc.) Write them down one at a time.

OPTION: If you prefer, you can make a boundary that no profanity will be included, although it may be useful to hear the real experiences students have.

2nd Column: Ask each student who has volunteered a "put down" to share how they felt when this label was used. *3rd Column:* Ask them what reason others may have had when using those terms on them. Write that in the 3rd column. Begin by modeling an example of your own. "I was missing a lot of baskets, playing basketball." Explain that sometimes bad names are used on us with no good reason, other than pure disrespect.

4th column. Invite the group as a whole to come up with a virtue others could have used instead of the negative label, one which would have "lifted them up" and helped them to focus on a virtue. e.g. "Use your determination." when you missed the basket. Write those in the 4th column.

Ask for a commitment: Ask the class, "How would our school be different if we use virtues to lift each other up instead of put downs to discourage and embarrass each other?" Ask for a show of hands of those willing to make a commitment to use only encouraging words for the rest of the day...then for the rest of the week.

Ask Closure and Integration Questions: "What was the most important thing you learned from this exercise?" "What did you appreciate most about this exercise?"

Give some Virtues Acknowledgments: "Ann, I want to acknowledge you for your courage to tell us your story." "Paul, you showed real excellence in coming up with the perfect virtue in a challenging situation." "Class, I respect the commitment you are showing by agreeing to use only encouraging words today! Our school will not be the same."

Key Point: Be moderate when you give Virtues Acknowledgements – three or four at the most. You may wish to use this exercise when teaching the virtue of Respect.

OPTION: Close the Shaming to Naming exercise with a song such as "I Think You're Wonderful" or "Home On the Range"

> Home, home in our school
> where we practice Respect every day
> where never is heard a discouraging word,
> when we study, work, and play.

(or something to that effect. Make your own lyrics based on the Virtue of the Week!) (See Resource Section for music by Jennifer Russell, Red Grammar, and Radha.)

Example of Excellence
Virtues Awards

Betsy Lydle Smith used this activity with 7th grade students in Bellevue, Washington.

Have a decorated shoe box in the classroom. Students nominate other students for virtues they see that student exhibit and tell how they saw it. At the end of the week, the teacher selects three or four of the nominees and awards each student with a certificate with student's name, class, teacher's name and date, and the words "We honor you for practicing the virtue of _____." Make sure that all students receive an award or two during the year. You can use Virtues Vouchers for this activity. Betsy says, "They loved it!"

School-wide Activities

"Virtue of the Week" Program

Introduce the "Virtue of the Week" at School Assemblies

- Create an overhead of the Affirmation or Signs of Success for the Virtue of the Week.
- Have a skit based on "What would it look like?" scenarios in the Virtues Section.
- Sing a song related to the virtue or weave the virtue into a well known song.
- Recite the Affirmation together.
- Have teachers acknowledge particular students for the Virtue of the Week by reading aloud Virtues Vouchers, with examples of students practicing the virtue. Have students stand when they are receiving their virtues acknowledgment. The student then gets to take the Virtues Voucher home.
- At the last assembly of the week, invite one of the classes or an individual student to choose the virtue of the next week.

Skits

Many schools offer student skits over the P.A. system, in school assemblies, and in the classroom. Often older students will perform for younger classes. Older classes can take turns being responsible for doing a skit at the beginning of each day, either over the public announcement system or in an assembly. They can role-play one of the scenarios from the "What would it look like?" section of each of the virtues.

Daily Readings

Each morning, a student reads from the virtue chosen for the week. Some schools read a section of the virtue each day in Assembly or over the P.A. system:

> Monday: What is the virtue?
> Tuesday: Why practice it?
> Wednesday: How do you practice it?
> Thursday: Signs of Success
> Friday: The Affirmation.

Quiet Time - A Virtues Morning

Some schools follow the reading by one minute of silent reflection throughout the school to focus on the Virtue and what has been read.

Focus on the Affirmation Each Day

Read the Affirmation at the beginning of each day, with all students reciting it aloud. It is helpful to have the Affirmation posted in classrooms or in the assembly as an overhead slide or large poster.

Group Discussion

Following the daily reading or skit, or at a time when students are ready for a peaceful break in regular academics, invite them to share their own experiences of being treated without the Virtue and then with the Virtue, for example, times they have experienced intolerance and tolerance in their lives. **IMPORTANT: Set a boundary before the discussion begins that no names are to be mentioned.** You want to avoid backbiting during all discussions.

Virtues Rap

Have a class compose a rap song on the Virtue of the Week and present it at Assembly.

Computer Posting

If you have a computer system in your school, put a quotation from the Virtue of the Week on as a screen saver to pop up when people turn on the computer.

Post Virtues Banners and Posters in Hallways

Place in a central hallway a banner of the Virtue of the Week. For example, "Our School (Scout Troop, Camp, etc.) is a PEACE Zone: We give up the love of power for the power of love." or "INTEGRITY: We walk our talk." You can invite students to make more elaborate posters for the classroom, using the Signs of Success of each virtue or Poster Points given with each virtue. Some teachers have one poster per week which remains displayed in the classroom to illustrate the Virtue of the Week.

Signs of Virtue

Some communities highlight a virtue per week or per month with the participation and sponsorship of local businesses. Have students take signs with one line definitions of the Virtue of the Week out into the community to go into store windows, on bank displays, sides of buses etc.

Chapter Summary:
Speak the Language of Virtues

✓ Acknowledge virtues when you see them, particularly the emerging growth virtues.

✓ Guide students to practice a virtue when you know they are about to need it.

✓ Correct misbehavior by naming the virtue involved – replace shaming with naming.

✓ Focus on what you DO want, not what you don't want.

✓ Use virtues language to be specific.

✓ Name the act, not the actor.

✓ ACT with Tact in student and staff evaluations – make a positivity sandwich.

✓ Use a multi-sensory approach in introducing virtues into your regular curriculum and through games, songs and special activities.

✓ Have a "Virtue of the Week" Program.

Virtues Voucher

_____ showed _____ when s/he _____
Name   Virtue   Action

_____

_____

Date: _____   **Signed:** _____

Virtues Voucher

_____ showed _____ when s/he _____
Name   Virtue   Action

_____

_____

Date: _____   **Signed:** _____

Virtues Voucher

_____ showed _____ when s/he _____
Name   Virtue   Action

_____

_____

Date: _____   **Signed:** _____

Virtues Voucher

_____ showed _____ when s/he _____
Name   Virtue   Action

_____

_____

Date: _____   **Signed:** _____

Hug Note

Give A Hug!

To: _____ for

Growing in the Virtue of _____
by _____
_____

Excelling in the Virtue of _____
by _____
_____

Signed: _____

Hug Note

Give A Hug!

To: _____ for

Growing in the Virtue of _____
by _____
_____

Excelling in the Virtue of _____
by _____
_____

Signed: _____

Hug Note

Give A Hug!

To: _____ for

Growing in the Virtue of _____
by _____
_____

Excelling in the Virtue of _____
by _____
_____

Signed: _____

Hug Note

Give A Hug!

To: _____ for

Growing in the Virtue of _____
by _____
_____

Excelling in the Virtue of _____
by _____
_____

Signed: _____

2 Recognize Teachable Moments

"Life is for learning our lessons."
Tlingit Elder

 ## Look for the Lessons

Every day, during classes, in the lunch room and in the playground, there are Teachable Moments. These are moments in which students can be helped to *master* their virtues and to understand the *meaning* of

- what they are learning
- what they are doing
- how they are interacting with others.

At the heart of meaning – at the core of why we do things – there is always a virtue. Students do not necessarily need special classes on character. In fact, it is best if most of their lessons on virtue occur within the context of daily learning and living. Virtues are the best tools for developing social skills, since they embody the *reason* one must interact well with others – to be kind, to be caring, to be a good friend, to be respectful and so on.

Ask virtues-oriented questions on subjects you are teaching.

> "What virtues did you notice in this historic event we just read about?"
> "In the book we read, what virtues did you notice in the main character?"
> "What do you think gave her the courage to do what she did?"
> "What could the main character have said or done instead of running away?"
> "What virtue would have helped him to do that?"

Even very young children can identify the virtues in a story when a teacher asks, for example, "What virtues would Peter Rabbit be acknowledged for?" "Which virtues does Peter need to be called to?" "What virtues might Mother Rabbit be acknowledged for?" "What was Peter's teachable moment? What virtue did he need to learn?"

Children can role play the characters, giving each other virtues acknowledgments and corrections in the Teachable Moments.

Teaching Tip

Link Teachable Moments about virtues to history, literature, and other academic subjects.

"Intelligence plus character – that is the goal of true education."
Martin Luther King, Jr.

Help Students Connect Personally to Lessons

Value is added to a lesson when you invite students to connect the Teachable Moments they see in the lives of individuals or characters they are hearing or reading about to their own experience. Helpful questions to ask are:

- When have you had similar challenges?
- What virtues did you need at those times?
- When have you experienced courage in your own life?

Support Mastery and Meaning

Teaching Tip

There are two ways to Recognize Teachable Moments:

1) Acknowledge effort in acquiring a virtue.

2) Remind or call a student to accountability for a virtue which is needed.

Virtues are the curriculum of character and Teachable Moments are the lesson plans.

Recognizing Teachable Moments is intimately linked to Strategy 1: Speak the Language of the Virtues. It is an attitude toward life as a process in which each of us is a life-long learner. Some of the most important lessons students receive in school go beyond academics. Teachable Moments are moments of awareness — awareness of the *meaning* of what is happening and the virtue which is at the heart of it. It is asking the questions: What happened? What can be learned from this? What virtues need to be practiced?

Recognizing Teachable Moments is a perspective in which we see the "stuff that happens" day-to-day as grist for the mill of character. Virtues are the content of our character, and Teachable Moments are the "lesson plans" for shaping our virtues. Our courage grows when we are afraid and "do it anyway." Our excellence is developed when a task is challenging and we give our best to it. Our responsibility, forgiveness and determination grow when we own up to a mistake, and then make it right. Speaking about virtues in Teachable Moments stimulates mastery of our inherent character traits and attaches meaning to our actions.

When a normally aggressive child behaves peacefully, that is a Teachable Moment in which to acknowledge their peacefulness. This increases their awareness that they are growing stronger in a challenging virtue. "You were very peaceful during recess, Malcolm." When the same child "forgets" about peacefulness and acts aggressively, that is a Teachable Moment in which to remind him to behave peacefully: "How can you get your friend's attention peacefully?"

Turn Stumbling Blocks Into Stepping Stones

Students' awareness of their inner strengths is greatly enhanced whenever a teacher recognizes the context or meaning of a situation in light of the virtues, and when the teacher respectfully guides them to call on that virtue. Self-esteem grows as children make choices to do the right thing. Making the most of the Teachable Moments that occur every day also builds morale because it takes the sting out of making mistakes. When we are really challenged by life, that is the best time for us to hone our virtues. Sometimes mistakes are our best teachers.

Positive encouragement by focusing on students' "growth virtues" supports them to keep improving in an area that is challenging for them. It draws their awareness to what they are doing right. If you feel the growth shows real effort, send home a "Virtues Voucher" or a "Hug Note" (found on pages 25 and 27).

When a student who has problems with self-discipline by talking too much in class has a less disruptive day, catching them in an act of self-discipline encourages mastery. "Jane, I noticed your self-discipline today. You were quite attentive."

"A teacher who can arouse a feeling for one single good action... accomplishes more than he who fills our memory with rows and rows of natural objects, classified with name and form."
Goethe

Be a Teacher, Not a Preacher

The number one challenge most teachers have is student discipline. How do you get students to behave so that you can teach them? How can you keep your attention balanced between the kids who have behavioral problems and the majority who are easier to teach? It is easy to succumb to the habit of preaching at students to embarrass them into behaving properly. The practice is generations old. However, lecturettes and "guilting" simply don't work very well or for very long. It is especially important not to use the Language of Virtues to moralize. e.g. "Why can't you be more peaceful?", which is shaming. What works far better is calling them to their virtues – their self-discipline, their respect, their cooperation. "How can you be more peaceful?" is a way to show respect for the student and respect for the Language of Virtues.

One of the greatest gifts you can give your students is your commitment to bringing out the best in them. When you see times of misbehavior, forgetfulness, or disrespect on the part of a student as a Teachable Moment in which to inspire them to call on a virtue, everything changes. Most of the time, a

Teaching Tip

Recognizing Teachable Moments is a way to refocus behavior on the virtue that is needed. When a student is acting in an unacceptable way, tactfully call them to a virtue or ask them what virtue they need.

Example: Student is being aggressive: "You need to remember to be Gentle." Student is "zoning out": "Focus, Amos. Be Purposeful."

student's resistance melts, and something inside them resonates with the virtue you have named. For example, if a student has an over-stuffed desk, use it as a Teachable Moment. Instead of criticizing, ask "What would help you to keep you desk orderly?"

Asking "What virtue do you need?" can help students to recognize the Teachable Moment, whether they are facing an academic challenge or at a time when they need to change their behavior. For example, if a student is irritable, ask "What virtue do you need today?" and "How can I support you?"

It can be helpful to have visuals of the virtues around, such as a poster listing the virtues (See Resource Section) or the names of individual virtues as posters with colorful borders.

What Virtue Did You Forget?

Ray Tufts, while serving as assistant principal at an alternative school in Renton, Washington, with high risk students, many of whom had been expelled from other schools and had criminal records, found that Recognizing Teachable Moments helped students save face when being disciplined. He put a Virtues Poster with the 52 virtues in every class room and had one in his office.

When a student was sent to his office for discipline, he would first companion them to hear the story of what happened from their point of view. Then he would point to the Virtues Poster and ask, "What virtues were you forgetting?" or "What virtues would have helped you to do the right thing?' The student identified one or two virtues. Ray then invited the student to make reparation and asked "How can you fix this by using these virtues? What would that look like?" The student left with a sense of encouragement rather than feeling shamed, having recognized a Teachable Moment.

Ray says: "Public schools know how to set boundaries, but they don't know how to establish relevant consequences. They are obviously ineffective because they don't change behavior. They're not using the problems as a 'Teachable Moment'. For example, I can't believe that schools are still using suspension as a punishment for misbehavior. What does that teach? If you want a week off, misbehave! Companioning takes time, but then the kid realizes that you care about his moral development. He learns that misbehavior is an indication that he forgot a virtue – not that he lacks it – and he can change his behavior by knowing the virtue he needs to practice, so he can succeed next time he's in a similar situation. You want to create an environment so supportive that the student doesn't want to disappoint you."

"In all situations, it is my response that decides whether a crisis will be escalated or de-escalated and a child humanized or de-humanized."
Haim Ginott

You want to create an environment so supportive that the student doesn't want to disappoint you.

Use Virtues, Not Labels

How easy it is to slip into shaming or embarrassing a student who has consistently failed to turn in homework, and brings it in one day. For example, a teacher might be sarcastic: "Hey, 'Day Late', it's about time you remembered your homework." Instead, the teacher has the opportunity to recognize the student's mastery at that moment, by saying "Niki, good reliability! You turned in your homework on time." In speaking the Language of Virtues in this Teachable Moment, you are reinforcing the practice of the virtue the student has shown and are giving them an anchor for the meaning of what they have done. The meaning is in their reliability, or self-discipline, or orderliness – the personal practices which produced the act itself. The value of this approach is that it goes way beyond managing behavior in the classroom. It inspires students to act on the gifts within.

Help Children to Balance Their Virtues

"We have to deeply touch ourselves and each other so that these things do not become trite, campy, or dated. The question at the base is 'Who are we and what are we here for?'"
Ann Bock

If a student is strong in one virtue, he or she may need help in balancing it with a complementary virtue. For example, you would not want to reinforce excessive "teacher's pet" behavior even if a student is being helpful to you personally. This behavior isolates the student from others and is a manifestation of people-pleasing. You would call on your own tact and while acknowledging the student's helpfulness, encourage them to be friendly to others or generous in giving others a chance to be helpful. When you see such a student reaching out to others, that is when a Virtues Acknowledgment, such as "You were being friendly today" is helpful in cultivating the balancing quality that the child needs.

 Rename and Reframe

> ### Example of Excellence
> **Rename and Reframe**
>
> **Joyce Boykin** is a primary school teacher in the Solomon Islands. She has transformed her students by renaming and reframing their personality traits into virtues of character. She is an excellent model of a teacher who "ACTs with Tact". For example, students in that culture are trained to "be seen and not heard", so they tend to be shy and quiet in the classroom. Joyce wanted to encourage them to be assertive and offer their opinions. So, she acknowledges them for being peaceful and obedient instead of shaming them by calling them "shy" and then calls them to their less developed virtue of assertiveness and confidence.

To Rename and Reframe, here are four simple steps.

1) Think of the student you have, whose behavior challenges you.
2) Rename their basic character trait as a virtue.
   (e.g. stubbornness = determination; talking back = honesty)
3) Identify the virtue you want to encourage them to practice.
4) Put it into a positive sentence.

Example: With an active, restless student, "Enoch, you have great enthusiasm. Now you need to be purposeful and focus on your reading." With a student who tends to talk back, "Maria, I appreciate your honesty about your opinion. How can you say that in a more respectful or courteous way?"

Be a Conscience Maker, Not a Conscience Breaker

One of the goals of a virtues-oriented educator is to help students build a strong conscience. Conscience is the regulator of character, the still small voice that keeps us doing right and warns us against doing wrong. Punitive approaches to character building – the historic precedent in schools throughout the world – have produced a combination of

- fear of authority
- people-pleasing
- rebellion
- free-floating guilt.

Many young people today believe that something is right "as long as you don't get caught". We are in danger of a moral morass with so many youth failing to grasp the importance of taking personal responsibility for their actions by practicing honesty, integrity, reliability and other virtues. In some schools and programs, where authority is used too harshly, students tend to be extremely passive, and only the most confident succeed.

Shaming Discourages Excellence

Many First Nations aboriginal children in the United States, Canada, and Australia, were taken from their families and placed in residential schools in the early 1900's. Discipline was so harsh that, according to Charlotte H., a member of the Tlinget nation in Canada, "You learned systematic mediocrity, so that you wouldn't be noticed. You did not want to draw attention to yourself, so even academically you wouldn't exceed or fail, just be as mediocre as possible. Of course, that underscored their belief that Indians are intellectually inferior. We were just trying to be as invisible as possible to avoid kneeling on a stone floor for hours or having our heads shaved." Shaming children in any way has a similar impact – it discourages excellence.

The Virtues Project advocates an educative approach to character building in which a healthy conscience is stimulated and nurtured. The Teachable Moment for those who work with children is to recognize teaching behaviors that are shaming and those that are empowering. The Language of the Virtues is a tool with which teachers can respond in an empowering rather than a demoralizing way.

"As a teacher, I possess a tremendous power to make a child's life miserable or joyous.

I can be a tool of torture or an instrument of inspiration.

I can humiliate or humor, hurt or heal."
Haim Ginott

Example of Excellence
Sometimes It Takes Some Looking

From Tammy Goff, fifth grade teacher in Lantern Lane Elementary School in Missouri City, Texas.

"We had a new student in our fifth grade this year. He had many, many problems. He was very impulsive, quick to get into a fight or argument, would never hold himself accountable, constantly blamed others, never had his homework, constantly earned after-school detentions – you get the picture.

Halfway through the school year his teacher began to allow more time for students to give one another virtues acknowledgments after the morning announcement about the Virtue of the Week. For several weeks, students raised their hands, acknowledged someone in the class for a virtue and then wrote the virtue on a gem shape kept on the class bulletin board. In all that time, no one acknowledged this boy.

One day, he raised his hand and asked, "Can I acknowledge myself?" His teacher said, "Of course you may, Fred." He did, and said something quite accurate about himself. Then classmates began to notice little things he did and also started to acknowledge him. Gradually he became more responsible. He was in far less trouble. I cannot say he was a model honor student, but the change was dramatic from the standpoint of all staff members who interacted with him. Best of all, his vision of himself improved. He was empowered."

Conscience Makers and Conscience Breakers

The Virtues Project strategy of Recognizing Teachable Moments replaces practices that demean and demoralize students with practices that empower them to build a strong conscience.

Habits that Break Conscience

Shaming (Communicating worthlessness)

Demeaning

Humiliating

Sarcasm and cruel teasing

Name-calling or negative labeling

Beating or hitting

Overprotecting or Excuse-Making

Using excessive punishment

Ignoring efforts to improve

Habits That Make Conscience

Using Time Out constructively (e.g. Replace "Naughty Chair" with "Courtesy Chair")

Naming virtues when you see them practiced

Calling students to a virtue when it needs to be practiced

Listening to offenders' point of view

Stopping negative behavior and refocusing on the Virtues Vision statement

Giving consequences when they are called for

Providing the opportunity to make amends

Noticing and acknowledging efforts to improve

Recognize Teachable Moments ....

Example of Excellence
Virtues Charts

Geoff Smith of the Ludgvan Primary School in Cornwall, England uses Virtues Charts with 9 and 10 year olds in his school. He begins with a Virtues Sharing Circle about the Virtue of the Week. "We use circle time to encourage class discussion and problem solving. I strongly feel that the virtues encompass these objectives but perhaps more importantly, maintain a positive focus to the activity."

"In order to encourage the recognition of virtues in others, I use Virtues Vouchers (see page 25) which children can fill in, detailing the virtue they observed in another, and post into a "Virtue Box". This gives them further material with which to encourage each other during Circle Time. I also use a Friendship Chart (see page 51 in the Activities Section following)."

Example of Excellence
"SNECA"

SNECA (created by Madison C. Munroe, 3rd grade teacher in Little Rock, Arkansas). When misbehavior occurs, remember how to turn caterpillars into a butterflies.

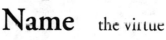

Stop the behavior

Name the virtue

Explain briefly how this behavior affected others

Consequence give an immediate consequence

Amends encourage the child to make reparation.

Recognize Teachable Moments with Special Needs Students

Teachers and aides working with special needs students, even individuals who are severely intellectually challenged, find that they are very responsive to virtues language. Whenever you see progress made by one of these students, use a virtue in your acknowledgment. "Sally, you were really persevering in putting your sweater on today. It was hard but you did it!" When things aren't going so well, use the virtues language to define the Teachable Moment, and to invite the student to call on one of her virtues: "Sally, be patient. You can do it." If Sally throws down the sweater in frustration, you can say "Sally, putting on that sweater is hard, isn't it?! What would help you find the perseverance to try again?"

Ask Closure and Integration Questions

Asking questions which encourage closure and integration at the end of a class, activity or lesson helps students to glean the Teachable Moments or lessons of that activity. These are not closed questions calling for a yes or no answer such as "Did you like that activity?" or "Was that helpful to you?" Rather they are open-ended questions which help students to <u>integrate the meaning</u> of what has occurred. Most closure and integration questions are worded positively. Positive wording helps students integrate thinking and feeling, head and heart.

"What was most helpful?"
"What did you appreciate about this class?"
"What was meaningful to you about this story?"
"How was this for you?"
"What is clearer for you after this lesson?"
"What do you think was the most important thing you learned today?"

Involve the Family

Schools that are most successful in character education encourage parental involvement. When children set character development goals, encourage parents to send in examples of times when children are "caught in the act" of practicing one of these virtues.

There are creative ways to involve families in a vision of virtues in school. Let families participate in focusing on "The Virtue of the Week" and actively contribute their own creativity to it.

Send home Virtues Vouchers or Hug Notes. Think of the difference it will make to the self-esteem of parents when you send a note home about a child's behavior, and instead of attacking their character by listing their faults and failings, you encourage them to develop their character by naming the virtues they need to be "working on". Sending home a Virtues Voucher will give the parents an anchor for their own self-esteem, because when their child shines, it reflects on them too! You can take it one step further and encourage parents to spot it in their child and report back to you! This spreads the virtues-oriented mentorship you are providing. It models for the parent a face-saving way to bring out the best in their children.

Example of Excellence
Family Time

This example comes from Colegio Bolivar in Argentina.

Each week one student's family takes responsibility to make a ten minute presentation on the Virtue of the Week. Families do skits, make videos, create posters, and compose songs. Then they come to school and teach them to their child's class. Afterward, the family is given virtues acknowledgments and appreciations by the class.

 # Activities

"Virtues in Me" Book

At the beginning of the year, have students make a "Virtues In Me" book. Modify this so that it is appropriate for younger and older students. Have children paste a photograph of themselves on the cover of their books, or draw a self-portrait if a photograph is not available. If possible, use a Polaroid camera to take a picture of each child. Then have them decorate the cover. Some ideas are:

- Make a Virtues Acronym of their name, e.g. **MARGERY**. Make this the opening page in their "Virtues in Me" book.

  > **M**erciful
  > **A**ssertive
  > **R**esponsible
  > **G**enerous
  > **E**xcellent
  > **R**espectful
  > **Y**owie what creativity!

- Write and draw two to four of their best developed virtues (Strength Virtues), as well as two to four virtues in which they need to grow and develop (Growth Virtues).

- Write a poem or story about a Strength Virtue or a Growth Virtue.

- Make a family tree showing Strength Virtues they feel each member has.

- A goal sheet showing:

  1. A Growth Virtue they want to work on.
  2. What actions will they take?
  3. What will it look like, sound like, and feel like?

Ray Tufts used Virtues Interviews at an alternative school in Renton, Washington.

Afterward he asked "What did you appreciate about this exercise?" a bit worried about how his students would react. "The first time I did this in class, I thought, 'This is kid stuff, they won't like it.' I had them do an exercise where you interview each other, look for the virtues in each other, and then introduce your partner by describing their virtues. In that 15 minutes the room was just intense, they were so in tune with it. Afterwards I asked a closure and integration question 'What did you think of that?' One big kid, a kid whose clothing and posture were very defiant, he stood up and said, "I really like this, because it makes you think of your real self.' Another girl said. 'I want to change my virtues.' She had decided there were qualities that would make her a better person and she wanted to start developing them right away!"

Virtues Interview

This activity is ideal for the beginning of the year, to set a tone of virtues awareness.

See next page for Student Activity Sheet. Instruct students to be present to each other with great respect and deep listening without teasing, interrupting, advising or comparing. They need not take any notes. Just listen and be really present. When the activity is completed, ask a closure question such as: "What did you appreciate about this activity?"

Student Activity Sheet

VIRTUES INTERVIEW

Choose a partner and take turns interviewing one another. Do not write or take notes. Just be present and listen.

1. Name someone you admire. This person may be a figure in history or a person in your life. What is the core virtue this person practices? What attracts you to this virtue?

2. Name one of your own strength virtues, one which is strong and well-developed in you. Say a few words about how you live it.

3. Name a virtue you need to grow, one that is under-developed in you. Say a few words about how it is needed in your life.

4. What is one of the biggest challenges in your life right now? What virtues would help you to meet this challenge?

5. What are your hopes for this school term?

6. What is a source of Joy in your life at this time?

7. Virtues Acknowledgment.

Interviewer, please give your partner a virtues acknowledgment by telling them a virtue you notice in them and specifically how you see it. "I want to acknowledge you for the virtue of _____ and the way you show it is _____."

Darkest Moments/Shining Hours

Teaching Tip

Use the **ART** of Boundaries:

Assertiveness (by doing what's right for you),

Respect (by listening and being present without teasing, comparing, advising, or interrupting) and

Trust (by keeping confidential any information shared).

(This exercise can be done in Circle Time for the whole class or in small groups of three to five.)

1. Describe one of your darkest moments (during your holiday, at school this week, with your friends). What virtues were needed?

2. Describe one of your shining moments. What virtues were involved?

3. As each person in your group finishes sharing, the others are to give them a virtues acknowledgement. "I saw your virtue of _____ in the way you _____."

Best Friend Brainstorm

Brainstorm the qualities of the most disappointing friend you ever had or could have and the qualities of the best friend you ever had or could have. Ask the group afterward how these qualities relate to virtues. Write on a board or flip chart the virtues they come up with, first for the disappointing friend, then for the best friend.

Key Point: Virtues are the basis for character, and good character is what makes for good relationships.

Virtues Integrity Profile

This can be done very simply with younger children and in a more detailed form for older students. Encourage 90 Day Goal Setting. Every three months have students revisit and revise their personal and academic goals, including the virtues they want to develop.

Student Activity Sheet

Name: _____ Date: _____ Period: _____

How Am I Doing?

(An honest look at my _____ Quarter of my _____ Year)

1. How well did I meet my expectations for myself this quarter?

2. How could I have been a better student?

3. My most important learning so far this year of school is:

4. My most important learning so far in this class is:

5. In my opinion, this class would be better if:

6. Two things I would do if I were the teacher are

     a.

     b.

7. In my opinion, my most outstanding virtues are:
_____ and _____.

8. I am still working to grow in the following virtues:
_____ and _____.

Adapted from Anne Bock, Sequoia Junior High School, Kent, Washington, U.S.A.

Virtue of the Day Reflection

(This is an exercise designed by Joyce Boykin of the Solomon Islands in the South Pacific.)

One of the ways to recognize Teachable Moments is to be aware of the ways we are practicing a particular virtue and ways we have yet to practice it. Joyce has two cans in her classroom. Can #1 contains small cards with the name of each student. She takes one out, reads aloud the student's name and then places his or her name card in Can #2. This student gets to pick the Virtue of the Day in her classroom. She does this activity at Virtues Circle Time, which is scheduled mid-morning as a way to help children become peaceful and focused. They sit on a mat and do the following:

1. Read the definition of the Virtue of the Week from a Virtue Card or from this Guide.
2. Have a brief class discussion of the virtue, describe when they have seen it in others, a public figure they know who practices it, or how they practice it themselves.
3. Ask students to close their eyes while you read "Signs of Success" from the virtue page, slowly and one at a time. The reason for this is to preserve modesty, and eliminate competition. Instruct them to raise their hands when they recognize that they are practicing a Sign of Success most of the time, and to keep their hands down if they are not.
4. Read each Sign of Success and pause afterward. Let them know "Oh, this one is a challenging one for most of us." "Lots of you are doing this." "Most of you, etc."

At the end of the day, Joyce stands by the door, smiles and acknowledges each student for a virtue she noticed in them that day.

Team Teaching

Have students form teams and each take a virtue. They are to:

1. Create a name for their team incorporating a virtue. e.g. "Purposeful Porpoises", "Respectful Raspberries", etc.

2. They will make a T-Chart as follows:

Purposefulness

Is Not	Is

3. They then read the Virtue definition to the class, "What is Kindness?", and share their T-Chart

4. Role Play the Virtue under "What would it look like if...?" scenarios found on the first page of each Virtue.

Example of Excellence
A Personal Virtues Poster

At Paekakariki Primary School in New Zealand the teachers of the Bilingual Unit work together with 40 children ages 5-12, delivering a comprehensive program which includes instruction in Maori as well as English. These two teachers use virtues in their program both in Maori and in English. At the beginning of the year, Miki Reikihana, who teaches the older children, worked with them about setting goals and developing qualities of character.

1. He posted Virtues Cards (See Resource Section) on the wall, and each day reviewed the characteristics of particular virtues that he felt were important in his classroom.
2. Then he had the children choose two or three virtues that they wanted to practice during the year and create a poster with an illustration of themselves practicing these qualities.
3. Underneath the poster, the children wrote in English or Maori an affirmation for themselves. Examples: "This year I will practice being respectful and assertive." "This year if I see people fighting I will try to help them calm down, and bring them to other people who are respectful and friendly."

"I use the strategies of The Virtues Project to create a peaceful, harmonious environment for my children. Perhaps the most important benefit it has brought to me is my own sense of peacefulness. It's easier to understand what the children's real needs are and how I need to respond. This has relieved a lot of stress for me."
Mika Tawhara-Tamihana

Walk About

Walk about your classroom or the playground or anywhere you are on duty. Be on the lookout for virtues that students are practicing, go over to them and give them a simple Virtues Acknowledgment. Examples:

> "You two are playing so peacefully today."
> "That is a really creative sand castle you built."
> "I see you are using lots of self-discipline today, focusing well on your work." "That is a friendly thing to do."

Then be on the lookout for virtues that are needed.

> (To students wrestling and getting rough) "You two need to be peaceful."
> (To a student who seems distracted) "Please call on your Determination to finish your assignment."
> "Be Respectful. Watch your language."

Some teachers give out Virtues Tickets to children who have been caught in the act of practicing virtues. Teachers who report using Virtues Tickets add that it is important to give all the children a Virtues Ticket. After the children become used to this process, they will ask for extra tickets so they themselves can catch the teacher and other children in the act of committing virtues!

Magic Box

This exercise was adapted by Beth Lew of Paekakariki, New Zealand from a popular Theater Sports game. It works very well in exploring a virtue with children or adults.

Model it first. "What's in My Box? Peacefulness." Begin by speaking briefly about what peacefulness is and how this virtue helps you in times of confusion, sadness, or anger.

Introduce the game by pretending that you have a box in front of you. Model how big it is with your hands and describe what your box looks like, what it is wrapped with, the colors, the texture. Then open your box and find something that will help you find peacefulness the next time you are feeling confused, worried, or annoyed. Tell about the item, what it looks like, feels like, sounds like, smells like – whatever is appropriate and adds to the concreteness of the image. Tell in what way this thing will help you to find your own peacefulness. Then close the box again. Explain that this is a magic box that can change its shape and size and the gift that is within it. Everyone that holds it will find something special just for them. Then pass the box to the next person.

Mind Map Virtues to Solve Problems

1. Have students write a brief description of a problem or concern on a slip of paper and place it in a box.

2. Choose one situation.

3. On the board, have a student create a Mind Map with the situation in the center.

4. As a group, brainstorm six virtues needed to solve the problem. Place them around the problem.

5. Brainstorm specific things to say or do under each virtue.

Virtues Celebrity Party

1. Think of several famous or well-known people who are recognized for their positive qualities. They can be people from a faith tradition or historical figures or famous people of any kind.

2. Make a name tag for each person, or have the students make them.

3. Choose a group of actors with the rest of the group as audience. Have each child pick one of the name tags and put it on. Each person pretends s/he is that person and must act like that person, picking one virtue that most exemplifies that person's character.

4. Have some dress-up clothes available, including hats, scarves, wigs, caps, jackets, to help them get into the character. Pretend that all the characters are at a party together. They must interact using the virtue they have chosen for the person they are pretending to be. After they have been at the party and interacted for five to ten minutes or so, freeze the action. The audience must guess which virtue each character was acting out. For example, Martin Luther King Jr. might act out courage, Mother Teresa compassion, etc.

Virtues "Vibes"

Creativity supplied by Ann Bock of Sequoia Junior High School, Kent, Washington.

Each student takes a sheet of paper, folds it into quarters, and puts their name on one panel. Then they add three virtues or "gifts" the world needs now on the other three panels. A hole is punched in the center and the sheet is hung from the ceiling with yarn. It will vibrate in the air, causing virtues "vibrations" to fill the classroom.

Symbols of Virtue

Children learn about virtues through visual symbols. Invite them to think creatively about symbols for each "Virtue of the Week". For example, the Bridge of Compassion or a Rainbow of Respect. Decorate your walls with their creations.

Student Activity Sheet

Instructions: Each day, fill in the name of at least one person with whom you were friendly in one of the ways listed on the chart below. In the bottom column, show how you were a friend to yourself. Recite the affirmation "I Am Friendly" each morning.

Friendship Chart

Week of _____

	Monday	Tuesday	Wednesday	Thursday	Friday	Weekend
Shared some time with						
I listened to						
I helped						
I asked someone about her/himself						
I found something I like about myself						

I am friendly.
Today I will smile and say hello to other people,
I will share myself and show interest in others.
I like myself and I know I can make new friends.

School-wide Activities

Community Service Project

Plan a service project for your community that involves the entire school. This is best if it comes from the students themselves. This is a significant opportunity for students to learn that through Idealism, Service and Unity, a small group of people can make a big difference.

Example of Excellence
"The Gift of Service"

This project was shared by Jan Maslyk, a teacher in Morinville, Alberta, Canada

"In June, Service was our last virtue for the year. Our practice of Service culminated with a school-wide effort to raise money and collect school supplies for a very poor special needs school of 54 students in Grenada, South America. The sister of a teacher in Grenada lives here in Morinville and she approached us just as we were looking for a final project! We talked to the teacher in Grenada over the intercom and all our students from Grades 1-5 listened as she described her wonderful students but just how poor they were and how they lacked even story books with all the pages in them. They had to color with little bits of wax crayons and write on every piece of paper or cardboard they could lay their hands on.

Our students were swept away with the gift of giving and raised $500.00 in two weeks and collected 52 boxes of books, school supplies, paints, and lots more! Further, what was also amazing was that I called a Canadian airline and they said yes to shipping $1700.00 worth of supplies for free! In this economic climate this is just about unheard of anymore. We were all very happy and in awe of how something good gives impetus to more 'goodness'. We will continue to phone and correspond with her this year."

Gem Tag Day

Every student, teacher and administrator wears a nametag in the shape of a gem with only their name on it. As the day goes on, people "catch each other committing virtues" and write the virtue they notice someone practicing on their gem tag. This builds self-esteem. Have students make one for their parents, siblings and household members and do the same for them.

Guest for the Day

Have a guest from the community come to speak to classes or at an assembly. A fire-fighter, police officer, artist, sports figure, musician, etc. Ask students to name the virtues they feel are essential to this person's success. Invite students to do this in the form of Virtues Acknowledgments to the guest. They will probably want to come back next year and do it again! Once in a while, have one of the teachers, a kitchen worker, or someone else who works in your school or program serve as the "guest speaker".

Career Day

When you have a day dedicated to learning about careers, have each guest speaker wear a gem-shaped name tag and speak about the virtues they need to do their jobs with excellence. Also, encourage teachers and students to fill the guest's gem tags with virtues they notice in them and the work they do.

The Virtues Club

Susan Lake, a board member and long time volunteer of The Boys & Girls Club of the Twin Cities, Minnesota, shares how they are applying The Virtues Project.

"Here is how we are incorporating The Virtues Project into the clubs in the Twin Cities. I cannot tell you what an exciting process this has been for me. To see it coming together is a dream come true!"

- When a child or youth (6 to 18 years old) joins a Boys & Girls Club (Cost $2.00 per year), the first step is an orientation tour for the child/youth and parent(s). They receive information on sports programs, Camp Voyager, Kaleidoscope Theater, Kids Cafe and, of course, The Virtues Program. Children choose which venues they want to participate in. If they choose to participate in The Virtues Program – and the parents are willing to support them – they will be given a copy of *The Family Virtues Guide* and a deck of Virtues Cards for home use. There is general participation in The Virtues Project by all staff and Club members. A Virtue of the Month poster is displayed in the club. The staff focuses on this Virtue all month applying the Five Virtues Strategies.

- For those children who voluntarily select The Virtues Program, a class is given once a week. The class size is limited to 20 and always has a waiting list. Our boundary is that if a participant misses two classes, they must return to the waiting list and someone on the waiting list is let in.

- Each child is given a "Virtues Passport". This IS the most important part of the program. It looks like a blue passport with their picture, and their date of "departure" (when they began the program). Children work on one virtue each month for a year. They have their passport "stamped", if they have completed their commitment, at the end of the month.

Program Steps are:

1. Each participant enlists four adults sponsors to observe and support them for the entire month (two from B&G Club, 2 from the community at large – minister, parent, teacher, coach, etc.)
2. Sponsors agree to observe the young person as much as possible during the month and encourage them to demonstrate the Virtue of the Month in every way.
3. Youth are presented with Virtues Tags they have earned, to be threaded on a "bathtub" chain and worn as a necklace. The tags are different shapes and colors with the virtues inscribed on them.
4. An Honors Banquet is held at the end of the year and every youth participating in The Virtues Program is recognized. Also their parent(s) are awarded a special Virtues Bracelet.

Character Trait of the Week

Write the virtue on the line below. Using a dictionary or Virtues Sheets, write the definition of the character trait:

_____

_____

_____

Fill in the blanks. Make your answers thoughtful! You may be asked to explain your choices. These will be shared in class. Do your best!

This virtue is _____.   *(Color)*

If it was a flower, it would be a _____.

It is a _____.   *(Animal)*

A time of day that reflects this virtue is _____.

When I think of this virtue, I think of _____.
                                             (Season)
It tastes like _____.

This virtue is _____

_____.   *(Your own idea)*

<u>Looks Like</u>   <u>Sounds Like</u>   <u>Feels Like</u>

Adapted from Toowoomba Anglican Academy, Australia and Citrus Heights District, California, U.S.A. (thanks to Jo Williams).

Chapter Summary:
Recognize Teachable Moments

✓ Connect virtues with academic lessons.

✓ Catch them doing it right. Notice and acknowledge efforts to improve.

✓ When a virtue is missing, call students to accountability. Ask tactfully "What virtue do you need?"

✓ Be a teacher, not a preacher. Invite respect by giving respect.

✓ Be a conscience maker, not a conscience breaker. Avoid habits that shame and humiliate. Use virtues, not labels.

✓ Use time out constructively by having students refocus on the virtue needed (the "Courtesy Corner", not the "Naughty Nook").

✓ Help children to learn which virtues balance each other: Truthfulness and Tact, Forgiveness and Justice, Compassion and Assertiveness.

✓ Recognize Teachable Moments with special needs students – it will empower them.

✓ Ask closure and integration questions at end of a lesson plan or the end of the day. "What did you appreciate most...?"

✓ Involve the family in focusing on virtues. Send home Virtues Vouchers and Hug Notes. Invite parents to make presentations on the Virtue of the Week.

3 Set Clear Boundaries

"The moral state of our children has become a national emergency."
Marion Wright Edelman,
Children's Defense Fund

Create a Safe Haven

What are teachers to do?

> ... when violence and heroism are merged in the images children see in films and television
> ... when the leading cause of death of youth aged 15 to 24 in North America is murder
> ... when students show flagrant disrespect to teachers
> ... when fights between students are life threatening
> ... when violence occurs unpredictably in peaceful rural towns.

Clear boundaries based on respect, peace, and justice are like a fence of **safety**, within which there is **freedom**. The virtues of peace, justice, respect, caring, kindness, gentleness and so on are the guideposts. The consequences are the wire and wood. A student who breaks through the boundary meets the consequences and is then **invited back** to the safety of the boundaries. **Establishing boundaries based on virtues** helps to create safe havens, where students feel free to learn and teachers feel free to teach.

If students don't feel safe, they are not free to learn. If teachers don't feel safe, they are not free to teach.

A Virtues Project school offers

Naming virtues, not shaming
Mentorship, not censorship
Reflection, not rejection
Restitution, not retribution

Fences of Safety

A middle school began the year without the fencing in place around the play ground. Teachers noticed that kids gravitated toward the middle of the yard, playing within a rather small radius. Once the fence went in they played throughout the yard. The boundary gave them a sense of safety. That is the main purpose for setting boundaries.

A Holistic Approach

The most holistic approach to preventing violence is to create a culture of character, an atmosphere of inclusive friendliness, mutual trust, caring, and kindness where these virtues are valued as much as academic achievement. Integral to a culture of caring is a disciplinary system based on peace and justice, focused not on retribution but restitution. The way authority is used – the leadership style of teachers and administrators – is the key in creating a culture of character.

An Educative Model of Authority

The Virtues Project teaches that authority should never be a power struggle, never be about dominance or people-pleasing. The core principle of virtues-based discipline is:

ALWAYS USE AUTHORITY IN *SERVICE* OF LEARNING.

The most empowering way to use authority is by seeing it as mentorship for learning. Authority can be used to help children develop virtues which are the life skills they need all their lives: Cooperation – getting along together; Justice – treating yourself and others fairly; Peacefulness – solving problems without violence; Kindness – treating each other in a caring way; Respect – everyone is valued.

Authority needs to be used to develop the gifts within, just as a good coach uses discipline to help an athlete develop all of his or her talents and strengths. The authority of a mentor is not abused in service of an adult's need to be in control. It is used to build champions.

The goal of effective authority is to enable children to develop their own inner authority, a sense of personal responsibility and accountability. It empowers them to make conscious moral choices.

Discipline as Transformation

Michael C. Seltz, Vice Principal of the Robert Frost Middle School in Livonia, Michigan shares a Virtues Project approach to discipline.

Frost has initiated a discipline program unlike any other in the District. Discipline is viewed here as a positive opportunity to teach behavior for living, not as punishment. The framework for this education are the virtues, including such frequently called upon character-builders as respect, obedience, self-discipline, detachment, honesty and responsibility.

Each incident that involves a discipline referral or report is typically channelled through my office. The framework for intervention involves first refocusing the student's energies away from a defensive posture and into self-reflection. The student is given an explanation of the missing or misapplied virtue that resulted in the office referral and then is encouraged to examine that particular virtue in depth.

Students are given packets which borrow heavily from Virtues Project materials. A paraprofessional is available to assist students in completing them.

The Virtues Packets:

1) Give the definition of the virtue in question (What is kindness?).

2) Ask the student to apply the virtue to a variety of situations (What would kindness look like if...?).

3) Invite the student to re-enact the situation which got them into trouble by correctly applying the virtue to the situation. This is done in writing.

4) Once the packet is complete, the student must then discuss the problem and solution with a counselor and parent.

5) All parties sign the completed packet.

6) Finally the student returns to whomever s/he has offended or hurt, or to the person who made the referral, and discusses the matter with them. At this point apologies and/or reparations are made, as directed by the Assistant Principal, with input from the offended staff member.

In serious or repeat behavioral matters, the Assistant Principal contacts parents by phone. The Language of Virtues again provides the framework for the discussion. Parental reaction has been notably more peaceful and less defensive using this approach. Suspensions were reduced last year by more than 40%.

Authority is Leadership

We have to give up being a pal who sometimes educates in order to be an educator who sometimes can be a pal.

The element which most shapes the culture or climate in a classroom is the *leadership style* of the teachers and administrators. Do they use their authority to overpower or to empower? Are they merely punitive or are they educative? If we are willing to accept the responsibility of *leadership as service*, we must sacrifice the wish for our students to like and agree with us at all times. A good coach doesn't consult an athlete about whether he feels up to a regimen of running every morning at five o'clock. A good coach takes the responsibility to take the athlete to the edge.

There is a lot of confusion among teachers about an appropriate way to use authority. It is almost a dirty word in some education circles, being associated with an outmoded *authoritarian* approach. In the educative model of authority, the boundaries are rules for living – not mere retaliations or punishments.

Don't put kids down. Lift them up.

"Don't lock them up. Lift them up."
Jesse Jackson

The language of virtues is specific, clear, and most important of all, easily internalized. It builds authentic self-esteem without over-dependence on approval. General terms, even when they are positive, do not hit the mark. Terms such as "Good girl," "That's a boy," "Good on you," "Great job," are too general for students to internalize. These terms promote people-pleasing as they only indicate that you are pleased with the student, without giving them any specific information about what they did that was "excellent", "helpful" or "creative". Giving a specific virtues acknowledgment is different than making general statements of praise which can create guilt. It is not helpful to label a child in any way, positive or negative. We don't say: "You're such a kind boy". We say "It was kind of you to show our new student where to sit. I'm sure it made him feel welcome."

Dominance taken to the extreme is cruelty masquerading as authority.

Authority as Abuse

I remember a third grade teacher whom we all called "Mrs. Axe". On the first day of school each year, she would spot the unsuspecting sibling of one of last year's "worst behaved" students, drag the poor child to the front of the classroom by the scruff of his or her neck and say "I had your brother in here last year. He was a holy terror. I put him in his place and made his life miserable, and I'm putting you in your place right now! Get up to the front where I can watch you." What injustice, prejudice and abuse. What negativity!

Authority used harshly does not show students what we DO want them to do, only models violence to them. Some schools around the world continue the practice of caning and humiliating children for not giving correct answers.

Old Men with Big Ears

In Fiji, The Virtues Project is being taught in many villages. In one village, during a Virtues workshop, a group of elders were asked to draw self-portraits of themselves as children. They all drew stick figures with large ears. The facilitator noted that they did indeed have quite pendulous ear lobes. "What does this depict?" the facilitator asked. The elders replied, "When we were small, our ears were pulled so fiercely and so often that they are quite oversized." There was laughter at that moment, but later, an elder began to weep and said, "How I wish I could raise my children over again, with the virtues instead of violence. All they really need is clear boundaries."

"We love working with virtues in our school. Most people believe the only way to respond to middle school students is with Gestapo tactics."
Tammy Goff, 5th grade teacher, Missouri City, Texas

A classroom without boundaries is a leaderless group.

In other places, the pendulum has swung to passivity, or the over-democratization of the classroom, where students are given too much freedom, with frequent arguments occurring and teachers unwilling to set limits, unaware of how helpful the exercise of their authority would be.

A student without boundaries is like a person without a job description.

The energy has nowhere to direct itself. Most students want to do a good job, be a "good" student, but without clear expectations or boundaries are uncertain what that looks like. Can you imagine showing up for a new job one day and the boss says, "Do a good job." and then leaves, without filling you in on what a good job would look like?

If there is a lack of clear, just and loving authority in the classroom, kids will BECOME the authority.

Many schools have found that boundaries based on virtues call deeply to the students' spirit, including the "tough" ones. They show remarkable willingness to follow the rules when there is no shaming in the classroom but rather the naming of virtues like respect, consideration, peacefulness, and caring. The best results are achieved not when authority is repudiated but when it is used in light of its true purpose – to create a safe, orderly place to learn.

What is Your Leadership Style?

One way to view authority and leadership is on a continuum of effectiveness from the least effective to the most effective.

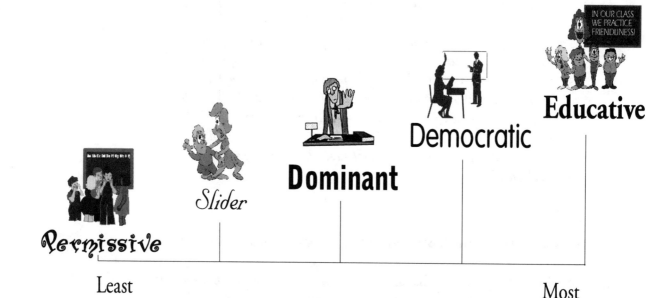

Least   Most

What elements of the following describe your style? What do you want to keep? What do you want to change?

Permissive Pal

- It is important to me to be a friend to my students.
- I often have difficulty getting students' attention.
- I go with the flow and prefer not to have class rules.
- I don't often structure my lesson plans or daily schedule.
- I often feel behind and overwhelmed.
- I resort to videos or films to distract the students when they get restless.
- I sometimes have to call in a Dominant Dictator to restore peace.

Intent: To be a pal to students, to maintain spontaneity, fun and creativity.

Main Refrain: "What do *you* want to do?

Results: Chaos reigns. Classroom tends to be noisy, messy, a difficult place to learn, over-stimulating to both teacher and student. Teacher and students get irritable and exhausted.

Leading Virtues: Kindness, Friendliness

Challenge Virtues: Assertiveness, Orderliness

Side-stepping Slider

- I start off permissive but slide to dominance when things get out-of-hand.
- I have no consistent approach to discipline.
- I sometimes feel controlled and tyrannized by students.
- I feel angry when students abuse the freedom I give them.
- There is chaos in my classroom most of the time.
- I often feel hurt and misunderstood.
- I often feel my class is out-of-control.
- I resist being too authoritarian.

Intent: To protect students' self-esteem; to be loved and valued by students. To prevent oppressive methods of discipline.

Main Refrain: "I don't understand why you kids can't behave!"

Results: Classroom is often disorderly and chaotic, students are disrespectful. An atmosphere of frequent stress, especially for students with learning challenges.

Leading Virtues: Gentleness, Kindness, Love

Challenge Virtues: Confidence, Assertiveness, Orderliness

Dominant Dictator

- Control is my goal.
- Criticism is my method.
- I am often sarcastic. "If you can't remember to bring your homework, then you can't remember to eat your lunch."
- I sometimes resort to physical force.
- I Frame, Shame and Blame students. "Listen, Bozo, if you have better things to do, maybe you ought to go do them."
- I use punishments and suspensions frequently.

Intent: To maintain control. To maintain high standards of excellence.

Main Refrain: "Because I said so."

Results: While there may be more quiet and stability in your classroom than some others, there is also a constant tension in your relationships with students. You have to continually accelerate your punishments to keep an upper hand. You feel exhausted. They resent you and you resent them. You often fantasize about a different line of work.

Leading Virtues: Orderliness, Excellence

Challenge Virtues: Respect, Kindness, Trust, Assertiveness without bullying.

Democratic Diplomat

- I consult students about every decision.
- I give choices without boundaries.
- Sometimes my students seem overloaded by choice and responsibility.
- There are frequent debates and arguments, but isn't that healthy?
- There is sometimes too much talking in my classroom.
- Tasks often take too long and sometimes don't get done.

Intent: To show justice and equality above all; to empower students to think for themselves.

Main Refrain: "What do you think?"

Results: Equality at the cost of effectiveness and efficiency. Classroom is animated and engaging, Students learn to think for themselves and resolve conflict equitably. However, students sometimes feel anxious without sufficient structure or authority. Learning and curriculum content is sometimes short-changed.

Leading Virtues: Justice, Creativity

Challenge Virtues: Assertiveness, Orderliness, Moderation

Empowering Educator

- I focus on virtues to remedy any conflict or behavior problem. "How can you express your anger peacefully?"
- Our class boundaries are clearly posted on the wall.
- I give choices within boundaries.
- I give immediate consequences if boundaries are violated.
- I always call "perpetrators" back to the virtue after a consequence. "Are you ready to be peaceful now?"
- Most of the time I am able to balance caring and assertiveness.
- I show love and respect to my students.
- I expect respect at all times.

Intent: To permit freedom within boundaries, to create an orderly, joyful place of learning. To focus on the Teachable Moment and the child's capacity for character development.

Main Refrain: "What virtue do we need to call on?"

Results: Peaceful sense of relaxed order, enthusiasm in students and teacher, strong bond of affection between teacher and students and among students.

Leading Virtues: Confidence, Assertiveness, Kindness, Enthusiasm

Challenge Virtues: Determination to remain consistent in enforcing consequences of boundaries. Assertiveness about non-negotiables.

Establish Restorative Justice by Listening

When a child comes to you complaining of an injustice, listen. Restorative justice can be in the form of a brief intervention.

When a teacher or administrator identifies the virtues needed in a disciplinary situation, they are instantly helping to focus the student's awareness on *meaning* and *mastery*. What did the students' action mean? What was the meaning or intent behind their behavior? They always have a reason, and at times that reason needs to be heard *before* you can redirect them to a virtue they could have used to replace helpless anger or attention-seeking behavior. What virtue could the student have called on? Refocusing the student on the virtue is a non-shaming, empowering way to structure any disciplinary action.

"Unless restitution comes from inside the person it will not heal."
Diane Gossen, Founder of Making It Right

Example of Excellence
Listen First

Ray Tufts of the Renton Alternative School, Renton, Washington worked with some challenging students, among them high school drop-outs, gang members, and drug dealers.

When a fight broke out or a student was sent to his office for discipline, first he would say "I want to hear what happened, from your point of view." He listened. He reflected the feelings expressed. "So you were really angry when John stole your homework. Then you pounded him." Then, he would look up at the Virtues Poster and say, "What virtue could you have used to stay out of trouble? To handle that situation better?" "I guess I forgot peacefulness." "Yes, exactly. So, how could you have handled it peacefully and also been assertive in standing up for your rights?" "I could have..." The student would come up with a new idea based on the virtues and Ray would say, "Let's see how peaceful and assertive you can be the rest of today. And what do you need to do to make it up with John? What do you need from John?"

In this manner, students were able to master their inner gifts, learn to practice virtues and restore justice. The discipline problems at the school were reduced by more than half.

Teaching Tip

Don't tell them what to do, ask them how they want to be.

Example: Not "George, share those blocks with Jose." but "George and Jose, how can you play fairly with those blocks?" This is how you awaken the child's integrity, generosity, and confidence, not by giving quick solutions to problems but by inviting them to find virtues-based solutions.

Restitution, Not Retribution

"It is better to look for long term solutions than just remove the offender from the situation."
Diane Gossen

True discipline happens inside out instead of outside in. Children already have goodness – the virtues – within them. It does not have to be imposed from without – it can be awakened from within. Instead of using coercion and force, a teacher or counselor who expresses clear, firm expectations based on virtues will see excellent results. This approach builds self-esteem while eliminating and healing aggressive or disrespectful behavior.

The purpose of virtues-based discipline is restorative justice, not retributive justice. In retributive justice the teacher or administrator is a *detective* asking:
- What was the crime?
- Who did it?
- How should they be punished?

In restorative justice, the teacher or administrator is a *mentor* asking:
- What happened?
- Who was hurt? (including the perpetrator)
- What do they need?

Teaching Tip

Use your vision statement as a reference point for discipline. (see Chapter 4 for how to create a vision statement)

Example: Ask "What do we believe at our school about how teachers are treated?" " ...about how we treat each other?" "What would respect sound like (look like, feel like) in this situation?"

For full restitution to be made, the questions to be asked are:
- What virtue could have been practiced?
- What amends can be made?

(See the dialogues in Chapter 5 on Spiritual Companioning in conflict resolution.)

Restorative justice is a process which challenges us to reevaluate some traditional ways of handling discipline. These definitions may help to make the distinction between traditional retribution and the restorative justice approach:

- Retribution: to pay back, especially to punish.

- Reparation: to make amends, to compensate for something lost.

- Responsibility: to respond ably, to be accountable.

- Restitution: to give back something that has been lost or taken, to restore, to reimburse.

- Restoration: to give back, to restore health and consciousness, to rebuild.

- Reconciliation: to make friendly again, to settle a quarrel, to make content.

Many schools focus only on retribution, the one principle that does not restore justice, either to the offender or the victim of an offense.

In the ideal process of restorative justice, students:

1. Take responsibility for what they do in order to...

2. Make restitution which results in...

3. Reconciliation, which is to make friends again, which...

4. Restores the relationship and restores the offender to the community.

Forgiveness alone is not enough. Justice requires that there be some amends, fixing of the problem, with the offender taking responsibility instead of merely being punished. In the ideal situation, there is also reconciliation, restoring of friendship and contentment on all sides with the outcome.

> *"Restorative justice is much more than just forgiveness and redemption. It also involves reconciliation and the reparation of damaged relationships – relationships between victims, offenders and the community."*
> Evan Evans (serving time in prison for bank robbery and murder)

Example of Excellence
Restitution Works

Jeff Grumley, a restitution counselor, works with a large inner city school in Illinois.

He found in one large school that with the introduction of restorative justice in the discipline system, there was drop of discipline referrals from 4076 to 2438: 40% within two years! Academic performance rose 20% in those classrooms where the preventive approach of restitution was used by teachers over those that did not use it in their classroom management approach. As discipline problems decrease, learning increases. Jeff says: "Even though students had already received a consequence before I met with them the first year, over 95% students chose to 'make it right' and repair the damaged relationship with their teachers without any extrinsic motivation. There was no need to dangle a carrot in front of students like reduced suspension time as an incentive to mend broken relationships with their teachers and peers. Values or beliefs do not have to be implanted."

10 Guidelines for Establishing Clear Boundaries

The following virtues-based guidelines for setting boundaries are helping schools in many communities and cultures to significantly reduce discipline problems and aggression, at the same time creating a climate of kindness, gentleness, safety and self-esteem. One of the things needed in a discipline system based on Restorative Justice is some clear ground rules, including the "bottom line behaviors" which will not be tolerated in your school. Having these ground rules in place is an important way to create a safe haven.

1. Be Moderate

Pay attention to Prevention

Choose a few ground rules and make them stick. There should be no more than three to five. Your school Vision is your guiding light. Your boundaries are the behaviors that support those principles and include the bottom line behaviors that are not acceptable. Long lists of rules are too hard to learn and memorize. Keep your list of boundaries short and also measurable. For example,

Our School Vision: We show respect for ourselves and others by treating people, feelings, and things with respect. Together we stay safe.

Our School Rules: We have zero tolerance for:

1. Drugs and alcohol on our premises.
2. Damage to property.
3. Rough play, threats, harassment, weapons or anything resembling weapons.
4. Leaving school grounds without permission.
5. Throwing rocks or any other harmful object.

2. Be Specific

The ground rules for your classroom need to be relevant to your specific expectations. The rules for your school should be specific to the needs of your particular population, based on behaviors you see and the behaviors you want to see.

Leave Your Gang Identity at the Door

An inner city Boys & Girls Club in Minnesota has a boundary about leaving gang identity at the door so that within the program, everyone is united on a level playing field. Sheila Oehrlein, Club Director explains:

"The rule about hats varies at each of the clubs. One of the clubs has a ban on hats altogether. In the other two clubs, hats may be worn, but only if the bill of the hat is worn straight - back or forward. They cannot be worn cocked to either side. Hats, as well as bandannas (or 'rags' as they are commonly called) can be worn to indicate gang affiliation. By wearing a hat of a certain color, with the bill facing left or right, members can indicate which gang they belong to. They can do the same by rolling up a pant leg, which we also do not allow. We do not exclude known gang members from participating at the club, but we prohibit them from 'representing' their gang affiliations. The club is neutral territory, and cannot be claimed or marked as belonging to any one group or gang.

Members wearing their hats, pants, rags etc. inappropriately are asked to straighten the hat, remove the rag, or roll down the pant leg. If they refuse, they are asked to leave. Sometimes, we hold the item (hat or rag) until the end of the day if the member "forgets" and we have to ask her/him more than once or twice in a day."

3. Be Positive. Base Rules on Virtues

Avoid expressing rules in the negative. In your daily interactions, guide children to what you DO want them to do instead of warning them about what you DON'T want them to do. "Don'ts" put ideas in their heads!

Focus awareness on the virtues in your Vision Statement (See Chapter 4), which is your shared commitment to how you want to treat one another.

Positive rules DO help	_Negative rules DON'T help_
BE CONSIDERATE. Walk in the halls.	No running in the halls.
BE KIND to people, feelings and things.	No hurting people, feelings or things.
BE RESPECTFUL in actions and words.	No talking back to teachers or cursing.
BE CAREFUL. Stay safe.	No unsafe behavior.
WE ARE PEACEMAKERS. We use words instead of fists.	No fighting.

4. Give Specific, Relevant Consequences

"...let the punishment fit the crime."
William Gilbert

When a bottom line negative behavior occurs, that is a time to bring in a consequence. Make sure that whatever consequence occurs is very specific and *fitting* to the offense. It is best if the consequence is in the form of amends, chosen by the student. For example, if someone puts gum under their desk, they are violating "Respect for things." Ask them how they feel it would be fair to make amends. (e.g. Check for gum under all the desks in the class and clean it off?) Be sure it is fair and in proportion to the "crime". Children tend to come up with overly harsh and punitive amends for themselves, so be sure they are being fair to themselves. Here are some examples of amends that are fitting and fair:

- Destruction of property - replacement of property.
- Punching – apology and doing a service for the person.
- Dropping someone's lunch on the floor – giving up one's own lunch.
- Leaving school grounds – buddy to accompany for two days.

Serious infractions of school boundaries need to have pre-determined consequences such as:

- Time with the Assistant Principal.
- Notification of parents.
- Suspension, either in school or out of school with a plan for mentorship and restoration such as described above (page 59) in Frost Middle School.

5. Use Consequences which are Educative, not Punitive: Restorative, not Retributive

"If the child isn't stronger by the amends that they make, it isn't restitution."
Diane Gossen

The goal of correction is to restore justice and to restore the child to the community or to the group, to repair the relationship, not isolate the perpetrator, to build character in the long term, not just get rid of the problem and the perpetrator.

Transformational Time Out: Replace the "Naughty Chair" with the Courtesy Corner. Focus on Time Out as a recovery in order to rejoin the group and recover their courtesy, respect, cooperation or whatever virtue they have momentarily forgotten or failed to practice.

Give Restorative Suspensions: When an in-school suspension is called for, give them a copy of the virtue they needed (from Section 2) and have them retell or rewrite how the event would have gone if they had practiced the virtue.

When an out of school suspension is needed, in addition to any legal steps that are necessary, offer the following:

- Provide a volunteer mentor to work with the individual who will:
  Do a "Virtues Pick".
  Do a Virtues Integrity Profile with the individual to assess their strength virtues and their challenge virtues.
  Help the student to make a plan for reparation.
- Student then returns to school with plan in hand.

> *"Central to the process of transformation and reconciliation is the relationship between victim, offender, and community."*
> Michael Hadley, Ph.D.

Example of Excellence
"I See You"

Alexina Keeling of Cleburne, Texas, to whom this book is dedicated, was a volunteer whom the principal of the school called on to mentor students when they were suspended from school. Alexina met with them, spoke to them of their innate virtues. She would always say "Do you know who you really are? You have many gifts inside." She would do Virtues Picks with them, read to them from *The Family Virtues Guide*, and help them work through how they could make amends. These boys had served time in jail in the past and were pretty hopeless before they met Alexina. After meeting with her they would come back to school restored and ready to restore justice to those they had offended. She made a big difference to youth with her service and encouragement.

---

6. Be Consistent

Assume that children will test the limits, sometimes forget the rules, or just be having a bad day. Regardless of the reason for the lapse, trustworthiness demands that the bottom line rules be automatically enforced. This is not a time for mercy, but justice. Students will only trust those rules that are constant and consistent. So, only make bottom line rules you can enforce.

Make reinforcement of the Vision and its boundaries a number one priority, particularly at the beginning of the school year. Bring parents and community members in as volunteers to help enforce boundaries during recess and in large classes.

7. Communicate Rules Clearly

Post the Boundaries and make sure that parents receive a copy. Use visuals as "noetic integrators" – the integration of meaning. Use humor. One test of effective rules is, how easy are they to memorize? Clever sayings or rhymes will help, such as, "On time every time." "We dare to care."

- Have a student handbook which has the school vision on an opening page, and gives the bottom line rules and consequences.
- When introducing the rules at the beginning of the year, remember to keep them short, sweet, and positive – focused on the virtues.
- After students have consulted on the shared vision, post it in hallways and common areas.
- Have students create posters with the vision statement.
- Ask students reminder questions, especially at the beginning of the school year.
    "When the bell rings, what do we do?" (We gather our things and get ready to leave.)
    "What virtues do we practice?" (Orderliness and courtesy.)

8. When Students Receive Consequences, Be Sure They Understand the Reason.

After a time out in the Courtesy Corner, always call them back to the virtue which lapsed. "What is a friendly, respectful way you could have gotten Mary's attention?" "Are you ready to be respectful now?" "Are you ready to play peacefully now?" "What will you do to make amends to Mary?" "I know you can do it." This tells them they belong in the group.

Reflection, not Rejection

Following a suspension, ask the student "What was your Teachable Moment in this situation?"(what did they learn), "What virtue did you need?" and then ask them to present their plan for restitution. This is NOT the time for a lecturette on why they should practice the virtue that was originally violated. It is a time to companion them about what they have learned, and to respectfully hear how they plan to make amends.

Boundaries Based on Virtues

Winnie Ponga teaches Japanese to young teenagers. She found she was needing to give detention to some youngsters because of their behavior. She remembered the process described in *The Family Virtues Guide* about what to do when children have received a consequence. She first would ask the children to tell her why they were in detention. Then she showed them the Virtues Poster and talked about how each person has virtues within them.

She asked the children to write on a piece of paper some virtues they saw inthemselves. Then she asked them what they thought they might do differently in class the next day so that they would not have to have detention again. They could talk about it first then write it down.

Finally, the children were asked to choose which virtues they would need the next day to help them. Winnie had excellent results in working with the children this way. The depth of understanding and ability to choose which virtues the children saw they would need was surprising. They chose Trust, Friendliness, Confidence rather than things like Responsibility, Peacefulness or Self-discipline. Winnie notes how important it is to acknowledge the children the next time they show effort in changing their behavior.

9. Make Bottom Line Rules Non-Negotiable

Ground Rules are your bottom line. They must be things that are non-negotiable so that everyone is clear that there is zero tolerance for them. Be sure to think about this before you make something a rule.

Example: Post only the positive Vision Statement on school walls. "Our school is a peace zone. We use peaceful language and work out problems peacefully." Also, send home a newsletter and give students a sheet called "Our Bottom Line" or "Boundaries Supporting Our Vision" which, as briefly as possible, list the behaviors that will not be permitted to breach school safety and integrity, such as making threats, carrying weapons, or destruction of property. Explain the consequences for infringement of the ground rules.

Example of Excellence

High Standards at Harlem Academy

Edward and Ann Carpenter had a dream of giving some real education to kids in the ghettos of New York. They began Harlem Academy. They recruited from the kids on the street, whom they called "5 per centers" because they had a 5% chance of making it to their 21st birthdays. They were drug dealers, gang members, prostitutes, into every kind of crime. The private school was funded and so enrollment cost nothing in terms of dollars. The cost of enrollment was willingness to commit 100% to the boundaries of the school, which included:

Cleanliness – Come dressed clean. Be clean and sober. Zero tolerance for drug usage in our school.
Reliability – On time every time.
Peacefulness –We are on each other's side. This school is a violence-free zone.

The Carpenters and their teachers did not hesitate to enforce the boundaries which were non-negotiable and whose consequences were immediate suspension or expulsion. Students learned quickly that the boundaries stuck. Those who remained, were on fire with commitment to the school and enthusiasm for what they were learning. Harlem Academy had 98% success rate in their students going on to a university. They taught history from the perspective of indigenous peoples, including feats of black individuals often left out of history books, helped students learn about their own cultural heritage, developed fierce pride and loyalty and awareness that there were options other than life on the street. The clarity of the boundaries was a major ingredient in the success of this project.

10. Make Your Expectations Clear

Practice the virtue of assertiveness in day-to-day interactions by:

1) Making your personal boundaries clear.
   "I will listen to whatever you have to say if you say it respectfully."

2) Making decisions without pressure.
   When you are undecided, take your time. "I'll think about it and let you know."

3) Giving consent within boundaries.

Say "Yes, if…" If, for example, students ask for a pizza party, rather than thinking to yourself "I'm already overloaded. I just don't have the time or energy for this," you can take some time to consider it and then say "Yes, if…You turn all your homework in on time for a week, I don't have to do the work, you raise the money for it, you organize the volunteers, it is on a Friday afternoon."

4) Using quick, gentle, *pre-agreed* ways to call students to attention.

You can waste a lot of breath yelling for them to be quiet or you can arrange a pre-agreed signal that whenever they see or hear it, they are to immediately "freeze", become silent, and turn their attention to you. Some ways to do this are:

    Ringing a chime or bell
    Playing music
    Raising your arm in the air (as soon as they see it they are to do the same)

When they are first learning the signal, acknowledge those that do it quickly for their excellence, cooperation or respect.

5) Acknowledging the cooperation of those who respond positively to a boundary.

When you have given the class a direction, such as bringing their attention back to you, acknowledge those who respond first – "Excellent cooperation, Maria, Karen, James. You're looking right at me." This is more effective than paying attention to those who have not yet responded – "Frederick, didn't you hear me? Stop what you're doing and pay attention."

6) Putting your regular expectations into clear boundaries.

If there are definite times you want complete silence, for example, tell them when those times are and have a signal for it, such as a sign you put up. Make sure to be moderate about this because noise and talking is a creative part of learning. Whatever matters to you, you are the manager of the classroom. Communicate your boundaries clearly and students will cooperate.

Taking Care of Materials

Radha, a Virtues Project facilitator and renowned composer of children's songs in New Zealand, has come up with excellent examples of how to set specific boundaries in the context of what children are doing:

<u>Books</u>

> 1) We take care of the books, so the pages are not ripped.
> 2) We keep the books clean – safe from drinks, paint, crayons, etc.
> 3) We return the books to the agreed area (shelf, mattress, etc.).
> 4) We share the books, and let others see the pictures.

<u>We practice Responsibility!</u>

<u>Examples of Virtues to Look for and Acknowledge in our Children</u>

> Gentleness – "You're being gentle with the books!"
> Orderliness – "Good! That was orderly of you to put the books away in such a neat order."
> Consideration – "That was considerate of you to move over so Alex could see the pictures!"
> Peacefulness – "I could see how peaceful and quiet you were during the story."

<u>Play Dough</u>

> 1) We keep the dough off the floor and in the right areas (table, play-stove, etc.).
> 2) We use our own dough, not taking other people's.
> 3) We keep the dough clean.
> 4) We respect our health by not eating the dough.

<u>We are respectful!</u>

<u>Examples of Virtues to Look for and Acknowledge in our Children</u>

> Cleanliness – "You're keeping the floor clean keeping the dough on the table and your hands clean by washing them after!"
> Creativity – "You are being creative with your play-dough, making something a new way!"
> Forgiveness – "That was forgiving of you to pardon John when he took some of your dough!"
> Patience – "I can see you're being very patient waiting for a turn with the dough."

Find the Natural Boundary

Safety Line

When I was teaching adults at a summer family conference center in Alberta, Canada, the word was spread that a moose and her calf were in the meadow. All the children came pouring out of their classes to see them. Moose can be dangerous, and like any animal, are especially prone to attack or trample anyone who gets near a calf. Teachers were yelling, "Don't get too close." While the children were stampeding closer and closer to the meadow, I looked around for a natural boundary and noticed the mown part of the grass just at the edge of the meadow. I called out twice: "Stop at the edge of the grass. Stay safe." I ran to the edge of the grass myself and lay down on my stomach to look at the moose. All the children did the same. Not one child stepped a foot over the boundary. It was quite a sight, too, watching the moose grazing on grass and low tree branches. They danced and pranced away on their delicate legs. Then, of course, I took the opportunity to acknowledge the children: "You were really respectful of the boundary and of the moose."

Keep Class Size Manageable

If possible have small classes. One of the general boundaries which is meeting with success is to have smaller school units and **smaller classes** so that teachers can get to know the children individually. This allows the teacher to have the energy to respond in empowering ways to them because they are not lost in a sea of faces. Nothing succeeds like a caring relationship between teachers and students.

"It don't mean a thing if it ain't got that swing."
Duke Ellington & Irving Mills

Discipline with Virtues is a Piece of CAKE!

There are many virtues a teacher needs to model each day in order to awaken those virtues within his students, and just for the sake of practicing them himself. Tact, respect, love, and creativity go a long way. The virtues are at the heart of good discipline.

The 4 ingredients that make DISCIPLINE a piece of CAKE!

C onfidence in using your authority in a mentoring way.
A ssertiveness in establishing your ground rules.
K indness in the way you treat students.
E nthusiasm for who and what you are teaching.

Activities

Discuss Assertiveness

Read the virtue, then discuss ways students can be assertive at school and at home. Distinguish between Aggression, Passivity and Assertiveness as explained in the virtue of Assertiveness in Section 2.

Discuss Stranger Danger

- What are some of our boundaries that keep us safe?
- What would you do if a stranger drives to school and invites you to get in his or her car?
- Who would you tell?
- How can you protect yourself from strangers on the Internet?

Vision and Boundaries Posters

Each classroom may have specific boundaries. Each teacher is free to set his or her own. Get creative with the rules by involving students in designing a border for the boundaries list. This gives them ownership. It is also helpful to have students create simple posters with your Vision Statement, to be prominently displayed. In fact, you may want to keep them focused on the positive by just posting your Vision Statement.

Restitution Fits My Mistake

Mark each restitution that fits the person's mistake with the word "Yes". Mark "No" if it does not fit. Remember restitution tries to put things back the way they were or better. If that is not possible, it tries to repair the need violated. Also, it helps the person get stronger in their area of weakness. Then write the virtue that was needed beside each example.

Action	Yes or No	Virtue Needed
1. I said a bad word so I will pick up the garbage. *(Does it fit?)*	——	————
2. I stepped on the plants so I will plant new ones. *(Does it fit?)*	——	————
3. I ripped up her paper decoration so I will give her mine and make a new one. *(Does it fit?)*	——	————
4. I pushed him so I will give him candy. *(Does it fit?)*	——	————
5. I took the teacher's time so I will help her in her room. *(Does it fit?)*	——	————
6. I took his pencil so I will clean the chalk board. *(Does it fit?)*	——	————
7. I took their ball at recess and ended the game. Tomorrow I will follow the rules. *(Does it fit?)*	——	————
8. I crashed into him on my bike so I will help setup bike safety week. *(Does it fit?)*	——	————

Adapted with permission from Restitution for Teens Video Guide Book by Diane Gossen. (See Resources)

Create a Peace Zone in Your Classroom for Solving Conflict

Use a special mat large enough for two or more to sit in a circle and have "Peace Talks". Put up a sign where the mat is located; "Peace Speaks" or "Peace Place". Teach children how to solve problems by focusing on the virtue involved, with both children taking turns. Put up a sign like this one:

Peace Place

1. Take turns *truthfully* telling your experience of what happened.
2. Listen *respectfully* to the other person's view.
3. Share how you *honestly* felt.
4. *Creatively* find a virtue you each need.
5. Use *Justice* and *Forgiveness* to decide what amends need to be made.
6. Practice *Commitment* to decide how to do it differently next time.

Congratulations! You have solved a problem *Peacefully*!

Class Clean-Up

- Keep a neat, orderly and pleasing classroom – it calms the mind and soothes the spirit.
- Have students create visuals or posters of a Vision Statement and the Boundaries. Hang in an open spot.

Send Home Virtues Vouchers and Hug Notes

Reward Effort and Improvement. Award special privileges to both those who excel in a particular virtue and those who show the most change and effort. You want to be fair and just to both the naturally excelling students and those for whom any improvement is a big effort.

School-wide Activities

Communicate Boundaries Clearly

1. Send home both the Vision Statement (next chapter) and the boundaries of your school in a bulletin or other form. Tell parents how important they are as helpers and mentors in keeping school a safe and enjoyable learning environment.

2. Sponsor a slogan contest reflecting your Vision Statement and Boundaries.

3. In a school assembly, have students do skits based on the School Rules.

Create Peace Squads

Set up Peace Squads of responsible students to keep the peace and detect and intervene in any conflict or roughhousing that occurs. Identify peacekeepers with a sash or a jacket so that other students can call on them when in trouble.

Example of Excellence
Kids Helping Kids

Brentwood Bay Elementary School in British Columbia, Canada has a peacekeepers group called "Ambassadors" who wear yellow jackets with the name "Ambassadors" on them. When any child feels picked on or in need of help, after they have used their "WIT" – 1) Walked away or 2) Ignored the aggressor, or 3) Tried to Talk it out, and the aggression persists, they call for one of the Ambassadors. The boundary for ambassadors is that if physical violence is involved, they obtain the help of an adult to intervene.

Carol Kenway, coordinator of the program, explains that this goes beyond a role of conflict management. "Our kids are really good at inclusion. If they see a student who is alone, they get games going, or invite them to just 'hang out' with them. They are wonderful with our special needs students as well."

Chapter Summary:
Set Clear Boundaries

✓ Base your discipline system on restorative justice.
✓ Always use authority in service of learning.
✓ See your authority as leadership and be aware of your own leadership style.
✓ Establish restorative justice by listening.
✓ Make virtues the reference point for discipline.
✓ When you set boundaries:

- Be moderate – have only four or five rules.
- Be specific – focus on the behaviors specific to your situation.
- Be positive – base rules on virtues and word them positively when you can.
- Give specific, relevant consequences for bottom line behaviors.
- Use consequences that are educative – not punitive; restorative – not retributive.
- Be consistent.
- Communicate rules clearly.
- When students receive a consequence, be sure they understand the virtue involved.
- Make bottom line rules non-negotiable.
- Be assertive in making your expectations clear.

✓ Find the natural boundary.
✓ Keep class size manageable.
✓ Create student Peace Squads to keep your school safe.

4 Honor the Spirit

"When I discover my 'why' to live, then my 'how' to live will just naturally follow."
Jim Paluch, Author

 ## Inspiring School Spirit

The word "spiritual" is now included in many education mandates as one of the aspects of a child's needs. Among the definitions of "spirit" in Webster's New World Dictionary is "essential quality", "animating principle", "life, will, thought." It defines school spirit as "enthusiastic loyalty". Other useful ways to think of "spiritual" in the context of education is that which pertains to:

- a sense of meaning and purpose
- beliefs and values
- mastery of the virtues in our character.

This chapter offers several ways to enhance school spirit and specific methods for addressing the spiritual needs of children in an inclusive and unifying way. In this multi-cultural world, focusing on virtues is a respectful way to address **meaning** and the **mastery** of character, which are basic elements of spirituality. Virtues give us a common language for addressing the spiritual dimension. This is essential in a pluralistic society in which children may or may not be religious, and if religious, are likely to be of different religions. Religion is a specific code or system of belief. Values are things we think are important and tend to be culture-specific. Virtues are universally valued by all cultures.

The most empowering way to create a safe, caring, respectful learning environment is not only to require it but to **inspire** it. We can inspire meaning and mastery as well as "enthusiastic loyalty" to our school or organization in many ways such as:

1. Seeing the potential virtues in all children
2. Creating shared Vision Statements
3. Modeling the virtues we expect children to practice
4. Sharing stories, which are the keepers of meaning
5. Focusing on virtues in the arts
6. Having ceremonies to mark beginnings, endings and special times.

See the Potential

"The wholly functioning human being seeks meaning in terms of his fellow human beings, but he does not find this meaning unless and until he learns to treat other humans with concern and respect." G. E. Rennie, Principal, Discovery School, Campbell River, BC, Canada

In speaking the Language of Virtues and finding the Teachable Moments each day, we are Honoring the Spirit in our students. The only thing which allows us to do those things is our willingness to look at every child in terms of their potential.

Example of Excellence
See the Potential

Dr. Magdalene Carney, in her early years as an educator, was assigned to an inner city classroom in Detroit in the middle of the year. All the principal told her was that the former teacher had left suddenly, and that this was a class of "special" students. She walked in on bedlam, spitballs flying through the air, feet on desks, the noise deafening. She walked to the front of the class-room and opened the attendance book. She looked down the list of names and saw beside them numbers from 140 to 160. "Oh," she thought to herself. "No wonder they are so high-spirited. These children have exceptional IQs." She smiled and brought them to order.

At first, the students failed to turn in work. Assignments that were handed in were done hastily and sloppily. She began to speak to them about their innate excellence, their giftedness, telling them that she expected nothing short of the best work from them. She kept reminding them of their responsibility to use all the extra intelligence they had been given. Things began to change. The children sat up tall, they worked diligently. Their work was creative, precise, original. One day, the principal was walking by and happened to look into the classroom. He observed students in rapt attention, composing essays. Later, he called Mag into his office.

"What have you done to these kids?" he asked. "Their work has surpassed all the regular grades." "Well, what do you expect? They're gifted, aren't they?" "Gifted?! They're the special-needs students – behavior disordered and retarded." "Then why are their IQs so high on the attendance sheet?" "Those aren't their IQs. Those are their locker numbers!" "Whatever," said Mag.

Create a Shared Vision Statement

One of the best ways to inspire true school spirit and high morale is to give children ownership in the school or class Vision Statement. This is done by involving them in shaping the vision. A classroom which has taken the time to form a **shared vision** of the virtues they choose to live by has a frame of reference – and a frame of "reverence" – for what is truly valued by the group itself.

1) Ask your class to consult together or form small groups to share the beliefs in their families about how people ought to treat each other. Write them down.

2) Ask them: how do we want to treat each other in our school?

3) Brainstorm the main themes or virtues of these beliefs and list on a board. e.g., "We respect each other." "We care about each other." "We play fair."

4) Ask the class to identify up to four virtues which capture their main beliefs about how we want to act toward one another in this class.

5) Create a <u>simple</u> sentence incorporating these virtues. Make sure all agree that this is the vision to which they can commit themselves.

> "We show kindness and respect for people, bodies, feelings and things. We enjoy learning."

A vision statement for the school can be established in a similar way or by reviewing the class vision statements and incorporating them in a few words for the entire school. It should be:

- Brief
- Easy to memorize
- Focused on virtues
- Posted where it can be clearly seen at all times

This example from a middle school in the United States is provided by Diane Gossen, author of *Restitution: Restructuring School Discipline*:

> "West School is a family committed to achievement through mutual dignity and respect."

"More important than being successful is being significant. Significance means making a contribution to others."
Steven Covey, Author, *Highly Effective People*

"An ounce of prevention is worth a pound of cure."
Anonymous

One-Minute Integrity Check

A Vision Statement is the guiding light for your discipline system, the reference point to turn to when someone has acted unkindly or thoughtlessly. Whenever we need to check our own integrity – how well we are reflecting the vision we have agreed to – we need only look at the Vision Statement and ask ourselves if our actions were in keeping with it. It serves as a reference point for daily Teachable Moments. For example, let's say your school Vision Statement is: "We are friends who treat each other with kindness. We treat people, things and feelings with respect and care."

Jim has just taken another child's pencil and won't give it back. Jim's teacher can ask questions such as:

"Jim, what do we believe about the way we treat people and things?"
"Jim, was that kind to take Manuel's pencil? Were you showing respect?"
"How could you have done that kindly?"
"How can you fix it now?"
"What will you do differently next time?"

You can also do an "Integrity Check" by having a poster of the 52 Virtues in your room and asking the class "Let's make an integrity check. What virtue do we need right now?"

School spirit grows when teachers share leadership with students, when discipline is not teacher-centered but virtues-centered. Taking the time, ideally at the beginning of the year, to create a Vision Statement for the classroom or for the entire school is an investment in a peaceful, joyful school environment. It provides a reference point for the code of behavior.

Example of Excellence
Making Choices

Edith Gulland, Victoria, British Columbia, Canada introduced a value system into her school, which helped children learn to make choices. One student made a poster, stating in his own words:

Making Choices

"A choice is a decision.
We make choices all our lives.
Our choices make us what we are."

Mark, Grade 2

Ms. Gulland said to another student in her junior year of high school:

"The value system seems to have been useful to you, Lewann."

Lewann: "It's like a new way of living. When I came to Discovery Passage School and I learned about the value system, I was living but not this life. This is a new life. It's like the tree reaching for the sky and everything around. In the old life I was like a tracking dog, able to do only one thing – think about the bird. People like a tracking dog are the same all the time. They are in the same place – doing and thinking the same things day in and day out. But people like the tree have to do something different every day to get these neat new feelings. His 'place' expands. It's like collecting knowledge."

Edith describes these as the steps in helping children develop the Value System (Shared Vision):

1) We make choices from among
2) alternatives in terms of
3) consequences because of what
4) we value (or prize or cherish).
5) We then publicly affirm our choice.
6) We then act according to our choices.
7) We then practice acting consistently with our choices until it becomes part of our habits to practice what we preach.

Model the Virtues You Expect Others to Practice

Being a model of virtues doesn't mean being perfect. It means you hold yourself accountable to the same vision statement that everyone has agreed to. Your saving grace, as a teacher, whom the children watch constantly to learn what is really important, is the practice of your humility. Whew! You don't have to be perfect. You only have to be willing to keep learning and growing, just like your students. Everyone has bad days. Sometimes that is a perfect time to model the virtue of humility and ask for the children's patience because you don't have much yourself that day.

Example of Excellence
A Model of Humility

Atusa R., a 6th grade teacher in Vancouver, Canada, tells of a time she lost her temper with her class. She came in the next day feeling very regretful about it and decided to apologize to her students. She said "I must apologize to you. I lost my patience yesterday and I am really sorry." "Mrs. R." one student said, "We forgot our obedience and we are sorry." "I promise to be more patient with you," she said. "We promise to be more obedient to you," the student said. The others nodded.

Atusa says they were about to present a skit on one of the virtues at a school assembly and did an exceptionally excellent job. "After that day, the bond in our class became so strong. It was wonderful. A Teachable Moment for all of us."

Story Together

"Whoever tells the stories defines the culture."
David Walsh

Stories, of course, always hold a group's attention, no matter what age they are. The magic words "Once upon a time ..." have all eyes and hearts focused on what comes next. Stories embody the values of our culture. Stories also help children to define their own values and become conscious of their virtues.

The sharing of personal stories about themselves, their own experiences, and their families is one of the ways to awaken students' sense of meaning. Inviting their personal stories during regular lessons on history or literature seasons those lessons with meaning. When personal stories are shared at Circle Time related to virtues such as the "Virtue of the Week", it supports a culture of character far more effectively than merely policing behavior.

Example of Excellence
"What Color Am I Today?"

Ann Bock, a teacher at Sequoia Junior High School in Kent, Washington, offered her students a very creative way to share their story, in terms of how they are feeling on a given day. Students could choose one or more sheets of colored paper in pink, green and blue and write the virtues which fit their feelings that day.

"I'm in the pink with (virtue) because..." meant they were feeling happy, confident, at home, comfortable with a particular virtue."

"I'm in the green, growing my (virtue), because..." meant they were feeling thankful for some growth or positive change in themselves.

"I have the blues with (virtue) because..." meant they were having a bad day, experiencing difficulty, not feeling well, or in some way challenged by a virtue.

Examples:

"I am in the green with Tolerance today because when someone ruined part of my lunch, I showed Tolerance by not getting in a fight with him."

One 6th grade student wrote: "I have the blues with peacefulness, because I am tired even though I got nine hours last night. I have a headache, an earache, a stuffy nose, a sore throat, I'm losing my voice...I am in the blue with peacefulness also because I have on a sweater, turtleneck and a fleece and I am still cold. I really wish that I was at home asleep instead of here at school. That's why I'm not peaceful."

Another student wrote: "I am in the green with tolerance today. I think I showed tolerance today when someone ruined my lunch and I showed tolerance by not getting in a fight with him. I am in the blue because of how mean and cold-hearted people can be."

A student wrote: "I am in the pink with unity. My unity comes from scouting with my troop. We do team working courses and building projects. I am in the pink with enthusiasm because I love to help out with what people need."

Virtues Pick as Storying Together

One way to "story together" (an expression in the Solomon Islands) is to do a Virtues Pick once a week, in which someone in the class pulls a Virtue Card (containing a definition of the virtue and Signs of Success), out of a box or bag, it is read aloud to the class and each person tells a story of a time he or she practiced this virtue. They can do this as a whole class or in small groups. You may want to follow this up with drawing or poetry writing about the virtue. This activity is meaningful to children and adults of all ages. More on this in the Activity Section at the end of this chapter.

 # Focus on Virtues in the Arts

Rivers of Respect, Cornucopias of Creativity

"The perception of beauty is a moral test."
Henry David Thoreau

In developing the virtues, it is very helpful to have visual cues in the environment. Noetic integration – the integration of meaning – occurs best when children create and see visuals of the virtues around them. Visual themes tied to the "Virtue of the Week" help to make virtues a natural element of the culture. According to Eugene Bedley, principal of El Camino Real School in California and a pioneer in virtues-based character education, children need symbols of the virtues to make them real – a bridge of compassion, a river of respect, or a road to respect, a heart of kindness. It is also helpful to hang Virtues Posters listing the 52 virtues described in this book.

Feature Virtues in the Performing Arts

Form a group of "Virtuous Reality Players" to write plays or put on plays that illustrate virtue. All meaningful plays do. This is a powerful way to reinforce the virtues in your environment. This activity goes well when you are studying historical figures.

Apply Virtues in Poetry

Author Shelley Tucker teaches many ways to connect virtues and creative writing. (See "Give a Virtue a Personality" work sheet in Activities section of this chapter.) Post virtues stories and poems on bulletin boards. Write poems about the virtues which are special about your school and post them.

Example of Excellence
Virtues Mural

The Petroglyph Elementary School in Albuquerque, New Mexico, under the guidance of art teacher, Sarita Birkey (originally from Nepal), organized an art project to promote multi-cultural awareness. One hundred 4th and 5th grade children painted a 40 foot long mural, while listening to music from Mexico, Nepal, Russia, England, United States, Malaysia, Africa, Israel, England and other countries. The theme of the mural was "Launching Virtues". Students painted a mural of hot air balloons of many colors and designs, each representing a different virtue, such as unity, caring, respect, courtesy, patience, etc. People of varied cultures launching the balloons from around the world were also featured in the mural.

Other learning activities were woven into the mural project. For example, before being introduced to the virtue of unity, they sang the "Hawaiian Unity Song". They discussed what is meaningful in their own lives about the virtue before painting it. They often discussed current trends and issues while they painted. Some students made a suggestion that they honor Israeli Prime Minister Yitzhak Rabin for his peace message to the world, after they learned that he had been assassinated. They decided to add a flag of Israel next to the flag of the United States painted on one of the balloon gondolas in the mural. They chose a world balloon and named it "Our mother Earth is the home of one human family." Some students wrote a story about the mural and shared it with the rest of the art class.

The activity cultivated an awe-inspiring sense of community and inspired such enthusiasm and creativity, that many students wanted to paint through recess. The students often spoke with wonder and appreciation during the project: "Oh, how beautiful your balloon looks!" "I didn't know I was a good artist." "Can I work with a partner?" "What a fun way to learn!"

Play Virtues Music

There are a number of excellent virtues CDs, some with song books, listed in the Resources at the back of this book. Singing a virtues song related to the Virtue of the Week at assemblies is another way to build school spirit.

Virtues in Ceremonies

Graduation: This is a perfect time to honor each student for one or more virtues he or she has contributed to the wellbeing of the school or virtues in which they shine. Let this also be a time when students honor teachers and administrators as well as community volunteers. The simplest way to honor someone is with a Virtues Acknowledgment. They can be written on gem shaped tags as a keepsake.

Awards Dinners: Include awards for virtues in addition to Excellence, such as Friendliness, Determination, and Caring.

Retirement: Virtues acknowledgments are also a meaningful way to honor a teacher or administrator who is retiring. Have someone record the acknowledgments and put them on a beautiful card made by the students.

Loss and Grief: If a student or teacher dies, having an honoring ceremony for them, by inviting various children and adults to tell stories about them and share the virtues they saw in them, is a healing way to bring closure.

Opening Circle: To open a retreat, the school year, or a camp, form a standing circle. Each person says their name, where they are from, and a virtue they bring to this gathering. "My name is Juan Lopez, I live on Delaney Street, and I bring Tolerance."

Example of Excellence
Trust Game

Janet Jackson of Taupo New Zealand created this exercise for Session 1 of the Standing Strong Program:
> "The aim is to become more familiar with each other by sharing about ourselves."

- Brief history of the Standing Strong Program.
- Brief introduction of the Facilitator/Tutor.
- Trust Game "Clever Brave and Strong".
  > "We're going to do this by sharing personal information about ourselves."
- History of my name:
  1) What is my name?
  2) Who gave me my name?
  3) What does my name mean?
  4) How do I feel about it?
  5) Something I want to share about myself...
  6) The Virtue I bring with me today is...

Example of Excellence
Honoring Each Other

Janine Roy of Rogers Elementary School in Victoria, British Columbia, Canada, shares two examples of how they are applying virtues. "After Linda came to our school in October 1998, our entire staff became committed to teaching The Virtues Project at our school.

• We posted each virtue on a card and displayed them in the main hall of the school.

• We dedicated a central bulletin board as our "Virtues Board" and displayed art work, stories and ideas about the Virtues.

• Every two weeks we select a virtue to focus on. We present it at our bi-monthly assembly in a variety of ways. I am always looking for inventive, meaningful ways to present the virtue. When we came to "Thankfulness" around Thanksgiving, I simply put a blank poster sheet and a pen on our "Virtues Board" in the main hall, and told the students that they could list things on the paper they were thankful for. This was everyone's bulletin board, and everyone was welcome to write on it. By the end of the first day, I was surprised to find that the paper was full and I had to put up more paper. Each day the page was filled with notes from students and staff about things they were thankful for. By the end of the week, the entire bulletin board was full and I had to post the filled charts on the walls around the bulletin board! It was a wonderful sight to see how thankful we all were for family, friends, and our school.

On the last day of school, as the Grade 7 students stood outside their classrooms teary-eyed about leaving our school and moving on to Junior High, one student took a virtues card – "Caring" – off the display in the main hall and attached the card onto a fellow student who really had embodied caring at our school. One by one, each student took a card and carefully placed it on another student, so that after a few minutes, every Grade 7 student was wearing a virtue. Arm in arm, they walked off wearing their virtues. It was an amazing sight! I hope you revel in these stories and savour our successes because they became possible because of The Virtues Project."

Closing Gratitude Circle: An excellent way to close a school year, a retreat or a camp session is with a Gratitude Circle. Everyone stands in a circle. Each person has their hands clasped in front of them, fingers laced together to form a gratitude "basket". Each is invited to say one word or phrase describing a gift they are taking from our time together. If they wish to pass they just wave their hands toward the next person. Examples of things people say are "Friendship", "Wisdom", "Kindness of my teachers", "Knowing myself". Optional: Then have everyone hold hands and play or sing a song.

Talking Stick: As a closing circle, you can pass any object, with each person who passes it to the next saying a Virtues Acknowledgment to that person.

Yarn Toss: Form a large circle. Someone holds a ball of yarn in one hand and holds and keeps the end in the other hand, then tosses it across the circle saying "I now commit to the virtue of ..." The person who catches it holds the line taut, keeps a hold on it and tosses the ball to someone else saying "I now commit to practice the virtue of ..." Alternative "I release (fear) and claim my (courage)." The tossing of the yarn continues until there is a large weaving across the circle. Children like to get under the canopy of yarn. Play a song when the toss is over while people wave the yarn canopy, moving it up and down.

Example of Excellence
The Gift of Virtues

Sue Ngametua, a teacher at the Leamington Primary School in Cambridge, New Zealand, did a special Virtues Acknowledgment session for her students at the end of the school year.

"I taught a virtue each week, after explaining what this involved to the principal and the parents of the children I was teaching. At our parent/teacher interviews half way through the year, the father of a student was so enthusiastic about my teaching virtues to his child, he said 'This is what school should be teaching! Each Monday we wait for our son to come home and tell us what the virtue of the week is and to hear all about it." At the end of the year I received a gift from this family – a beautiful handmade angel with stuffed wings, bearing a plaque saying No. 1 Teacher 1998.

At the end of the teaching year, each child took turns sitting at the front of the class, individually about five or six students each day, and the other children acknowledged that child with the virtues they had shown throughout the year. This is to be done for the teacher as well.

When finished, the child receives a written list of their virtues and then types them into the computer. Their name is written in bold letters at the top of the page, and the list of their virtues underneath. They choose a picture that relates to them, and put a border around it. It is then mounted on a coloured card and laminated. This is a gift to each person from the teacher and the class. I treasure my own!"

 # Activities

Virtues Picks

Using Virtues Cards when you are in a counseling session with a child or in a Virtues Sharing Circle can be an enjoyable and reverent way to focus on opportunities for action and change. Receiving a particular virtue is never a condemnation. It is either an invitation or an affirmation.

Individual Picks

This activity is helpful to adults as well as children. Take out the Virtues Cards. Shuffle them gently and have a student pick one without looking. They can be holding a question or problem in mind, asking "What virtue will help me solve this problem?" or simply be open to "What virtue do I need today?" Spend a few moments reading and reflecting on it. Keep it in mind throughout the day. If you are doing this with an individual student, you may want to pick one yourself to model how to do it. This, then, becomes a small sharing circle.

Virtues Pick Sharing Circle

You can do this in two ways:

1) Pick one virtue, read it aloud and invite each person to share a time he or she practiced this virtue or how it speaks to them today. Remember the boundaries of a Virtues Sharing Circle: Assertiveness – people can pass. Respect – listen in complete silence and be deeply present. Trust – What we say here stays here.

2) Have each person pick. Have the virtues in a small decorated box or bag and pass it around the circle, each person replacing the Virtue Card when their turn is over. Or you can fan the cards and have each person pick one. Create a small sharing circle of three persons or a whole group, depending on time available. While the others remain silent each person shares.

1. Reading the Virtue Card aloud or listening while someone else reads it.

2. Sharing how this virtue speaks to them in the light of what is happening in their life.

3. Sharing what gift this virtue offers, either as an affirmation of what they are already doing or as an invitation to do something new.

4. Others in the sharing circle remain silent and deeply present, and when the speaker is finished, they acknowledge the person for a virtue they see in him or her, relevant to what they have just shared. If time is limited, have only two people give acknowledgments.

5. Then the next person shares, and so on, until each person has had a turn.

Sharing Circles of three persons in a Virtues Pick take about fifteen minutes.

Gem Tags

Have children cut out various shapes of gems – pearls, diamonds, and so on from varied color construction paper, or have them color their own.
After the shape is cut out, have them print their name in big letters in the center of the gem tag.

Allow them to decorate them with glitter, glue, and colored markers. Explain that today everyone will wear their gem-shaped nametag to remind them that they have the gems of virtues within themselves.

Light a Candle

Some teachers find that just by lighting a candle for a special quiet time of reflection or story telling becomes a routine which students look forward to. You can do this as a way to start a virtues sharing circle or a special sharing time.

What Virtues Do We Bring?

This is an alternative to Light a Candle. Do it without the candle. Each person says something he or she is looking forward to from school this year and then says a virtue they bring to school or to this class.

"My name is Susan.
I look forward to math.
I bring the virtue of kindness."

As each person shares, the rest of the class says "Welcome, Susan." or "Thank you, Susan."

Inspirational Walk

Go for an inspirational walk around the school grounds. Find an object such as a flower, spider, tree, leaf, the sky, etc., and focus your attention deeply on it. You may wish to journal about it, or write a poem about it. What does the object say to you? What lessons does it offer? Ask "What is your gift for me?" "What virtue do you show me?"

Example: If you focus on ants, you may write a short poem about the virtues of Diligence and Unity and how they would help you in your life right now.

The boundaries for this activity are:

• Do this by yourself.
• Remain silent.
• Focus your full attention on the object.
• Use paper and pen if you choose to.
• Return to the classroom and write about your experience for a few minutes.
• Then share with a partner or in a small group what your experience was like.

Do this as a Virtues Sharing Circle, with complete silent attention to each other, followed by Virtues Acknowledgments after each person shares. "Kelly, I see your humility to learn from the ants."

Elders' Council

This is a form of problem-solving which calls on the wisdom of children to help each other with their problems. The following Example of Excellence illustrates how to do it.

Example of Excellence
Elders' Council

Mahshid Jones of Western Australia describes this reverent activity which her 6th graders created. Each week children anonymously write on slips of paper a problem they are facing. They place it in a Virtues Mail Box. Once a week, five elders appointed by the class from their classmates, don robes (dress-up clothes such as scarves and large coats brought from home) and sit in a semi-circle in front of the class. They pull slips from the mailbox, read the problem aloud to the class and then share their wisdom on what virtues will help to solve the problem. It is helpful to have a Virtues Poster hung in the room for the "elders'" reference.

Example of Excellence
Gem Pick 1

To address the tactile needs of children, Sue Hazelhurst of Australia created this activity.

Prepare a blackline master with the drawing of an outline of two people/children. Write underneath the first figure "This person is practicing virtues" and under the second figure "This person is not practicing virtues".

Ask each child to glue some glitter on the heart of each figure, and cover the second figure with tracing paper. Get each child to talk about what the activity represents to him/her. For me it represents an empowering image in that we all have the virtues inside us; we just need to polish them by using them.

My daughter once said she was too tired to practice courtesy (and say thank you). With the above picture in mind I acknowledged her tiredness but still asked her to find courtesy. I said "This is an opportunity to learn how to find courtesy even though you are tired – to dig deep, because I know it's in there." It took a while but she eventually found it and from this experience we both learned that she could overcome other emotions to practise a virtue. This leads to empowerment because she learned that she could choose how to behave in that situation and that I believed in her ability.

Example of Excellence
Gem Pick 2

This also comes from Sue Hazelhurst in Australia.

Fill two thirds of a container with rice (or similar) and add several pretend gemstones – the more the merrier. Ask a child to "Think of a virtue that is really easy for you to find today". Child responds with "Love". "Look, there it is right on the top; you pick out the gem of Love." Child selects a gem from near the top of the rice and is fascinated when you say that it is the Love gemstone. Now ask "Can you tell me a virtue that is really hard for you to find today?" Child says "Patience". "Okay, now I want you to put your hand deep into the container and see if you can dig down deep and find Patience for me."

Child pulls out a gem. "Wow, there is patience. I honor you for digging deep and finding patience." Do this activity with each child and then talk about how on some days it can be very difficult to find any virtues and we have to struggle all day and on other days it's easy.

My daughter (who is four now) said last week that she was digging to find a particular virtue and was just not quite reaching it. As she said this she was mimicking with her hand as if she was trying to reach into her heart to find the virtue but her hand just couldn't quite reach. This activity is great for children, adults and grandparents aged between 3 – 93. It can change the paradigm of many parents from thinking that they have to fill up their child with good behaviors rather than to draw forth those desirable ones which they already possess. I showed this activity to the principal of my daughter's school and he asked all the teachers to offer it to every child in the school.

To sum up, when we practice virtues our gems shine through and when we don't practice virtues it is hard to see them.

Personal Virtues Poster

Example of Excellence

Character Commitments

At Paekakariki Primary School in New Zealand the teachers of the Bilingual Unit work together with 40 children ages 5-12, delivering a comprehensive program which includes instruction in Maori as well as English. These two teachers use Virtues in their program both in Maori and in English. At the beginning of the year, Miki Reikihana, who teaches the older children, worked with them about setting goals and developing qualities of character.

1. He posted Virtues Cards on the wall, and each day reviewed the characteristics of particular virtues that he felt were important in his classroom.
2. Then he had the children choose two or three virtues that they wanted to practice during the year and create a poster with an illustration of themselves practicing these qualities.
3. Underneath the poster, the children wrote in English or Maori an affirmation or commitment for themselves. Examples: "This year I am practicing Respect and Assertiveness." "This year if I see people fighting I will try to help them calm down, and bring them to other people who are respectful and can help."

Example of Excellence

Virtues Success Posters

Janet Jackson, coordinator of the "Standing Strong Program" in Taupo, New Zealand, created a beautiful poster herself, which served as a model for the young women in her group. They followed her example and took hours to develop virtues posters, which she then laminated. Each poster gave a number of key words or points from the definitions or Signs of Success of the virtue found in this Guide. For these students, it was a reverent and deeply personal activity.

Personal Virtues Shield

1. In the upper left quadrant, write the name of a Strength Virtue – one in which you have excellence, one of your best. Then draw a symbol or picture to represent this virtue.

2. In the upper right quadrant, write a virtue in which your family shows excellence and draw a symbol or picture for it.

3. In the lower left quadrant, write the virtue "Joy" and draw a symbol or picture of what gives you joy.

4. In the lower right quadrant, write a Growth Virtue – one which is a challenge for you, one you need to grow and cultivate, and draw a symbol or picture for it.

5. In the center, draw a symbol that represents you. Example: If you love horses, draw a horse or a horseshoe.

6. In a Virtues Sharing Circle, or with the class as a whole, talk about your shield. Others in the circle give Virtues Acknowledgments to each person as he or she finishes sharing.

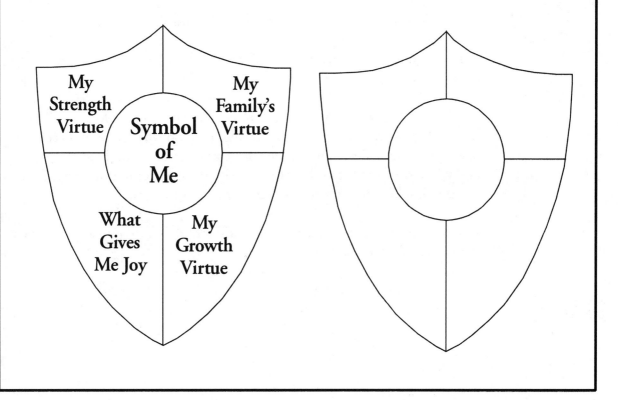

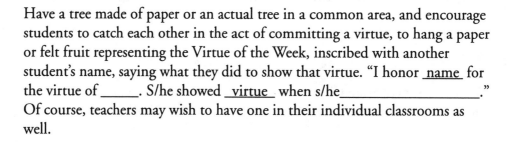

Virtues Integrity Tree

Have a tree made of paper or an actual tree in a common area, and encourage students to catch each other in the act of committing a virtue, to hang a paper or felt fruit representing the Virtue of the Week, inscribed with another student's name, saying what they did to show that virtue. "I honor _name_ for the virtue of _____. S/he showed _virtue_ when s/he_____." Of course, teachers may wish to have one in their individual classrooms as well.

Alternative for Younger Children: Create a Virtues Fruit Tree

Make a sign for the tree which says "Virtues are the fruits of good character". Construct the tree out of paper or felt. Have children cut shapes of fruits out of construction paper or felt. Write the names of virtues on each fruit. Assertive Apples, Kind Kiwis, Respectful Raspberries, Moderate Melons, etc. The names of children can be written on small leaves and when noticed practicing one of the virtues, the name of a student is attached temporarily to a particular fruit. Virtues Fruit stickers or badges with the name of the virtue reinforce an act of kindness or courage or generosity.

Key Point: Use stickers moderately or it will too easily turn into a competition for who has the most stickers.

Virtues Poetry

Give a Virtue a Personality

Choose a virtue _____ .

Then, answer the following questions pretending you are the virtue.
Be sure to write in complete sentences.
Example:
1. I am Creativity
2. I live in the sky, trees and wind.
3. My favorite colors move between the lines in a rainbow.

Choose a few or all of these questions to answer.
1. Virtue, what is your name?

2. Where do you live?

3. What are your favorite colors?

4. What clothes do you like to wear?

5. What is your job?

6. Who are your family and friends?

7. Where do you go on vacation?

8. What is your favorite holiday?

9. How do you feel?

10. How do you move?

Adapted from Shelley Tucker, author of "Painting the Sky: Writing Poetry with Children"

Virtues Songs

Sing a song about the "Virtue of the Week" in school Assembly. (See suggestions for virtues music in Section 3.)

Virtues Journals

Have students choose a virtue which is very important to them and create a journal. It can include drawings, thoughts, experiences, poetry and so on.

"The taste of peace is like..."
"The sound of peace..."
"The touch of peace..."
"The smell of peace..."
"The color of peace..."

School-wide Activities

Virtues Assemblies

Read a Virtues Affirmation and have students recite it aloud. Then have one minute of silence to reflect on the virtue. This sets a tone of reverence and peacefulness. For more ideas see Chapter 1.

Virtues Bulletin Board

Have a bulletin board for The Virtue of the Week in each classroom, in the library, or a common area with drawings, murals, poems, essays, and journal entries from students.

Make a Virtues Acronym of Your School Name

When making a Virtues Acronym use actual virtues words whenever possible, since they have a special meaning and exert a powerful influence.

South Central High School
    Service
    Caring
    Honor
    Spirit

Frost School
    Friendliness
    Respect
    Order
    Service
    Truth

A Virtues Garden

Create a Virtues Garden for your school. Patient Petunias, Respectful Raspberries, Determined Dahlias. The design, planting and maintenance and the beauty of the garden will add much to your school spirit.

Virtues Appreciation Party Day

This activity may be done sometime near the end of the year. Have each student, teacher, administrator, staff and volunteer on Virtues write their name on a Virtues Voucher (see page 25). Pass them around in paper bags or baskets at an Assembly. If you are in a large school, do this in smaller units to be sure everyone knows each other and can write a virtue they observed about whoever they receive. INCLUDE EVERYBODY! (every staff person and volunteer as well as students). After each person has filled one out, they are to find the person and give the Voucher to him or her. You can use gem-shaped tags and allow others to add virtues. This way everyone gets at least one appreciation.

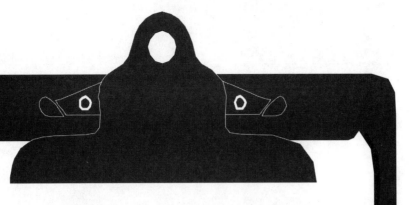

Chapter Summary:
Honor the Spirit

✓ See the potential in every child. Look for their virtues.

✓ Create a Shared Vision statement for your classroom and/or school. Use your Vision Statement and Virtues Poster to do one minute Integrity Checks. "What do we believe?" "What virtues do we need right now?"

✓ Model the virtues you expect children to practice.

✓ Focus on virtues in the arts.

✓ Share stories – the keepers of meaning.

✓ Have ceremonies at special times, such as the beginning and end of the school year.

5 Offer the Art of Spiritual Companioning™

"It's in everyone of us to be wise."
Proverb

 ## The Companioning Presence

The Art of Spiritual Companioning was best described by a young First Nations mother who used it as a communication tool with her two children but found the words "spiritual companioning" difficult to remember. On the third day of a workshop in Northern Canada she came in and said, "You know that thing worked so well with my kids! But I can't remember how you say it. I call it 'walk along'."

Companioning is walking along with another, not pushing or pulling them, but being present to them and offering them clarifying questions which help them to find their own wisdom. It is called "spiritual" because it goes beyond problem solving to the meaning, intent and virtues of a situation. It strengthens character by calling on the virtues at the heart of the matter. It is not about giving quick solutions. It is about listening so that the one being heard can hear himself and find his own clarity. It is a form of **reverent curiosity** based on the belief that the wisdom needed to resolve a problem, a loss, a disappointment is within us rather than something to be imposed from someone else. Spiritual companioning is given in a spirit of trust in the other person's process, seeing others as spiritual champions capable of learning their life lessons.

The best present you can give is the gift of your presence – your undivided attention. The quality of your attention is directly proportionate to the degree of your concentration, even if it is for a few moments. A caring presence is often the only thing someone needs to "feel better" in a moment of sadness or frustration. Feeling better is often just a matter of feeling heard, having an opportunity to empty one's cup. Always at the bottom of that cup is the pearl of truth. At times a more active and complete form of companioning is needed to empty the cup of confusion, sadness or anger, and then to reflect on the virtues needed to refill the cup and gain some resolution.

The quality of your attention is directly proportionate to the degree of your concentration.

Companioning is an empowering way to meet the needs

- to be seen
- to be heard
- to be taken seriously
- to tell our stories and have them valued
- to find meaning and purpose in what is happening
- to get to the heart of the matter

Companioning is useful when someone

- has been sent to you for discipline
- has strong feelings – sad, mad, glad, or scared
- is confused
- has a moral dilemma

SPIRITUAL COMPANIONING

IS NOT	IS
A fix	Walk Along
A rescue	Respect
Curing	Caring Presence
Advice	Listening
Sympathy	Compassionate Detachment
Telling	Asking
Victim-based	Virtues-based

 # Helping Children to Make Moral Choices

One of the most important ways to build character is to support a child's capacity to make moral choices. Spiritual Companioning is an art and a skill with which to support children to discover their own wisdom and discernment. It is quite a contrast to the typical approach taken by most caring people when a child has a problem to be solved or a strong feeling about something. Usually we try to solve the problem as quickly as possible – giving the child *our* wisdom – "Why don't you just...?" Or we resist and distract them from their strong feelings. "Let's get you some water." "Don't cry. It's Okay."

The Magic Word

The magic word in companioning is "What", and sometimes "How". Playing detective and asking Who, When, Where, Why questions is very time consuming and sets you up to be the judge, jury and problem solver. In companioning, the reference point is not your judgment but the heart, mind and character of the one being listened to. Follow their lead. If they say "This stinks", ask "What stinks?" If they say "I had the best holiday ever" ask "What made it the best?"

The Perfect Twin

I was asked to consult with a bright 6-year old who had suddenly stopped writing and was refusing to continue. When I sat down with her, she had a cynical look on her face and rolled her eyes as if thinking "Here comes someone else trying to force me to write." This is what transpired:

"Jean, I understand something is going on with writing?"
"Yes, and I know, I won't get a good job if I don't write."
"Well, maybe, but I'm interested in what you are feeling about it."
She looked surprised.

Jean: "I hate it."
"What do you hate?"
Jean: "That stupid black line."
"Oh, the black line."
Jean: "Yes I hate, hate, hate it."
(My voice getting intense to match hers) "What is it about that hateful black line?!"
"I can't make my letters the way I want them."
"How do you want them?"
"Like my sister's."
"Oh, your sister makes them the way you would like them."
"I hate that."
"What do you hate about it?"
She smiles a sly smile. "We're twins and I'm better at everything than she is, except for writing."
"Oh" I smile back. "What does it mean to you not to do something better than she does it?"
"I don't know. I just don't like it. And I'm never going to write again."
"Can you show me the black line?"

She pulls out a lined paper (with faint blue lines). The writing is in black ink. The straight parts of her letters are shaky.
"So, show me the black line."

She points to her letters. "They're yucky."
"How are they yucky?"
Jean: "All squiggly."
"Pretty squiggly."
Jean: "I hate that!"

I pounded on the desk with the flat of my hand. "Horrible squiggly black line."
She pounded and we chanted that for a while. Then we both laughed.

"What do you hate most about that black line, Jean?"
Jean: "I can't do them over if I make a mistake."
"So what would allow you to do them over?"
She thinks and then looks amazed. "A pencil with an eraser!"
"Will your teacher allow that?"
Jean:" Yes."
"I get the sense you are very confident in everything you do."
Jean:" Yes, I am."
"What would give you the confidence and humility to accept that it is okay to make mistakes? Or even not do every single thing better than your sister?"
She smiled and said, "It would be fair wouldn't it?"
I smiled back. "What has been helpful to you about talking?"
She said "Now I know what to do about mistakes and they're okay anyway."
I said "I know a little song: 'It's okay to make mistakes. That's the way we learn.'" She repeated it.

I said "Jean, I respect you for your sense of excellence – wanting to give your best to everything – and your creativity in thinking of a new way to write. And I appreciate your humility to realize you don't have to be perfect."
Jean: (with a huge grin)"Thanks!! Is listening the best thing you do?"

Jean's teacher reported that she had no further problems and that Jean was now using a pencil. Companioning took approximately 10 minutes. Hours had already been spent in parent teacher conversations and attempts to bribe, cajole and force Jean to write.

Spiritual Companioning is an attitude reflecting deep respect, which
• requires deep listening and concentrated attention
• will only be effective if you are free of an "agenda" or predetermined outcome
• is meant to support, not rescue or control
• uses receptive silence and questions skillfully
• requires trust in the other's process.

Prepare Yourself

To prepare yourself for spiritual companioning, you need to call on two virtues. They are Compassion and Detachment. Think of them as a protection, both for you and the person to whom you are listening. Compassion allows your caring to flow to the other person. Detachment keeps you from taking on their feelings or their problem.

The 7 Steps of Spiritual Companioning

There are seven steps in full spiritual companioning. You do not always need to use all of them, but when you are taking the time to companion someone, particularly in grief or with a moral dilemma, these are aspects of the process.

1. Open the Door

If you are initiating the conversation, ask door opening questions such as:

> "What's up?"
> "What's happening?"
> "What is it?"
> "What kind of day are you having?"

Physically moving closer to a person in a compassionate way or just turning your eyes to them giving compassionate attention is often the best way to open the door.

2. Offer Receptive Silence

Receptive silence gives others the space to speak fully, to tell you the whole story without interruption. Be fully present with deep concentration on the person.

3. Ask Cup-Emptying Questions

Your goal is help them empty their cup and get to the heart of the matter by asking questions that are open ended and show the utmost non-judgmental curiosity. Take your lead from the speaker. Use their words and their way of describing things. Don't turn the "volume" up or down. Meet them at their level of energy.

Use **"what"**, **"how"** and **"when"** questions, not **"why"**. Asking "Why are you crying?" or "Why did you do that?" can feel like an interrogation, or a request for an instant analysis. It creates defensiveness. It also encourages disconnection from feelings. Asking "Who" is not helpful as it is information-gathering so that you can make a judgment about the situation. Rather ask "What hurts?" "How does it hurt?" "When do you feel hurt?"

Ask **open-ended** questions. Don't put words in their mouth, such as "Are you scared?" "Are you having a good day?"

Examples:

> "What is that like for you?"
> "What worries you?"
> "How is that for you?"
> "What is your main worry?"
> "What does it mean to you?"
> "What is the hardest thing about this?"
> "When do you feel most (sad, discouraged, etc.)?"

Children often answer "I don't know." Ask "What don't you know?" or "What confuses you?" They often stop saying it when they trust that you really want to hear their truth.

4. Focus on Sensory Cues

Reflect their feelings, follow their lead, use their language, and concentrate on the sensory or perceptual cues – their body language. If they are blowing out their breath, ask "What are you blowing away?" If they are crying, ask "What are those tears?" If they are holding their arms around themselves, ask "What are you holding onto?" If they are describing something physical, like, "He hit me on my arm." look at the arm and if you notice anything, say it. "It looks swollen." or "It's red." Don't detract or distract – give attention. If they are describing something, repeat back to them phrases that describe their physical sensations. "When I jumped in the water, it went up my nose!" "Water in your nose!" and picture it happening as you speak. Be with them.

5. Ask Virtues Reflection Questions

In the cup-emptying part of companioning, you are following the other's lead. You are helping them get to the heart of the matter. After that, it is time for you to take the lead and help them refill their cup with their own virtues, to ask questions that lead them to their own answers. Help them to balance the virtues they need and reflect on what virtues will help them.

"What would be a kind and assertive way to solve this?"
"What does your integrity tell you? What feels like the right thing to do?"
"What would give you the courage to...?"
"What is a fair way for you to make amends?"
"What do you need?"
"How can I support you?"

6. Ask Closure and Integration Questions

These two questions help the person to integrate thinking and feeling and to reach closure.
"What has been helpful about talking?"
"What is clearer to you now?"

7. Give a Virtues Acknowledgment

Always end with a virtues acknowledgement. "I see your courage." "I honor you for your loyalty to your friend and your integrity to do the right thing." "You showed humility in taking responsibility for what you did."

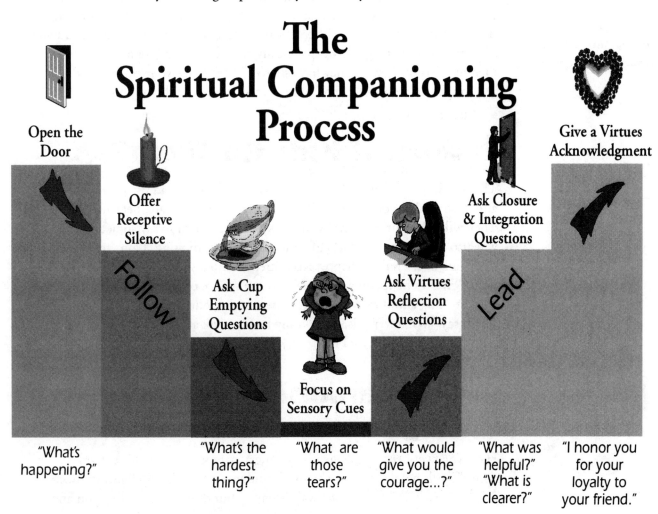

The Spiritual Companioning Process

Set Boundaries

Companioning is an attitude. Many companioning situations are very brief, such as looking at a wound and commenting on how it looks, "That's really swollen." or asking "How was that for you?" However, it is important to set boundaries around when you companion. Do not attempt to companion if you do not have the time or energy at that moment. If you have limited time but do want to offer your attention, set a boundary for how long you can listen and tell the person "I can spend ten minutes with you," or "I only have two minutes but I will give you my full attention for that time." Or you can choose to set another time to companion the person. When the ten minutes (or whatever your limit is) is almost up, **bring the process to closure** with a closure and integration question: "Our time is almost up so I want to ask you, 'What has been helpful about talking?'"

Always, always end with a virtues acknowledgement.

In a regular counseling session, set boundaries around **time** and keep them. Don't expect the person who is talking to do it. Take responsibility for allowing time for closure. Give a warning, "We have a few minutes left. What do you need to say?" Make sure to allow time for a closure and integration question "What's clearer for you after talking today?" And **always, always end with a Virtues Acknowledgement**, specifically related to what you have observed in them in relation to what they have shared. "I really see your courage for facing this tough problem." "I honor you for your honesty with yourself."

What If Kids Go Silent?

The best way to companion someone who is silent is to adjust your own attention so that you are focused in a warm, compassionate, detached way. They will feel your tension if you are waiting for them to say something. They will also feel the peacefulness of your silent companioning. Don't try to make them talk or keep them happy. Keep them company. Ask door opening questions. "What's happening with you?" If the silence continues, ask "What's the hardest thing about talking?" If you are running out of time and they are still silent, say "Whatever it is seems really hard to talk about. I just want you to know I'm here if you need me."

Companioning Someone in Anger

Have you ever been challenged by an angry parent whose child "can do no wrong"? Felt helpless when two angry students wouldn't stop fighting? Been angry yourself and felt no one was listening, but only stone-walling you and trying to calm you down? These are times when companioning can bring down walls of resistance and anger. Bear in mind that companioning is not agreeing or disagreeing. It is hearing someone's point of view fully, as a detached, compassionate listener, making no judgments, just totally curious to "hear it all". We do have to stop behavior if it is aggressive, but if someone raises his voice in anger, and you feel it is the appropriate time for you to companion him, ask cup-emptying questions. Bear in mind that most anger stems from helplessness and an individual feeling that their sense of justice has been offended.

Companioning is not agreeing or disagreeing. It is hearing someone's point of view fully.

> "I hate this f--ing school!"
> "What do you hate?"

This is not the time to give a lecturette about respectful language. Sometimes it is more important to hear the truth and companion the feelings. Most of the time, companioning calms the person quite quickly, knowing they are being heard.

Don't Get Furious, Get Curious!

If a child is expressing anger toward you, you want to avoid escalating the anger by reacting with your own. You need to model detachment and respect, especially at times like this. The companioning attitude can help. First, determine whether you want to companion them or to use this as a straightforward Teachable Moment and invite them to be respectful, cooperative or detached in accepting something you have said or done. You may decide to ask something like "I can see that you are upset. What would help you to detach and accept this situation right now?" If you decide it is a good idea to companion them, ask a cup emptying question and then listen – **don't argue or explain away their point of view.** Get curious about what their perception is. Companioning does not imply agreement with what the person is saying, only respect for their right to see it that way.

"That's not fair. I shouldn't have detention for this."
"What isn't fair about it?"
"I wasn't the only one that was doing it."
"You weren't the only one."
"Right."
"So, what would feel fair to you?"
"Give detention to all of us."
"John, I see your sense of justice here. I'll give it some thought. What I ask you to do is to think about your responsibility as a leader. How you could have been more responsible in this situation? Please write out your thoughts and we'll talk later."

A Fresh Approach to Conflict Resolution

Companioning is an excellent tool for keeping the peace, whether used by an adult or a peer. It is effective in violence prevention and conflict resolution. Many schools have Peace Squads or "Quality Control" Teams (Virtues being the great qualities the school is encouraging) made up of students. They wear identifying sashes or jackets and can be called on in any conflict situation. They also patrol, looking for ways to be of help.

Companioning may take more time than giving a quick consequence or an adult resolving the problem externally, but it is worth the time in prevention and character building. Sometimes it actually takes less time than traditional methods of stepping in when children are fighting. Companioning gives them virtues-based life skills which will help them manage themselves better in the future.

There are three basic companioning questions to ask when two individuals are fighting or in conflict.

1. Ask what happened:

   "What happened?" or "What's happening?" (Door Opener) Have them take turns and speak one at a time.

2. Listen to each person's feelings:

   "What are you feeling?" or "What did you want by doing that?" (Cup-Emptying)

3. Help them make amends:

   "What do you need?" "How can you make it right?" "What would be a peaceful way to do that?" "What would be fair to both of you?" (Virtues Reflection Questions)

When they do resolve their problem, honor each of them for a virtue they showed – for example, truthfulness for telling the truth, peacefulness for finding a peaceful solution, creativity for finding a new way to solve the problem, humility for accepting the Teachable Moment or responsibility for owning the mistake.

Peace Ambassadors

Brentwood Elementary, in British Columbia, Canada has student ambassadors go through several weeks of training in conflict resolution. When they come across conflict between students, (other than physical violence where an adult is summoned) they ask a series of questions:

1. Define the problem
    "What happened, John?" "Anne, now please tell what happened."
    "What did you want?" "What were you thinking when you took the ball?"

2. Repeat the problem back
    "You mean you wanted to play?"

3. Brainstorm solutions
    "What do you need?" "How can you solve this so it's fair to both of you?"

4. Agree on a solution

5. Ask them to report how it is working.

Here is an example of a Peace Squad coming upon two kids fighting over a basketball:

PS member: "What's happening? Please take turns and each tell your point of view. You first."

Student A (victim): "He grabbed the ball and I had it first."
Student B (perpetrator): "Did not"
PS: (Ignoring student B): "So he grabbed it? "
Student A: "Yeah and that's not fair."
PS: "You had the ball and it didn't feel fair to you, is that right?"
Student A: "Right."
PS: Turning to Student B "So, what happened?"
Student B: "I was just playing. He's a dweeb."
PS: "How did you feel he was a dweeb?"
Student B: "I was just kidding around."
PS: "So, you wanted to have fun with him?"

Student B: "Yeah."

PS: "So grabbing the ball didn't work?"

Student B: "No."

PS: "So what would have been a respectful way to get to play with him?"

Student B: "I could have asked instead of taking the ball."

PS: (To Student A) "How would you have liked him to show you respect?"

Student A: "Ask me, 'Can I play?' and if I want to I will."

PS: (To Student B) "What would respect look like if he didn't want to play with you?"

Student B: "Go find someone else."

PS: "Right on! Good flexibility. I want to acknowledge you both for your honesty in telling what happened, your assertiveness about your rights (addressing Student A) and your humility (addressing Student B) for owning your mistake. What would feel fair right now?"

Student A: "He can play."

PS: "Excellent friendliness!"

If bodily or property damage is involved or feelings are hurt, there need to be two distinct steps during the Virtues Reflection stage:

1) Ask both the victim and the perpetrator

"How could you have handled this...?"
Peacefully
Assertively
Kindly
Gently
Respectfully

2) Ask how amends can be made.

"How can you make it right?"
"How can you fix it in a just way?"
"What do you need from him to make amends?"
"How will you make amends?"
"What can you (the victim) do to help the unity between you?"

As a companion and a peacemaker, make sure that both the victim and the perpetrator are restored by the amends.

As a companion and a peacemaker, make sure that both the victim and the perpetrator are restored by the amends. Kids tend to be very punitive toward their own actions. Often, they will respond to "How can you make it right?" by saying they should receive the same abuse they gave. If they took someone else's lunch, they are apt to say they should go without lunch the next day. Guide them to come up with amends that repair the relationship and strengthens them as well as the victim, rather than retaliates against themselves for the crime.

Then, end with a Virtues Acknowledgment: "Thank you for being...

> Honest in acknowledging your part."
> Peaceful in working it out together."
> Responsible in the way you are being accountable for your actions."

Companioning as Problem Solving

Companioning helps in problem solving as it is solution-oriented rather than blame-oriented. It focuses on the virtues in the Teachable Moment, rather than just making the problem go away, which it usually doesn't! The following example from a Texas middle school illustrates it well.

Example of Excellence
A Miracle of Companioning

Tammy Goff was a 5th grade teacher in Lantern Lane Elementary School, Missouri City, Texas, when this occurred in her classroom. She and her principal had just returned from a Virtues Project workshop.

"My students were composing raps on racism as a culminating project for one of our novels. We discussed ahead of time what virtues would be needed in order to successfully complete the project. Enthusiasm was high on everyone's part. One group fell apart and found it impossible to do. I said to myself, 'OK Tammy, you have just finished Virtues training. If what you believe is ever going to work, now is the time to apply it.' So I did. I spent some time with the four students in this group and we companioned each other and, through listening, got to their concerns. After they got to the heart of the matter and did some virtues reflection, they were able to name some virtues which would help them complete the project and they set to work again. About 15 minutes later, as I worked with another group, I felt a tap on my shoulder. I turned around to see four beaming faces. They were completely finished, did an excellent job and felt completely happy with themselves for applying the virtues so well. Kyle, whose face I will always remember, looked at me in joyous astonishment and said, 'Mrs. Goff, these virtues are a miracle!'"

How To Hold a Virtues Sharing Circle

A Virtues Circle is one form of sharing circle. Make it clear that this activity requires great respect and trust. Have tissues available if the topic is personal. You may wish to choose a topic such as "What friendship means to me" or you may want to have a circle in which individuals share freely whatever is on their minds and hearts. Follow these guidelines:

1. Complete silence without any "cross talk" while each student is sharing. You may wish to use an object to pass, such as a feather or talking stick.
2. Set a time for each person to speak if your time is limited, e.g. one to three minutes each.
3. People have the right to pass.
4. The only time others can speak is at the end of each participant's turn by giving Virtues Acknowledgments. When each person is finished speaking, one or more in the circle will acknowledge the virtues they see in that person in light of what they have shared.
"I honor you for the virtue of ___ in the way you ____."
5. Confidentiality is of the utmost importance. All information shared is to be kept in complete confidence, saying nothing at any time about what anyone has shared.

Have the following boundaries:

Boundaries

1. **Respect:** We listen in complete silence as each one shares.

2. **Compassion and Detachment:** We have compassion for the feelings of others without taking their feelings on.

3. **Trust :** What we say here stays here.

4. **Appreciation:** We give each other virtues acknowledgments.

You may want to use a symbol for companioning, such as imagining a veil placed over the heart made of both compassion and detachment: The veil allows compassion to flow out but detachment keeps us from taking on others' feelings. Invite students to place one hand over their hearts before the circle begins, to remind them of the veil of compassion and detachment.

One-Minute Counseling Strategies

Set a boundary for yourself that you will only listen when you have attention to give. If you are too distracted, it's best to ask the child to be patient and wait until you have a free moment. If you do feel you have a bit of attention, it is honest to say "I have one minute to listen. I'll give you the best attention I can in that minute. What's happening?" Companioning gives new meaning to the expression "undivided attention."

Allow the child to empty her cup, then ask her "What virtue would help you right now?" or "What virtue do you need to call on?" If you feel you see a particular virtue needed you can ask "What would help you to have the (specific virtue) to solve this?" Here is an example of a primary student making snowflakes.

> "I can't do this. It's too hard."
> "What's hard?"
> "I don't understand it."
> "What don't you understand?"
> "How to cut the shapes."
> "What would help you to feel confident cutting the shapes?"
> "Show me."
> "Okay, now you try it. Good assertiveness to say what you needed."

Virtues Picks in Counseling

A Virtues Pick is a method being used by counselors to call on the positive qualities within the student. It can be a fun activity or a reverent one. Have a deck of Virtues Cards with brief definitions of the virtues. (See Resource Section for how to obtain a set.) After the student has shared a problem with you, have them pick a virtue which "can help you."

- Have them "blind pick" the virtue without looking and then read it aloud.

- Ask "How can this virtue help you? How does it speak to you?"

- When the child is finished sharing, give a Virtues Acknowledgment of a quality you see them beginning to grasp or one they are showing in relation to what they have shared. You may also want to pick a virtue and share with them.

Offer the Art of Spiritual Companioning ....

Companioning Grief

When a death or loss occurs it is important to provide a safe haven for the grief responses children and adults have. This is a time to use Receptive Silence for the most part. To just be with the person. They need to:

1. Empty their cup, including tears. If physical touch assists them in this process and is welcomed, offer it. Follow their cue. Put a hand on their shoulder or hold out your hand. If they move toward you, give more touch, if away, allow the space.

2. Talk about it. Often they will repeat the same story over and over. Encourage this by listening and repeating sensual cues. Student: "My Dad was just lying there. His eyes were open." Counselor: "His eyes were open."

3. Go into the pain with them through your attention, then lead them out of the pain, with a question such as "What do you need?" "What did you love most about your Dad?"

4. Always, end with a Virtues Acknowledgement. "I see how much you love your Dad."

Companioning in Catastrophe

If there is a catastrophic event, such as a fire, violence, or something involving the endangerment or loss of many people, people need a safe place to express their emotions. Set up Virtues Sharing Circles where each person who wishes to has an opportunity to say how this has affected them, their biggest concern etc. There need be no reply, just people acknowledging each person after he or she speaks either with "Thank you, John" or, if it feels right, a Virtues Acknowledgement from one or two people in the group.

Example of Excellence
A Healing Circle

I was keynote speaker at a conference called "Remember the Healing" for First Nations communities in British Columbia. On the second day of the conference, several members of a particular community were informed that three people in their small home town had just died, one of illness, two in accidents. I was invited to attend a special Healing Circle with Winston Wuttunnee, an elder who chanted and set a sacred atmosphere by burning sage. People needed to cry silently. A drummer joined the circle and played a grieving song. That released more tears. Then, when they were ready, each person was invited to speak of what was in their heart. Some wept and cried bitterly. Young students were present who seemed numb until they spoke in the circle. That released their tears. They spoke of the shock and the things they will remember about the friends and relatives they had lost. Sometimes people needed to be held and allowed to cry. This was a very healing and sacred experience for everyone present. It pointed out the need, after a catastrophe, to allow safe space for people to be and feel. The boundary of a Healing Circle, where people speak one at a time, is essential.

Companioning in Suicide Prevention

Counselors dealing with suicidal ideation or threats need to be able to help the person get to the heart of the matter. There is always an issue such as a failed relationship, anger at a friend or relative, a loss, a failure, a sense of isolation. Naturally you don't want to take on counseling responsibilities for which you are not prepared. However, in the course of counseling, there are times when you may find yourself in the position of dealing with suicidal statements. The goal, as in all companioning, is to help the person empty their cup and get to the pearl of truth which always lies at the bottom. When they can hear their own truth, it gives them freedom to choose another way to deal with it.

"I just don't want to live anymore."

"What don't you want to live with?"

"I can't eat. I can't sleep."

"What's keeping you awake?"

"My boyfriend left me. How could he do that?"

Receptive silence.

"What hurts most?"

"We were going steady and he just dumped me."

"Dumped you."

Tears.

"What is the hardest thing about being dumped?"

"I feel like nothing."

"What does that nothing feeling like? Where in your body do you feel it?"

"Here." Holding her stomach.

"Empty there."

"Yes. And it hurts!" (Cries again)

After sufficient cup emptying. You need to begin bringing her attention back out.

"What do you need to help you deal with this pain?"

"My friends."

"Friends help."

"Yes."

"Melissa, what would give you the courage to live through this?"

(Laughs) "Knowing it's not the end of the world."

"Can you assure me that you will do nothing to take your life?"

"I'm not sure."

"What's clearer for you after talking?"

"That I will live through this."

"I need you to promise that you will literally live through this."

"I promise."

"Melissa, I want to honor you for your courage to deal with this, and having the assertiveness to ask for help."

Companioning is, at the very least, the first step in any intervention.

Companioning is, at the very least, the first step in any intervention, as it honors the inner strengths of the individual, no matter how young, to examine their own experience, find their own answers, heal their own wounds, and learn healthy ways to handle life's challenges.

Activities

Sad-Mad-Glad-Scared Game

Make up cards with faces representing each of these words and the words as well. Place them in the center of a circle and model for students by doing this yourself.

1. Choose a card (they can be face up or face down).

2. With everyone listening in Virtues Sharing Circle format, say "I feel SAD when I..." or "I feel GLAD when I..." Say something specific, e.g. "I feel SAD when I have a cold and have to miss a day of teaching." (Only say it if it's true!)

3. After a few rounds of each person sharing after picking a card, have the person to the left acknowledge the person to their right for a virtue they noticed in them while they were sharing.

(Activity created by Judi Morin, S.S.A.)

Glad   Mad

Sad   Scared

Peer Peacemakers

Role play a situation in which two people are arguing. Two of you are the fighters and two are the Peer Peacemakers. Here are the steps for the Peacemakers to follow:

1. Open the Door: "What's happening between you? Please take turns."

2. Cup-Emptying: "What was (hardest, mean, unfair)" – take cues from the individual.

3. Focus on the sensory cues: "What happened to your body? Your ribs are sore?"

4. Virtues Reflection: "What virtue do you need from the other? What virtue can you call on for yourself?"

5. Restoration Commitment: "What do you need to make it right?"

6. Closure and Integration: "What's been your main Teachable Moment?" "What's clearer to you now?"

7. Virtues Acknowledgment of both parties.

Discussion Questions

How did it feel watching this?

What would have happened without this Peacemakers' help?

What was one of the effective things you saw the Peacemakers do?

What could they have done to improve their approach?

What was the best thing about the Peacemakers?

Describe a time you wish you had had the Peacemakers around to help.

School-wide Activities

Virtues-Based Strategic Planning

These questions may be used with strategic planning activities conducted with your school or club. These questions are effective with children and adults and reflect all five strategies of The Virtues Project:

- What are our strongest virtues at (name of school or club)?

- What virtues do we need to develop more (at our school or club)?

- What are the three main Teachable Moments facing us?

- What boundaries do we need to set to feel safe and learn well?

- Who/What isn't being heard?

- What needs to be heard?

- What did you appreciate most about this activity?

Chapter Summary:

Offer the Art of Spiritual Companioning

✓ Be fully present – it's the greatest present you can give.

✓ Don't try to fix or rescue. Give the student a chance to own and solve the problem and make moral choices.

✓ Use the magic words "What" and "How" to ask open-ended questions.

✓ Don't put words in their mouth. Listen to what they have to say.

✓ Respect and trust the wisdom others have to solve their own problems.

✓ Prepare yourself for counseling by using Compassion and Detachment.

✓ In counseling sessions, use the seven steps of Spiritual Companioning:

- Open the Door with open-ended questions.
- Offer Receptive Silence.
- Ask Cup-Emptying Questions.
- Focus on Sensory Cues.
- Ask Virtues Reflection Questions.
- Ask Closure and Integration Questions.
- Always end with a Virtues Acknowledgment. This restores dignity after someone has opened up to you.

✓ Set boundaries about your time and attention.

✓ Use companioning to diffuse anger by hearing the feelings and justice issues involved.

✓ Use companioning for conflict resolution, problem solving and strategic planning.

Section 2

● ●

Virtues:
The Gifts of Character

How to Use This Section

There are 52 virtues in this section, each containing the following parts:

- What is it?
- Why practice it?
- How do you practice it?
- Signs of Success
- An Affirmation

Daily Readings

One way to use these five parts is to read one per day in your classroom or over the P.A. system to stimulate awareness of "The Virtue of the Week" Program. See other ideas in the School-wide Activities in "Chapter One: Speak the Language of the Virtues".

Discussion and Role Play

The first page of each virtue also contains "What would (the virtue) look like if...?" scenarios. There are two ways to role play these:

1) Discuss what the situation would look like if the person were not practicing the virtue. Then have students role play the situation positively showing what it would look like if the virtue were being practiced. Some people believe that role playing is so powerful in internalizing an experience that it is best not to role play the negative situation first, but only to discuss it.

2) Alternatively, role playing "before" and "after" the practice of the virtue can be humorous and impress students with the negative consequences of failing to practice a virtue and the positive consequences of doing so.

Each virtue also contains an Activity Page made up of the following:

Virtues Activities

Activities with the virtue – some starter ideas for ways to focus on the virtue in your group or class.

Virtues Reflection Questions

These questions are designed to help students to reflect on the meaning and mastery of the virtues in their own lives and the feelings they experience with or without the practice of the virtue.

Drawing the Virtue

This feature has suggestions for art projects related to the virtue.

Poster Points

These are a list of phrases which students may find useful in creating a poster about the virtue. Of course, they may create their own.

Quotable Quotes

There are at least five quotes for each virtue, one or more of which you may want to hang in your classroom or read aloud each day of the school week. They are intended to inspire students and teachers to practice the virtue.

At the end of Section 2 is a poster of "Virtues: The Gifts of Character" which you may wish to copy or enlarge and have the children color.

Virtues: The Gifts of Character

Assertiveness

What is Assertiveness?

Being assertive means being positive and confident. It begins by being aware that you are a worthy person with your own special gifts. When you are assertive you think for yourself and ask for what you need. You have the self-confidence to tell the truth about what is just.

Why Practice It?

Without assertiveness, we would be passive, allowing others to bully us or lead us into trouble. We would have a hard time saying no. We would be afraid to tell if someone is hurting us. Without assertiveness, we might be too aggressive, bullying, fighting or trying to control others. When we are assertive, others respect us and we respect others. We stand up for what is right.

What would Assertiveness look like if...

- You start to feel inferior around some popular kids?
- An aggressive person starts to bully you?
- Your teacher asks the class for opinions about a story?
- A friend asks you to go somewhere you don't really want to go?
- A group tries to convince you to do something harmful?
- A stranger invites you for a ride?

Signs of Success

Congratulations! You are practicing Assertiveness when you...

- Think for yourself
- Share your own ideas and feelings
- Tactfully tell others what you really think
- Choose not to allow others to lead you into trouble
- Ask for what you want and need
- Expect respect at all times

How Do You Practice It?

When you are assertive, you are your own leader. You stand up and speak out. You don't accept unfair or hurtful treatment. You set boundaries about what you will and will not do, and get help when you need it. You share your true feelings – tactfully. You express your one-of-a-kind ideas, opinions and talents. You make a difference in the world in your own special way.

Affirmation

I am assertive. I think for myself and do what I feel is right. I am my own leader. I expect respect at all times. I freely express my own ideas.

Activities with Assertiveness

Mind Map

Make a mind map showing the personal boundaries you need in order to stay safe, to stay healthy, to get what you need, e.g. I walk away from trouble, I get help if I am threatened. I speak up about what I need.

Role Play

Describe a situation of someone being disrespectful, such as breaking in front of someone in line at a movie theater. First discuss what it would be like to be too passive, then discuss what it would be like to be too aggressive, then role play the situation using assertiveness, an approach which is firm but tactful and courteous.

Virtues Reflection Questions

- What happens to people that are too passive?

- What happens to people that are too aggressive?

- What is the difference between aggression and assertiveness?

- Name three things to do when someone is bullying you.

- What would you say and do if a stranger asked you to go with him or her?

- When do you find it difficult to say no?

- What are three ways to avoid a fight?

- What can a bossy person do to become more respectful?

- What can a bully do to become a friend?

Drawing Assertiveness

Draw a picture about "Stranger Danger".

Poster Points

- Expect respect.

- Express Yourself.

- Stand Up Speak Out.

- Set Clear Boundaries.

- Lead Your Life.

Quotable Quotes

"Since you are like no other being ever created since the beginning of time, you are incomparable." Brenda Ueland

"Yes, I can!" Sammy Davis Jr.

"This above all – to thine own self be true, and it must follow as the night the day, thou canst not then be false to any man." William Shakespeare, Hamlet

"If a man does not keep pace with his companions, perhaps it is because he hears a different drummer. Let him step to the music which he hears, however measured or far away." Henry David Thoreau

"No one can make you feel inferior without your consent." Eleanor Roosevelt

Caring

What is Caring?

Caring is giving love and attention to people and things that matter to you. When you care about people, you help them. When you do a careful job, you give it your very best effort. You treat people and things gently and respectfully.

Why Practice It?

Without caring, nothing and no one matters. If someone is hurt or sick, no one will help them. When people have an "I don't care" attitude, they do a sloppy or incomplete job. Things break and people are hurt. Caring people help others feel less alone. Because they care, others trust them. Caring makes the world a better and safer place.

How Do You Practice It?

You care for others when you show love and concern by doing kind things for them. Ask them how they are and what they think. When they are sad, ask "How can I help?" You handle things with control and gentleness. You give your best to everything you do. When you take care of yourself, you treat your body with respect. You keep yourself clean and healthy. You take care of your needs.

What would Caring look like if...

- You are doing a chore for your family?
- You notice that one of your friends looks sad?
- You come home after school and start talking to your mother?
- It is your job to take care of a pet?
- You are doing a school assignment?
- You feel upset about something that is hard to talk about?

Signs of Success

Congratulations! You are practicing Caring when you...

- Treat others, yourself and the earth with care
- Look at people and listen closely
- Handle things carefully
- Are gentle and loving with anyone or anything placed in your care
- Treat your body with respect
- Work with enthusiasm and excellence

Affirmation

I care for others and myself. I pay loving attention to the needs of people and animals. I give my best to every job.

Activities with Caring

Activities with Care

- Brainstorm everything a class or family pet needs.

- Do a project focused on caring for the earth, such as cleaning up a neighborhood street.

- Offer help to an elderly person.

- Think of someone in your class or your family and do caring things for them for a week. Then share what changes you noticed.

Virtues Reflection Questions

- How can you tell when others care about you?

- How do you feel when others act uncaring?

- Name three caring things you have done this week.

- Name a character from a book or story and describe what they care about most?

- Look at a newspaper or magazine and find stories about people who need care. Think of a way you and others can be of help.

- Name three ways you can care for the earth. (e.g. recycle, reuse, reduce)

Drawing Caring

Draw a picture of the people you care about. Draw a picture of people caring for the earth. Make a "Caring" Collage.

Poster Points

- Show that you care.

- Caring is a special way of loving.

- Yes, I care.

- Giving my best.

- Earth is our home. Let's take care of our home.

Quotable Quotes

"People don't care how much you know until they know how much you care." Unknown

"Charity begins at home." Terence

"Caring matters most." Hugel

"How shall we expect charity toward others, when we are uncharitable to ourselves?" Thomas Browne

"The care of human life and happiness, and not their destruction, is the first and only legitimate object of good government." Thomas Jefferson

"Every part of this earth is sacred to my people. Every shining pine needle, every sandy shore, every mist in the dark woods, every clearing and humming insect is holy in the memory and experience of my people." Chief Seattle's letter to President of U.S.A, 1885

Cleanliness

What is Cleanliness?

Cleanliness means washing often, keeping your body clean, and wearing clean clothes. Cleanliness in your mind is concentrating your thoughts on things that are good for you. You can "clean up your act" by deciding to change when you have done something you aren't proud of or have made a mistake. Staying clean also means keeping your body free of harmful drugs.

Why Practice It?

Keeping yourself clean makes you nice to be around. Cleanliness protects you from disease. Washing your hands before you eat and after you go to the bathroom keeps away germs that cause disease. When a room is clean and orderly, your mind feels clean and uncluttered too. A clean mind keeps you feeling peaceful.

How Do You Practice It?

Cleanliness is washing often and brushing your teeth. It is putting things away after you use them and keeping things in order. If you make a mistake, clean it up. Make amends and then act differently. Avoid looking at, listening to, or eating things that harm you. Only put into your body and your mind things that make you healthy.

What would Cleanliness look like if...

- You haven't been able to find your shoes for three days because your room is so messy?
- You notice that unwelcome thoughts are sticking in your mind?
- It is time for bed and you're so sleepy you don't feel like brushing your teeth?
- Your desk at school is cluttered with papers.
- Someone offers you drugs.
- You broke a promise to a friend.

Signs of Success

Congratulations! You are practicing Cleanliness when you...

- Keep your body fresh and clean
- Put things away after you use them
- Do your share to keep your home neat and clean
- Put only healthful things in your body
- Use clean language
- Clean up your mistakes

Affirmation

I keep myself fresh and clean. I put my things and my life in order. I am willing and able to clean up my mistakes.

Activities with *Cleanliness*

 ## Activities with Cleanliness

- "Clean Up Your Act"
  - Name a mistake you have made that you regret. How did you feel afterwards? How did it affect others?
  - Describe how you could have cleaned up the mistake? What could you have said or done to make amends?

- Choose a school or neighborhood area and clean it up.

- Study pollution in your local community or elsewhere in the world. Define ways this can be changed or cleaned up.

- Talk about physical health and hygiene.

 ## Virtues Reflection Questions

- What does it feel like to be in a messy room?

- How does it affect your mind? Your sense of well-being?

- How does it feel to be in a clean, orderly room? What effect does this have on your ability to think clearly?

- Brainstorm what to do and say when another student or an adult is selling drugs.

 ## Drawing Cleanliness

Draw a picture of a child or animal that has become dirty. Draw a second picture showing the figure clean and neat again.
Draw three ways you keep your body clean.

 ## Poster Points

- Clean body. Clean thoughts. Clean slate.

- I clean up my mistakes.

- Drug Free Zone.

- Garbage in, garbage out.

- The earth is our home. Let's keep it clean!

 ## Quotable Quotes

"Our eyes may see some uncleanness, but let not our mind see things that are not clean. Our ears may hear some uncleanness, but let not our mind hear things that are not clean."
Shinto saying

"Clean and sober." 12-Step Program

"Bid them wash their faces and keep their teeth clean." Shakespeare (Antony & Cleopatra)

"Let me remember that there is nothing more soothing than the sound of running water, even if it is only in my bathtub."
Anne Wilson Schaef

"Live pure, speak true, right wrong..."
Tennyson

Commitment

What is Commitment?

Commitment is caring deeply about something or someone. It is the willingness to give your all to a friendship, a task, or something you believe in. It is the ability to make decisions and follow through on them. It is keeping your promises.

Why Practice It?

Without commitment, we just drift along, with no idea where we are going. We change our minds. We give up easily if things get too hard. We break our word. We give up on people we care about if they disappoint us or make a mistake. When we are committed, people can count on us to keep our promises. With commitment we can achieve great things.

How Do You Practice It?

Commitment is thinking carefully about what you want to do, deciding to do it, then giving it 100%, holding nothing back. You don't allow problems to stop you. You go the extra mile. You only make promises you can keep. Being a committed friend is choosing your friends wisely, then sticking together through good times or bad. Commitment makes you trustworthy. It leads you to success.

What would Commitment look like if...

- You are doing a chore at home?
- You promised to bring in some materials for a class project?
- You fall asleep before finishing an assignment that is due tomorrow?
- Someone asks you if you will take responsibility for a big job?
- Your friend does something annoying and won't apologize?
- You want to learn a new sport but worry you may not be good enough?

Signs of Success

Congratulations! You are practicing Commitment when you...

- Think before you make a promise
- Keep every agreement you make
- Make decisions confidently
- Go the extra mile
- Give 100% to everything you do
- Are faithful to people you care about

Affirmation

I practice commitment. I make good decisions and give my all to whatever I do. I keep my agreements. I am a faithful friend.

Activities with Commitment

Make a Commitment

Choose a virtue and make a commitment to practice it for a week. Share with your class at the end of the week how it felt and what changed as a result.

Virtues Reflection Questions

- Name some athletes who show commitment. How do they express it?

- What does it feel like to be able to count on someone completely?

- What does it feel like when someone breaks a promise?

- How do you decide what promises you want to make?

- How do you know when you do not want to agree to something?

- What are you committed to?

- What virtues help you to keep your agreements?

Drawing Commitment

Draw your idea of something you really want in your life.

Poster Points

- Go for it!

- Give 100%.

- A Promise Keeper.

- Always a friend.

- Dreams do come true.

Quotable Quotes

"Until one is committed, there is hesitancy, the chance to draw back, always ineffectiveness. Concerning all acts of initiative and creation there is one elementary truth, the ignorance of which kills countless ideas and splended plans: that the moment one definitely commits oneself, then Providence moves too. All sorts of things occur to one that would never otherwise have occurred." Johann Wolfgang von Goethe

"Commitment isn't something that just happens by chance. Commitment is a capacity, and it grows as a muscle grows, by being exercised." Charlotte Jollo Beck

"Put your heart, mind, and soul into even your smallest acts. That is the secret of success." Swami Sivananda

"Nothing deflates commitment faster than broken agreements." Gay Hendricks and Kate Ludeman

"Never doubt that a small group of thoughtful, committed citizens can change the world. Indeed it's the only thing that ever has." Margaret Meade

Compassion

What is Compassion?

Compassion is having kind feelings toward someone who is hurt or troubled. It is caring deeply and wanting to help, even if you don't know them. It is being kind and forgiving to someone who has hurt you.

Why Practice It?

When people feel hurt or in trouble, they often feel alone. Feeling alone can make things even worse. Without compassion the world is a hard and lonely place. Being compassionate helps us to feel less alone. Compassion helps us to be understanding of others and ourselves.

How Do You Practice It?

Compassion begins by noticing when someone seems sad or troubled. Put yourself in their place and ask how you would feel if it were happening to you. Think about how you can help. Take time to listen, and then say kind things like "What are you sad about?" and "How can I help?" Be forgiving when others make mistakes. Be a friend when someone needs a friend.

What would Compassion look like if...

- Your dog is caught up in his leash?
- A friend is confused about what the teacher said?
- Your mother is sick in the hospital?
- A new student is lonely and feels left out?
- Your father seems really tired after work?
- Your brother's best friend just moved away?

Signs of Success

Congratulations! You are practicing Compassion when you...

- Notice when someone is hurt or needs a friend
- Imagine how they must be feeling
- Take time to show that you care
- Ask how they are and listen patiently
- Forgive others when they make mistakes
- Do some service to help a person or an animal in need

Affirmation

I have compassion. I notice when someone is hurt or needs my help. I take the time to show that I care.

Activities with Compassion

Service Project

- As a group, think of a way to serve people in your community who may be lonely or need some help.

- Look up newspaper articles that show people in need. Decide on a project you can do to help.

- Write a letter to someone who is sick at home

Virtues Reflection Questions

- What does compassion feel like inside?

- When have you felt compassionate towards someone you didn't know?

- What does it feel like to be lonely?

- Name three ways you can help a new student to feel less lonely?

- What would you do to be helpful and show compassion if your parent were in hospital?

Drawing Compassion

Draw a picture of a compassionate person helping a person or animal in trouble.

Poster Points

- My heart is full of compassion.

- Do for others what you would have them do for you.

- I care.

Quotable Quotes

"If your compassion does not include yourself, it is incomplete." Jack Kornfield

"Walk a mile in my shoes." Song

"To 'listen' another's soul into a condition of disclosure and discovery may be almost the greatest service that any human being ever performed for another." Douglas Steen

"...no man can live for himself alone." Ross Parmenter

"[Man] is immortal...because he has a soul, a spirit capable of compassion and sacrifice and endurance." William Faulkner

"The individual is capable of both great compassion and great indifference. He has it within his means to nourish the former and outgrow the latter." Norman Cousins

"Don't do unto others as you would have them do unto you. They may have different tastes." George Bernard Shaw

"Let no one ever come to you without leaving better and happier." Mother Teresa

Confidence

What is Confidence?

Confidence is having faith in something or someone. It is a kind of trust. When you have self-confidence, you trust that you have what it takes to handle whatever happens. You feel sure of yourself and enjoy trying new things. When you are confident in others, you rely on them and confide in them.

Why Practice It?

Without confidence, fears and doubts hold us back. We feel worried and uncertain, and afraid of making a mistake. With confidence, we try new things and learn all the time.

How Do You Practice It?

Practicing confidence is knowing you are worthwhile whether you win or lose, succeed or fail. You feel sure of yourself and gladly learn from your mistakes. You don't allow doubt or fear to stop you. You try lots of new things and discover what you are best at. You think positively. You have confidence in life, trusting that all things work together for good.

What would Confidence look like if...

- Your friends invite you to play a game you have never played before?
- You are asked to give a speech in front of your class?
- You try out for a sport and don't get picked?
- You did something that really upset your mother?
- You received a very low score on a math test?
- You see someone with lots of friends and wish you were one of them?

Signs of Success

Congratulations! You are practicing Confidence when you...

- Remember that you are worthwhile whether you succeed or fail
- Are willing to try new things
- Discover your talents
- Learn from your mistakes
- Are free of worry
- Think positively

Affirmation

I am confident. I love to try new things and I give them the best I have to give. I appreciate my gifts. I welcome new possibilities.

Activities with *Confidence*

Activities with Confidence

- Invite your students to set a goal of meeting one new person they have been wanting to get to know. Ask them to describe how a confident person would go about getting to know someone new.

- Ask them to reflect on something new they would like to try.

- Ask them to journal about the smell, the taste, the feel, the sound of confidence.

Virtues Reflection Questions

- Name one of the most confident people you know. What do you think gives them confidence?

- When do you most need your confidence?

- When do you feel most confident?

- What are you best at? What gave you the confidence to do it the first time?

Drawing Confidence

Draw a picture of yourself doing something with confidence.

Poster Points

- Think positively.

- Go for it!

- Why not?

- Just say YES!

Quotable Quotes

"We learn wisdom from failure much more than success. We often discover what WILL do by finding out what will NOT do." Samuel Smiles

"If we are not fully ourselves, truly in the present moment, we miss everything." Thich Nhat Hanh

"Only a person who has faith in himself is able to be faithful to others." Erich Fromm

"You see things; and you say 'Why?' But I dream things that never were; and I say 'Why not?'" George Bernard Shaw

"Shoot for the moon. Even if you miss it you will land among the stars." Les Brown

"Dream lofty dreams, and as you dream, so shall you become." Anonymous

"Everyone has inside of him a piece of good news. The good news is that you don't know how great you can be! How much you can love! What you can accomplish! And what your potential is!" Anne Frank

Consideration

What is Consideration?

Consideration is being thoughtful about other people and their feelings. It is thinking about how your actions affect them and caring about how they feel. It is paying attention to what other people like and don't like, and doing things that give them happiness.

Why Practice It?

When people behave selfishly and don't practice consideration, other people feel hurt. If we play music too loud, or forget someone's birthday, or leave things around that people can trip on, we are being inconsiderate. When we are considerate, others know they are important to us. We bring them happiness, and they feel like making us happy too.

How Do You Practice It?

Consideration begins by noticing what people need and thinking about how your actions are affecting them. You care about how they feel. You act as if other people are just as important as you are. You do little things to bring happiness to others. In giving a gift to someone, think carefully about what would please that person. Give tender attention to people who are sad.

What would Consideration look like if...

- Your brother is feeling bored because he is sick and has to stay in bed?
- You and your parents have very different tastes in music and how loudly it should be played?
- Your best friend's birthday is coming up?
- You are entering the front door at school and realize someone is right behind you?
- Your teacher is carrying an armload of materials?
- You have just come home from school and your grandmother is taking a nap?

Signs of Success

Congratulations! You are practicing Consideration when you...

- Respect other people's needs and feelings
- Consider others' needs as important as your own
- Stop and think how your actions will affect others
- Put yourself in other people's shoes
- Give tender attention
- Think of little things to bring others happiness

Affirmation

I am considerate of others. I stop and think about how my actions affect them. I do thoughtful things that bring happiness to others.

Activities with *Consideration*

Activities with Consideration

- Make a Mind Map of the people you care about most and thoughtful things you can do to bring them happiness.
- Spend a day being considerate of everyone who crosses your path. The next day share what that felt like and what effect it seemed to have with your friends, at home, on the street, in school.
- Think of someone who needs help or kindness and do something thoughtful.
- Choose a counselor, teacher, or administrator and without telling them anything, do considerate things for that person for a week. At the end of the week, ask them what they noticed.
- Secret Pal: Each student draws a name out of a box and does something considerate for that person during the week. At the end of the week, everyone finds out who their secret pal was.

Virtues Reflection Questions

- What is one of the most considerate things anyone ever did for you?

- What was the best surprise you ever received?

- What is one of the most considerate things you have ever done for someone else?

- How can you tell what is the best gift to give someone?

- Name three considerate things you can do that will make a big difference to your family.

- Commit to doing them! After a week, report on the differences you noticed.

Drawing Consideration

Draw a picture of yourself doing something considerate for someone at home.

Poster Points

- Consider this.

- Do unto others.

- Give a little.

- A little consideration goes a long way.

- Consideration brings happiness.

- Give surprises.

Quotable Quotes

"Let them at all times concern themselves with doing a kindly thing for one of their fellows, offering to someone love, consideration, thoughtful help." 'Abdu'l-Baha

"Try a little tenderness." Song Title

"The best portion of a good man's life, his little, nameless, unremembered acts Of kindness and of love." William Wordsworth, "Lines Composed Above Tintern Abbey"

"No one can sincerely try to help another without helping himself." Anonymous

"Life lived just to satisfy yourself never satisfies anybody." Vic Kitchen

Cooperation

What is Cooperation?

Cooperation is working together for the good of everyone. It is a willingness to respect others and to follow rules which keep everyone safe and happy. Cooperation is being helpful to one another, sharing the load. It is joining others in order to do something that cannot be done alone.

Why Practice It?

Without cooperation, people disturb others. They don't care about the rules, and they don't seem to care about others. When we work together, we can often accomplish more than each of us could do alone. When we cooperate, we can do great things.

How Do You Practice It?

Being cooperative is being willing to go along in order to get along. We are respectful of the rules. We consider other people's needs. We look for ways to be helpful, and we ask for help when we need it. Cooperation helps us bring together the ideas of many so that a new idea can come to light. Working together, we can make any place a safe and happy one.

What would Cooperation look like if...

- You have a project to do for school and don't have all the information you need?
- You notice that there is some bullying going on in the playground?
- You need to move something heavy?
- You are asked to participate in a group discussion?
- A new teacher seems nervous and doesn't know the rules yet?
- You don't agree with something your teacher has asked the class to do?

Signs of Success

Congratulations! You are practicing Cooperation when you...

- Work well with others
- Freely offer your help and ideas
- Follow the rules
- Do your part to keep a safe, happy environment
- When you disagree, do it peacefully
- Ask for help when you need it

Affirmation

I am cooperative. I work and play well with others. I respect the rules. I keep myself and others safe.

Activities with *Cooperation*

Trust Walk

Form pairs and blindfold one person. The other is to lead them gently and carefully around the room, making sure they do not bump into anything or anyone. Then they change roles.

Yarn Toss

Make a design out of yarn or string by forming a circle and tossing a ball of yarn across to others. Hold onto one part of the string while tossing the ball and keep holding the parts of the string that come to you. Option: As each individual tosses the yarn, they say aloud a virtue they like to practice. "I like Cooperation." "I like Kindness."

Cooperative Hide and Seek

(From *The Joyful Child* by Peggy Jenkins)

Two children, hand in hand, begin as the seekers, and each time they find someone he or she joins hands with them. The game ends with all children holding hands.

Virtues Reflection Questions

- When have you needed someone else's help to do something difficult?
- When have you helped someone else to do something they could not do without you?
- Describe what it is like when there is no cooperation in a group.
- Describe what it is like when there is cooperation in a group.
- What can you do with others you cannot do yourself?
- Name three things that can be done cooperatively to stop all bullying.

Drawing Cooperation

In a group, using a large sheet of paper, make a mural or drawing of people doing things together. Decide who will draw what before you start. Come up with one general idea and then give each other the freedom to be creative in your own ways.

Poster Points

- Go along to get along.
- Together we can do great things.
- Be a safe-keeper.

Quotable Quotes

"We must help one another; it is the law of nature." French Proverb

"By uniting we stand, by dividing we fall." John Dickenson (The Liberty Song)

"We must try to trust one another... and cooperate." Jomo Kenyatta

"Cooperation is doing with a smile what you have to do anyway." Anonymous

"Asking for help does not mean that we are weak or incompetent. It usually indicates an advanced level of honesty and intelligence." Anne Wilson Schaef

"Oh, I get by with a little help from my friends." Paul McCartney

Courage

What is Courage?

Courage is personal bravery in the face of fear. It is doing what needs to be done even when it is really hard or scary. Courage is going ahead even when you feel like giving up. Courage is needed in trying new things. It is admitting mistakes and then doing the right thing. Courage is the strength in your heart.

Why Practice It?

Without courage, people would only do what is easy. No one would try new things. Everyone would do what everyone else is doing, to avoid standing out – even if they knew it was wrong. Fear would be in charge. With courage, you can face any situation. Courage helps you to do great things.

How Do You Practice It?

Courage helps you to do the right thing. When you feel afraid, name the fear and then let it go. Then do what you really want to do. Admit mistakes and learn from them. Keep trying. Stand up for what you know is right even if all your friends are doing something wrong. Ask for help when you need it. Let courage fill your heart.

What would Courage look like if...

- You are asked to speak at a school assembly?
- All your friends want you to try something, like stealing or smoking, and you feel it is wrong?
- You see another child being teased or hurt by other children?
- You do something you are sorry for, like breaking one of your mother's plates and no one knows who did it?
- You feel scared of the dark when you're trying to go to sleep? (What help do you need?)
- You want to learn a new sport, like swimming, but it is scary.

Signs of Success

Congratulations! You are practicing Courage when you...

- Do what is right for you even when it is hard or scary
- Find strength in your heart even when you are afraid
- Are willing to try new things
- Admit mistakes and learn from them
- Make amends when you do something wrong
- Ask for help

Affirmation

I have courage. I am willing to try new things. I admit mistakes and learn from them. I listen to my heart. I have the courage to do the right thing.

Activities with *Courage*

Courage Collage

Make a collage of pictures of people showing courage.

Courage Commitment

Each person (including the teacher) chooses something that will require courage to do and sets a goal to do it in the next three days. At the end of the week, share your experiences with one another. It might be calling someone and clearing up an old problem, it might be trying a new activity, like skating, that you have never done before. The boundary is that it must keep you safe, and not be foolhardy. Even if it doesn't go just right, share the Teachable Moment together.

Virtues Reflection Questions

- When in your life have you needed the most courage?

- What helps you when you feel afraid?

- Name three people you know or from history who had great courage.

- What jobs require physical courage?

- What jobs require other kinds of courage?

Drawing Courage

Draw a picture of yourself doing something that requires courage.

Poster Points

- Do the right thing.

- Feel the fear and do it anyway!

- My heart is full of courage.

- Brave heart.

- Take a risk.

Quotable Quotes

"We cannot escape fear. We can only transform it into a companion that accompanies us on all our exciting adventures." Susan Jeffers

"Heart, be brave. If you cannot be brave, just go. Love's glory is not a small thing." Rumi

"Life shrinks or expands in proportion to one's courage." Anais Nin

"With courage, you will dare to take risks, have the strength to be compassionate and the wisdom to be humble. Courage is the foundation of integrity." Keshavan Nair

"Life is either a daring adventure, or nothing." Helen Keller

"Look fear in the face and it will cease to trouble you." Sri Yukteswar

"If you don't go out on a limb, you're never going to get the fruit." Anonymous

"If you think you're too small to do a big thing, try doing small things in a big way." Anonymous

Courtesy

What is Courtesy?

Courtesy is being polite and having good manners. It is a gracious way of speaking and acting which gives others a feeling of being valued and respected. It is greeting others with respect. "Please", "Thank you", "Excuse me", "Hello", "Goodbye", "You're welcome" are not just words. They are courteous expressions that show people you respect them and care about them.

Why Practice It?

When a person doesn't practice courtesy, people feel insulted and disrespected. They think this person is rude and ignorant, not caring about anyone or anything. Practicing courtesy gives people a sense that they are valued. Courtesy is like a magnet. It makes you attractive to others.

How Do You Practice It?

Courtesy is remembering your manners. Speak politely. Wait your turn. Instead of interrupting someone, say "Excuse me," and then wait patiently for them to give you their attention. Greet people pleasantly. When you are courteous, you make requests instead of demands. Bring courtesy home. Your family needs it most of all. Courtesy helps life to go smoothly.

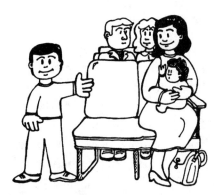

What would Courtesy look like if...

- You are meeting someone for the first time?
- Your mother is having a conversation and you want to speak to her?
- You are at a birthday party and the cake is being served?
- You answer the phone and the caller asks to speak to your sister?
- You have walked into class late?
- Your feel annoyed at your brother?

Signs of Success

Congratulations! You are practicing Courtesy when you...

- Show others that you value and respect them
- Remember to treat elders, parents, teachers, and children politely
- Think about how your actions affect others
- Eat, speak and move graciously
- Make requests instead of demands
- Greet people with a smile

Affirmation

I am courteous. I speak and act in a polite way.
I show others that I value and respect them.

Activities with *Courtesy*

Phone Courtesy

1) Have a phone-answering role play. Show discourteous ways to answer the phone first, then courteous ways (a) at home (b) at a friend's house (c) at an office.
Have students practice with a partner until they come up with expressions with which they feel comfortable, then do it for the class. (e.g., "Jones residence, Chris speaking.")

2) If you answer the phone and someone wants to speak to the adult in the house, and she has said she does not want to talk to anyone, what is a courteous and honest way to tell that to the caller. (Avoid lying and saying "She's not home". Could be an expression such as "She's not available right now." or "She can't come to the phone at the moment. May I take a message?")

Virtues Reflection Questions

- How do you and your friends show courtesy when you greet each other?

- How does it feel to you when someone is not courteous? When someone is courteous?

- How does it feel to you when you are not courteous? When you are courteous?

- How do people tend to react if you disrespect them by forgetting courtesy?

- What can you do if you have "slipped" and forgotten to be courteous?

- Who in your family needs more courtesy from you?

- What is the difference between making a demand and making a request? (You may want to role play the "before" and "after", first without courtesy, then with courtesy.)

Drawing Courtesy

Draw a picture of two animals greeting each other without courtesy, then greeting each other with courtesy.

Poster Points

- Remember your manners.

- Courtesy smooths the way.

- Smile! It's easy.

- Take courtesy home.

- Just say, "please".

Quotable Quotes

"Life is not so short but that there is always time enough for courtesy." Ralph Waldo Emerson

"If a man be gracious and courteous to strangers, it shows he is a citizen of the world." Francis Bacon

"Use a sweet tongue, courtesy, and gentleness and thou mayest manage to guide an elephant by a hair." Sa'di

"Politeness is to do and say the kindest things in the kindest way." Anonymous

"Most smiles are started by another smile." Anonymous

"Of all the things you wear, your expression is the most important." Janet Lane

Creativity

What is Creativity?

Creativity is the power of imagination. Creativity is a way to develop your special talents. It is seeing something in a new way, finding a different way to solve a problem. Creativity is using your imagination to bring something new into the world.

Why Practice It?

Without creativity, life would be boring. There would be no inventions or advancement in the world. Things would just stay the same. We wouldn't have cars, planes, computers, dance or music. The arts bring joy to the world. Sciences bring cures for disease and new ways to get things done. Creativity helps us to be all we can be.

What would Creativity look like if...

- You wish you could play an instrument?
- You get an idea for designing a new toy?
- The method you use for cleaning your room takes too long?
- You wonder if you could write a poem?
- A friend is having a birthday and you don't want to spend much money on a gift?
- You are spending too much time watching television?

How Do You Practice It?

You practice creativity by developing your gifts to the fullest. Find out what interests you and what you are good at. Learn and practice, so your talents will get better and better. Do ordinary things in creative ways. Expose yourself to beauty in nature and in the arts. Be open to inspiration. Remember to take time for dreaming.

Signs of Success

Congratulations! You are practicing Creativity when you...

- Discover your gifts
- Use knowledge and training to develop them
- Think of new ways to make things work better
- Use your imagination
- Take time for dreaming
- Do things in your own creative way

Affirmation

I am creative. I have special gifts and I am willing to develop them. I use my imagination. I am open to inspiration. I am happy to be myself.

Activities with *Creativity*

Activities with Creativity

- Write a poem or a make up a song. Create a dance. Make up a skit.

- Tell a progressive story, by starting it and allowing different students to finish it. "Once upon a time there was a _____ and (he, she, it) was very _____ ... and they lived happily ever after."

- "Thingamabob": Take some ordinary objects such as discarded cereal boxes, macaroni, toilet paper rolls, etc. and have students make one large interesting object out of them, or each do one small creation.

- Read "Stone Soup" by Marcia Brown and talk about how creativity saved the soldiers.

Virtues Reflection Questions

- Name three people in history who have done creative things that have made a big difference in our lives today.

- What does your mother create? Your father? Your teacher?

- What are some new ideas you have come up with?

- What is a talent you would like to have? How will you find out? How can you develop it? Read a story about someone such as Thomas Alva Edison, Albert Einstein or Madame Curie and ask the group to say what about them was creative?

- Describe a problem you know about. What is a creative way to solve it?

Drawing Creativity

Draw a picture of yourself doing something creative (dancing, singing, doing a science project, coming up with a new invention).

Poster Points

- Express yourself.
- Be all that you can be.
- Discipline in service of a vision.
- One of a kind.
- A gifted child.
- Expose yourself to beauty.
- Play with ideas.

Quotable Quotes

"Without this playing with fantasy no creative work has ever yet come to birth. The debt we owe to the play of imagination is incalculable." Carl Gustav Jung

"...Whatever you can do, or dream you can...begin it. Boldness has genius, power, and magic in it." Johann Wolfgang von Goethe

"A man's life is dyed the color of his imagination." Marcus Aurelius

"There comes that mysterious meeting in life when someone acknowledges who we are and what we can be, igniting the circuits of our highest potential." Rusty Berkus

"Insanity is when we keep doing the same things expecting different results." Albert Einstein

Detachment

What is Detachment?

Detachment is experiencing your feelings without allowing your feelings to control you. It is choosing how you will act in a situation rather than just reacting. With detachment you are free to do only what you choose to do. Detachment is using thinking and feeling together, so you can make smart choices.

Why Practice It?

People never know what to expect from someone who is not detached. Without detachment, you just react and let your feelings control you. Anger can pop out without warning. With detachment you don't have to react. You can decide what you are going to do. Detachment brings self-confidence. It helps you to be moderate. It helps you to be your best self.

How Do You Practice It?

Detachment helps you to decide how you are going to act, even when you have very strong feelings. It is like going to a calm, peaceful place within your mind and looking at what is happening without getting swept away. Whenever you have a strong feeling about something or someone, stop and ask yourself "What am I feeling?" and "What do I really want to do?" Take time out when you need it. Look. Choose. Act.

What would Detachment look like if...

- Your mother asks you do to some chores and you feel like playing video games instead?
- Your sister takes your best sweater without asking and you feel really mad?
- You really want to join a team and it doesn't happen?
- Someone teases you or tries to start a fight?
- You see that half of a cake is left and you feel like eating all of it?
- You are really upset because your best friend disappointed you?

Signs of Success

Congratulations! You are practicing Detachment when you...

- Take time out before doing something you would be sorry for
- Look at your feelings before deciding how to act
- Use thinking and feeling together
- Act instead of react
- Reflect before taking action
- Choose to do what is right

Affirmation

I am detached. I am aware of my feelings and choose my actions with detachment. I do what is right for me. I choose to be my best self no matter what happens.

Activities with Detachment

Activities with Detachment

- Make a list of the things that annoy you. Set a goal to detach from each of these and think about what will help you to detach. Don't name names. This list is just for you.

- Name three life situations that need detachment in order to live happily. (e.g., Someone who has a chronic illness, or is in a wheel chair).

Virtues Reflection Questions

- What are some of the hardest times for people to be detached?

- Name a time you needed lots of detachment.

- What are the best things about detachment?

- What happens if we don't practice detachment?

- What would you change in your life and your behavior if you only had one week to live?

Drawing Detachment

Draw a scene of yourself showing detachment.

Poster Points

- Look. Choose. Act.

- Smart choices.

- I don't react. I act.

- Detach and go within.

- Stop and think.

- Use thinking and feeling together.

Quotable Quotes

"Never undertake reflection and action independently." Pablo Friere

"Let go and let God" Alcoholics Anonymous

*"He who binds to himself a joy doth the winged life destroy,
but he who kisses the joy as it flies
lives in eternity's sunrise."* William Blake

"You always have the choice to take all things evenly, to hold onto nothing, to receive each irritation as if you had only fifteen minutes to live." Tolbert McCarroll

"When there is something wrong with everyone, there is something wrong with you." Anonymous

"Life is like an orchestra – if a man wants to lead, he has to turn his back to the crowd." Lawrence Welk

"Do not look back in anger, or forward in fear, but around in awareness." James Thurber

Determination

What is Determination?

Determination is focusing your energy and efforts on a task and then sticking with it until it is finished. Determination is using your will power to do something when it isn't easy. You are determined to meet your goals. Even when it is really hard, or you are being tested, you still keep going.

Why Practice It?

Without determination, things don't get done. People give up easily and don't ask for help when they need it. With determination, even the hardest task becomes a challenge we are willing to accept. We do things that matter in the world. With determination, we can make our dreams come true.

What would Determination look like if...

- You are trying to learn to ride a bike?
- You are doing a really hard homework assignment and it is due tomorrow?
- You are building a model for your Dad's birthday and it gets complicated?
- You want to become good at a sport or art?
- You decide to work on a new virtue and keep slipping into your old habits?
- You are doing a job for your mother and TV distracts you?

Signs of Success

Congratulations! You are practicing Determination when you...

- Believe what you are doing is important
- Set goals for yourself
- Focus your attention on what you are doing
- Resist being distracted
- Keep going if it gets difficult
- Ask for help when you need it
- Finish what you start

How Do You Practice It?

Decide what is important to you. Then use your will power to make it happen. Finish what you start. If obstacles come up, deal with them, and get back on track. If you get discouraged or distracted, remember your goal. Ask yourself "What do I need?" Then start again. It feels good to meet your goals!

Affirmation

I am determined. I set goals and keep going until I achieve them. I get things done. I stay on purpose.

The Virtues Project

Activities with Determination

Song

"The Itsy Bitsy Spider went up the water spout. Out came the rain and washed the spider out. Out came the sun and dried up all the rain And the itsy bitsy spider went up the spout again."

Puppet Play

Using puppets, tell a story of a very discouraged animal who never gets anything done and a friend who encourages the animal to be determined. Show the puppet changing from giving up to having enthusiasm and determination. Example: Character has a hard job to do and feels like giving up. Winter is coming and a bear needs to dig his den. An ant needs to gather food.

Stories of Determination

The Ant and the Grasshopper.
Tell a story about Helen Keller.

Virtues Reflection Questions

- Name a character from a book who succeeded because of his or her determination.

- Name an historical figure who showed great determination. (Examples: Helen Keller, Albert Einstein, Rick Hansen.)

- What would it be like to play a sport without determination? With determination?

- When have you needed the most determination?

- What is your biggest distraction? What helps you to resist it?

- Name three of your personal goals in life.

Drawing Determination

Draw a picture of yourself having achieved one of your life goals with determination.

Poster Points

- I set goals.

- I get things done.

- Keep on keepin' on.

- I finish what I start.

Quotable Quotes

"Keep on keepin' on" African American Proverb

"An eagle misses seventy per cent of his strikes. Why should I expect to do better?"
Sophy Burnham

"Just do it!" Anonymous

"The difference between determination and stubbornness is that one comes from a strong will and the other from a strong won't."
Anonymous

"Strong reasons make strong actions."
Anonymous

"Character is a perfectly educated will."
Novalis

Diligence

What is Diligence?

Diligence is working hard and doing the best job you possibly can. When you are diligent, you take special care to do things step by step. You think and move carefully to make sure things will turn out right. Being diligent is being industrious, giving all you have to give to whatever you do.

Why Practice It?

Without diligence, people act lazy and don't get much done. They act as if what they do doesn't count, rush through it or just do the least amount possible. Diligence helps you to get things done with excellence and enthusiasm. Diligence leads to success. When you are diligent about the things you do, people rely on you and trust you to give your best effort.

How Do You Practice It?

You practice diligence by deciding what you can do and then giving it all you have to give. You treat each action as important and do things carefully, one step at a time. You don't rush through things. You give them your full attention. Diligence takes patience. When you work hard, you can accomplish wonderful things.

What would Diligence look like if...

- You are washing the dishes for your family?
- You are doing an assignment you find boring?
- You want to be a musician?
- Some friends ask you to come out when you have a job to do?
- You feel like taking a break in the middle of a job?
- You have an idea for something you want to build?

Signs of Success

Congratulations! You are practicing Diligence when you...

- Pay attention to what you are doing
- Do things carefully, step by step
- Practice to the point of excellence
- Give your absolute best to what you do
- Work hard
- Don't give up

Affirmation

I am diligent. I work hard. I work carefully. I give my best to whatever I do.

Activities with Diligence

Activities with Diligence

Give students a task that involves intricate sorting, such as different shapes of beads, or a sewing project. Invite them to do it with diligence.

Virtues Reflection Questions

- What do dishes look like when they are done without diligence?

- What do dishes look like when they are done with diligence?

- What difference could diligence make in your future success?

- Name three successful people and describe how they showed diligence in their careers.

- Name some jobs in which diligence is essential.

- What would it be like if people did a rushed, careless job of
  - building a bridge
  - performing an operation
  - painting a house
  - working in a laboratory.

Drawing Diligence

On one side draw someone doing an important job without diligence, on the other with diligence.

Poster Points

- Giving my best.

- Giving my all.

- A careful and thorough worker.

- Hard work leads to success.

Quotable Quotes

"Learning is not attained by chance, it must be sought for with ardor and attended to with diligence." Abigail Adams

"Diligence is the mother of good fortune." Cervantes

"Failure and success are not accidents, but the strictest justice." Alexander Smith

"Everything comes to the one who waits, if he works while he waits." Anonymous

"Luck is what happens when preparation meets opportunity." Elmer Letterman

"The trouble with opportunity is that it often comes disguised as hard work." Anonymous

"Genius is 10% inspiration, 90% perspiration." Thomas Alva Edison

Enthusiasm

What is Enthusiasm?

Enthusiasm is being inspired – full of spirit. It is being cheerful and happy. It is doing something wholeheartedly, with zeal and eagerness – giving 100% to what you do. Being enthusiastic is being excited about something, looking forward to it. It comes from having a positive attitude.

Why Practice It?

Everything becomes boring to a person without enthusiasm. A person without enthusiasm becomes boring, too. Enthusiasm is catching. When you are enthusiastic, other people like to be around you. Enthusiasm makes life more enjoyable.

How Do You Practice It?

Enthusiasm is a positive attitude. When you enjoy whatever you are doing, even the dullest job can be fun. Use your imagination to find ways to enjoy what you are doing. Take time for simple pleasures and enjoy the wonders of life. Show enthusiasm to others by celebrating with them when something wonderful happens. Your enthusiasm shines through your smile.

What would Enthusiasm look like if...

- You particularly like a dish your mother or father cooks?
- You like a new song a friend played for you?
- Your brother did well in a sport?
- You are bored and tired of sitting around at home?
- You look outside one night and see the stars?
- You have a big chore to do for your family?

Signs of Success

Congratulations! You are practicing Enthusiasm when you...

- Let yourself enjoy looking forward to something
- Think of imaginative ways to get things done
- Do things wholeheartedly
- Smile, laugh and enjoy what you do
- Enjoy the wonders of life
- Are full of positive spirit

Affirmation

I am full of enthusiasm. I look on the bright side. I give 100% to whatever I do. I use my imagination. I am open to the wonders in store for me today.

Activities with *Enthusiasm*

Activities with Enthusiasm

- Do a game such as musical chairs, once without enthusiasm, once with. Then talk about how it felt different each time.

- Take a simple object, like an apple or a chair and describe it twice: First, as if it is the most boring thing in the world and second, as if it is the most delightful, wonderful thing.

Virtues Reflection Questions

- How do people without enthusiasm look, sound, act? (Their faces, their movements, their voices)

- What do enthusiastic people look like?

- What activity do you do with enthusiasm?

- What are you enthusiastic about for the future?

- What kinds of work or careers require enthusiasm?

- What difference can enthusiasm make if you have a boring job to do?

- What helps you get back to enthusiasm when you are bored or sad?

Drawing Enthusiasm

Draw something you are really looking forward to doing when you are older.
Draw a picture of a bored, boring person and a cheerful, enthusiastic person.

Poster Points

- Wow!

- That's great!

- Full of spirit.

- Simple Pleasures.

- What a great day!

- Life is fun.

Quotable Quotes

"Enthusiasm, n. 1.a. Rapturous interest or excitement. b. Ardent fondness. 2. Something that inspires a lively interest. [Greek enthousiazein, to be inspired by God]."
The American Heritage Dictionary

"When an optimist gets the worst of it, he makes the best of it." Anonymous

"Life is fun." Benjamin Hoff

"To be successful, the first thing to do is fall in love with your work." Sister Mary Lauretta

"It don't mean a thing if it ain't got that swing." Duke Ellington and Irving Mills

"Man is just about as happy as he makes up his mind to be." Abraham Lincoln

"All that we need to make us really happy is something to be enthusiastic about."
Charles Kingsley

Excellence

What is Excellence?

Excellence is doing your best. It is giving your very best to any task you do or any relationship you have. Excellence is effort guided by a noble purpose. It is a desire for perfection. The perfection of a seed comes in the fruit. When you practice excellence, you bring your gifts to fruition.

Why Practice It?

Excellence is the key to success. People who don't practice excellence just do things half way. Usually they don't have very exciting or fruitful lives. Doing your best helps you find out what talents you have. You may discover something no one has ever thought of before. When you practice excellence, you can make a difference in this world.

What would Excellence look like if...

- You are cleaning up the classroom?
- You are learning to play a new instrument?
- You keep arguing with your friend?
- You get tired in the middle of a job?
- You compare yourself to others?
- You realize that you have made too many promises and have too much to do?

Signs of Success

Congratulations! You are practicing Excellence when you...

- Give your best to whatever you do
- Give your best to relationships
- Set noble and realistic goals
- Remember to plan and practice
- Don't try to do everything
- Develop your special gifts

How Do You Practice It?

When you practice excellence, you are not content to give less than your best – to big things and little things. You give careful attention to every job, and to the people you care for. You learn from your mistakes, so you can do better next time. Day by day, you strive to improve. We can't excel at everything. Discover your own talents and give them your best.

Affirmation

I give my best to the work I do. I give my best to others. I dare to set noble goals. I choose excellence in all things.

Activities with *Excellence*

Make an Excellence Mobile

Using a coat hanger, cards and string, make a mobile about yourself listing your most excellent virtues – those that are your strengths – as well as things you do with excellence.

Virtues Reflection Questions

- Name a time that you needed excellence but chose to give up instead.

- Name a time you chose to practice excellence.

- Name a character from a story or lesson you have been learning. How did they show excellence? What difference did it make?

- How would things have turned out without excellence?

- List the names of three famous people who excel in their field. How do they show it?

- What do you think they have done to become excellent?

Drawing Excellence

Draw yourself doing some of the things you do best.

Draw people doing three different kinds of work. (for example, nurse, farmer, house builder) Write or tell what would happen if they didn't practice excellence. Then write or tell what would happen if they did practice excellence in their work.

Poster Points

- It's okay to make mistakes. That's the way we learn.

- At my best.

- The key to success.

- Day by day I'm getting better and better.

- Excellence in all things.

- Growing our gifts.

Quotable Quotes

"I do the very best I know how – the very best I can; and I mean to keep doing so until the end." Abraham Lincoln

"Dost thou reckon thyself a puny form, when within thee the universe is folded?" Imam Ali

"May you discover your own special abilities and contribute them toward a better world." Charlene Costanzo

"Attention to little things is a great thing." St. John Chrysostom

"It's a funny thing about life: if you refuse to accept anything but the very best you will very often get it." W. Somerset Maugham

"When love and skill work together, expect a masterpiece." John Ruskin

"The oak sleeps in the acorn; the bird waits in the egg...dreams are the seedlings of realities." Anonymous

Flexibility

What is Flexibility?

Flexibility is being open to change. It means not always having to have your own way. It is being open to the opinions and feelings of others. With flexibility, you are willing to change your mind. If something doesn't work, you try a new way. Flexibility is making changes for the better.

Why Practice It?

Without flexibility, people keep doing things the same old way when new ways are needed. They become rigid. They get angry and upset when things don't go their way and try to control other people. When you are flexible, you adjust and adapt. You bend like a tree in the wind. You keep making positive changes.

How Do You Practice It?

When you practice flexibility, you let go of bad habits and learn new ones. When you see a need for change, look inside and find the virtue you need. Then practice it little by little, day by day. Try new, creative ways to get things done. Accept the things you cannot change. Go with the flow. When you are flexible, you enjoy surprises.

What would Flexibility look like if...

- You keep making the same mistake over and over?
- You decide you want to change one of your habits?
- Your family had something fun planned and it was cancelled at the last minute?
- You notice that some of your friends are avoiding you?
- The way you are doing a job isn't working very well?
- You can't stand the way one of your friends is acting?

Signs of Success

Congratulations! You are practicing Flexibility when you...

- Learn from your mistakes
- Are willing to change bad habits
- Try imaginative new ways to do things
- Don't insist on always getting your own way
- Can adjust when something unexpected happens
- Go with the flow. Trust the unexpected.

Affirmation

I am flexible. I keep changing for the better. I look for new ways to do things. I welcome surprises.

Activities with Flexibility

 ## Flexibility Chain

Have children make a chain by holding hands, then get themselves into a knot, by stepping over hands etc. or weaving in and out. Then have them straighten out the chain without dropping hands.

How Many Ways?

Put on some music and ask everyone to do one motion trying to be as different from each other as possible, e.g., hands clapping, turning in a circle, bending knees up and down.

Tell a Story with Puppets

Have children divide into groups and make puppets, then have a show in which one puppet is very rigid and wants everything to go his or her way. A friend shows him how to become flexible and how friends like to be around someone who can be flexible.

 ## Virtues Reflection Questions

- What is it like to be around people who are not flexible?

- Name some habits or ways of behaving which do not show flexibility.

- Name some actions that do show flexibility.

- Name some sports or arts that require flexibility. Do some stretches and toe touches.

- Discuss how many ways you could prepare or cook a vegetable you like to eat. (e.g. boil, bake, fry, eat raw, in strips, whole, mixed with other vegetables).

 ## Drawing Flexibility

Make two drawings on a sheet of paper: First, draw a tree that is likely to be blown down in a windstorm. Then, draw a tree that is likely to survive the storm, (e.g., oak and willow).

 ## Poster Points

- I bend but do not break.

- Go with the flow.

- I welcome surprises.

- Change for the better.

- Day by day, little by little.

 ## Quotable Quotes

"Go with the flow." Anonymous

"I bend but do not break." Jean de la Fontaine

"A man should endeavor to be pliant as a reed, yet hard as cedar wood." The Talmud

"Do I contradict myself? Very well then I contradict myself. (I am large, I contain multitudes)." Walt Whitman

"I learned when hit by loss, to ask the right question: 'What next?' instead of 'Why me?'" Julia Cameron

"Change is just an attitude away." Anonymous

Forgiveness

What is Forgiveness?

Being forgiving is giving someone another chance after they have done something wrong, knowing that everyone makes mistakes. It is making amends instead of taking revenge. It is important to forgive yourself, too. Forgiving yourself means to stop punishing yourself or feeling hopeless because of a mistake. Forgiveness is moving ahead, ready to act differently, with compassion for yourself and faith that you can change.

Why Practice It?

Everyone does hurtful things at one time or another. If someone is not forgiving, others feel worried around that person. Without forgiveness, we judge and criticize others instead of giving each other a chance to improve. Forgiveness is the best way to encourage ourselves and others to take responsibility for our actions, to try harder and to change for the better.

How Do You Practice It?

Forgiveness is having the courage to face a mistake that you or someone else has made. You may feel sad, guilty or angry. Let your feelings come, and then let them go, like leaves passing by in a stream. Avoid revenge. Decide what amends need to be made. If someone repeatedly hurts you, forgiving them won't help. You need to stop giving them chances to hurt you. Humbly learn from mistakes. Sometimes mistakes are our best teachers.

What would Forgiveness look like if...

- Your friend accidentally broke one of your belongings?
- Your mother is late picking you up from school?
- You did something you feel is very bad?
- Your brother repeatedly takes something of yours without asking?
- A friend lost her temper at you and later apologized?
- You decide you want to stop the habit of criticizing?

Signs of Success

Congratulations! You are practicing Forgiveness when you...

- Remember that everyone makes mistakes
- Take responsibility for your own mistakes
- Share your feelings without taking revenge
- Stop giving uncaring people the chance to hurt you
- Accept people without judgment or criticism
- Make amends instead of punishing yourself with guilt

Affirmation

I am forgiving of others and myself. I am willing to give and receive amends. I learn from my mistakes. I have the power to keep changing for the better.

Activities with Forgiveness

Forgiveness Fire Circle

This powerful ceremony has been done with all ages, from pre-school through adult. There are alternatives without fire. If fire is not available, have each person shred their paper and release it into a basket. Have someone agree to take them and burn them.

1. Read from this Guide about the virtue of Forgiveness and say that all of us have done things we regret or are sorry for.

2. Set a boundary that silence will be kept throughout this exercise. There will be no sharing. It is to be done privately and individually. No one else will look at what we are putting on paper.

3. Pass out slips of paper and invite individuals to write or draw something they feel very guilty about. Do one yourself.

4. In a safe, outside area, have a small fire. With older children, you can invite some to be the fire makers, and some to be responsible for dousing the fire with water afterward. All is to be done in complete silence. Have wood, paper, kindling, matches available. Form a circle and say "When you are ready, release your mistake to the fire of forgiveness. If it is appropriate in your setting, say a prayer for forgiveness. "Forgive us these mistakes. Make them our teachers. Help us to replace them with new ways of being and acting."

5. Come back in and invite each person to write or draw a commitment. "I commit to..." involving a virtue and an action which will replace the mistake. It could be a form of making amends. Close with a closure and integration question "What did you appreciate about this exercise?"

Virtues Reflection Questions

- When do you find it most difficult to forgive? What blocks you from being forgiving? What would help you to replace those habits with true forgiveness?

- What virtues help you to keep from retaliating when someone hurts you?

- Name three things you could do to make amends if you break a promise to your mother?

- When a friend hurts you, what amends do you need them to make?

Drawing Forgiveness

Draw two scenes: (1) friends not being forgiving, (2) friends being forgiving.

Poster Points

- Starting over.
- A clean slate.
- Turning the other cheek.
- To err is human, to forgive, divine.

Quotable Quotes

"Forgiveness is not an occasional act, it is a permanent attitude." Martin Luther King

"It is by forgiving that one is forgiven." Mother Teresa

"To err is human, to forgive, divine." Alexander Pope

"One of the most important trips a man can make is in meeting the other fellow halfway." Anonymous

"If you haven't forgiven yourself something, how can you forgive others?" Dolores Huerte

Friendliness

What is Friendliness?

Friendliness is being a friend. It is taking an interest in other people. It is going out of your way to make others feel welcome or to make a stranger feel at home. When you are friendly, you happily share your belongings, time, ideas, and feelings. You share the good times and the bad times together. Friendliness is the best cure for loneliness.

Why Practice It?

Friendliness keeps you and others from feeling lonely or left out. It helps people feel that they belong. When something good or bad happens, it feels good to share it with a friend. Friendships don't just happen — they are made by people who are willing to be themselves with each other.

How Do You Practice It?

Friendliness begins with liking yourself and believing you have something to share with others. Be kind to people you don't know. You can be friendly just by walking down the hall, looking into people's faces, and smiling. They will probably smile back. Show your friends you are glad to see them, by asking how their day is going and sharing your news with them.

What would Friendliness look like if...

- You see someone who is new at school looking lonely?
- You wish you could make friends with a popular student at school?
- Your parents invite a family to dinner whom you have never met?
- One of your friends looks like she has been crying?
- You are walking past someone who looks strange and dresses differently?
- You wish you had more friends?

Signs of Success

Congratulations! You are practicing Friendliness when you...

- Like yourself and realize you have a lot to offer
- Smile and greet someone you don't know
- Get to know someone and let them get to know you
- Show an interest in others
- Show caring when a friend needs you
- Are friendly to people who look and act different

Affirmation

I am friendly. I smile and greet people. I show an interest in others. I like myself and know that my friendship is worth a lot.

Activities with Friendliness

A Friendly Week

Make a commitment together as a class to be friendly to at least one new person a day for a week and share about it on the last day of the week. Questions to ask are:

- What was hard about it?
- What was easy about it?
- How did it feel to be friendlier?
- Did you meet anyone you would not have met before?
- How has your friendliness helped make our school/club/camp a better place?

Virtues Reflection Questions

- What are some of the challenges or obstacles to being friendly?

- What are the characteristics of a best friend?

- What would a good friend do if someone was sad?

- How can you be friendly with someone without making it into a "best friends" situation?

- What happens when cliques form and they are unfriendly to everyone else?

- Name three things you can do to have more friends.

Drawing Friendliness

Draw a picture of people being friendly.

Poster Points

- A friend through good times and bad.

- Always a friend.

- Friendliness is contagious.

- There are a lot of interesting people out there.

Quotable Quotes

"Don't walk in front of me
I may not follow
Don't walk behind me
I may not lead
Walk beside me
And just be my friend."
Albert Camus

"The friendship that can cease has never been real." St. Jerome

"The best way to have a friend is to be one." Peggy Jenkins

"A friend loves you enough to support you and to confront you." Anonymous

"The world is like a mirror
Reflecting what you do,
And if your face is smiling
It smiles right back at you."
Unknown

"To be a friend, remember that we are human magnets; that like attracts like and that as we give we get."
Wilfred Peterson

Generosity

What is Generosity?

Generosity is giving and sharing. It is giving freely because you want to, not with the idea of receiving a reward or a gift in return. Generosity is being aware that there is plenty for everyone. It is seeing a chance to give what you have and then giving just for the joy of giving. It is one of the best ways to show love and friendship.

Why Practice It?

Without generosity, people act uncaring, refusing to share their belongings, their time, and their friendship. People who need help feel helpless because no one will give them what they need. When we give freely, especially if a sacrifice is involved, our spirit grows strong. When one person is generous, other people want to be generous too.

12

How Do You Practice It?

When you are generous, you think of ways to share what you have. You think about what people need and do things to give them happiness. You share your time, your ideas, your things, or your money. When you give away something that is really special to you, that is a very generous way to show love. It feels good to give freely, just for the sake of giving.

What would Generosity look like if...

- A friend comes over to play the day after your birthday and you have a new toy?
- Someone who has broken your things before wants to borrow your favorite thing?
- Your father is cooking dinner and needs someone to set the table, and you're watching a good TV show?
- A student in your class has forgotten her lunch and doesn't have any money?
- Someone's birthday is coming up and you wonder what to get him?
- You learn that there are children somewhere who are hungry and do not have enough clothing?

Signs of Success

Congratulations! You are practicing Generosity when you...

- Are thoughtful about the needs of others
- Notice when someone needs help
- Give freely without expectation of reward
- Give fully without holding back
- Are willing to make sacrifices for others
- Use wisdom about sharing treasured belongings

Affirmation

I am generous. I look for opportunities to give and to share. There is plenty of time for thoughtfulness. I give freely, fully, and joyfully.

Activities with *Generosity*

Generosity List

Make a list of ways you can be generous
• with your time and energy
• with your belongings
Think of something generous to do for someone in your family and do it!

Gift Wish Box

Decorate a small recycled box or tissue container. Make some paper hearts and write on each of them some gifts you wish to give others, such as an act of service (washing the dishes, setting the table), or a toy you are willing to share for a day. Let someone take a heart out of the box, and then be generous!

Virtues Reflection Questions

● When do you find it most difficult to share? When do you feel like sharing?

● How do you feel when someone does not share with you? How do you feel when someone does share with you?

● What helps you to be generous?

● Who is it hard to be generous to? Who is it easy to be generous to?

● Have you ever sacrificed something that was important to you? How did that feel?

● When is it important to balance generosity with assertiveness about what you choose to share?

● What boundaries do you need to set with people who are not gentle with your things?

● Name three ways you can be generous at home today.

Drawing Generosity

Draw three of your favorite things. Are these things to share or things to keep only for your own use? (Deciding that is up to you!) Include one thing that you are willing to share.

Poster Points

● Giving freely, giving fully.

● Giving joyfully.

● Sharing yourself.

● The more we give the more we have.

Quotable Quotes

"What goes around comes around." Unknown

"One of the marks of true genius is a quality of abundance." Catherine Drinker Bowen

"A man of humanity is one who, in seeking to establish himself, finds a foothold for others and who, desiring attainment for himself, helps others to attain." Confucius

"A cheerful giver does not count the cost of what he gives. His heart is set on pleasing and cheering him to whom the gift is given." Julian of Norwich

"The more one gives, the more one has." Chinese Proverb

"Whatever you give to others is also a gift to yourself." Sanaya Roman

Gentleness

What is Gentleness?

Gentleness is acting and speaking in a kind, considerate way. It is using self-control, in order not to hurt or offend anyone. You can be gentle with people and animals in the way you touch them and the way you speak to them. You handle things carefully so they will not break or be hurt. When you think gentle thoughts, it makes the world a safer, gentler place.

Why Practice It?

Without gentleness, things get broken and people feel hurt. It is easy to become too rough or say things we are sorry for. People are very sensitive beings. Many things are delicate and fragile, but feelings are the most fragile of all. When you are gentle, people and things stay safe.

How Do You Practice It?

Gentleness is moving wisely, touching softly, holding carefully, speaking quietly and thinking kindly. You have to think about being gentle. Otherwise, it is easy to become too rough, move too fast or say hurtful things. When you feel mad or hurt, instead of hurting someone back, talk things out peacefully. When you think kindly and gently, people will see the gentleness in your eyes.

What would Gentleness look like if...

- You want to touch or hold a baby?
- You have something to tell your friend and worry that his feelings might be hurt?
- You are setting the table with your family's best dishes?
- You walk into your classroom and start to slam the door?
- You find an injured animal?
- You're wrestling too roughly with a friend?

Signs of Success

Congratulations! You are practicing Gentleness when you...

- Make it safe for people and animals to be around you
- Touch carefully
- Speak with a soft voice
- Express your feelings peacefully
- Take time out when you don't feel gentle
- Think gentle thoughts that make you smile inside

Affirmation

I am gentle. I think, speak and act with gentleness. I show care for people and for everything I touch.

Activities with *Gentleness*

Activities with Gentleness

- Bring a small animal into class and have students take turns holding it gently.
- Invite students to write or tell a story about a bully who learns to be gentle.
- Take a few quiet moments, to stroke the back of your hand with your fingertips very, very gently, as if you were stroking a kitten. Then reverse and stroke the other hand. Notice how gentle you feel now.

Virtues Reflection Questions

- When is it most important to be gentle with people?

- How does it feel when someone is rough or unkind to you?

- How does it feel to be rough and unkind?

- Name three things you need to remember if you are going to handle something delicate?

- What do you need to remember when you pick up a baby?

- What other virtues can help you to be gentle?

- How would you keep your gentleness if you felt annoyed when someone bumped into you?

- How could you tell your friend something that isn't pleasant for him to hear? (e.g., he needs a bath, she is coming over to your house too often, you feel like being with someone else for a while.)

Drawing Gentleness

Draw a picture of some baby animals that need lots of gentleness.

Poster Points

- *Easy does it.*

- *Gentle as a dove.*

- *Soft as a feather.*

- *Taking care.*

- *A light touch.*

Quotable Quotes

"Use a sweet tongue, courtesy, and gentleness, and thou mayest manage to guide an elephant by a hair." Sa'di

"I want a kinder, gentler nation." George Bush

"The great of earth, how softly do they live." Ruth Tenney

"There is certainly something in angling...that tends to produce a gentleness of spirit, and a pure serenity of mind." Washington Irving (referring to fishing)

"The gentle mind by gentle deeds is known." Edmund Spenser

"The quality of mercy is not strained, It droppeth even as the gentle rain from heaven Upon the place beneath: it is twice blessed; It blesseth him that gives and him that takes." William Shakespeare (The Merchant of Venice)

Helpfulness

What is Helpfulness?

Helpfulness is being of service. It is doing useful things for people, such as things they cannot do for themselves, something they do not have time to do, or just little things that make life easier. It is important to be helpful to ourselves too, by taking care of our bodies. There are times when we need help from others. That is a good time to ask for help.

Why Practice It?

We all need help sometimes. We need people to teach us, and people to give us their strength or ideas. Sometimes we just need a friend to talk to. If there were no helpfulness, there would be no cooperation. When we practice helpfulness we get more done. We make each other's lives easier.

How Do You Practice It?

When you are helpful, you care about others. You don't wait to be asked. You notice what needs to be done and just do it. If you cannot figure out what someone needs, ask them "How can I help?" or "What do you need?" Remember to help yourself by eating healthy foods, exercising and getting plenty of rest. And remember to ask for help when you need it.

What would Helpfulness look like if...

- A friend is carrying a whole pile of books?
- It is time for dinner and your mother could use help?
- You notice that a friend looks sad?
- Your best friend asks you if he can copy your homework?
- An older person just slipped and fell?
- You see a student surrounded by a group who don't look friendly?

Signs of Success

Congratulations! You are practicing Helpfulness when you...

- Notice when someone needs help
- Do a service without being asked
- Give people what they need, not always what they want
- Listen to someone who needs to talk
- Care for your own needs
- Ask for help when you need it

Affirmation

I am helpful. I look for ways to be of service. I care for others and myself. I look for helpful ways to make a difference.

Activities with Helpfulness

Making a Difference

Discuss what would be helpful to your school and design a project to make a difference. Remember to ask permission before you do it.

Virtues Reflection Questions

- How are you helpful at home?

- Describe a time you helped an animal.

- Name three ways you could be more helpful at home.

- How would you be helpful to a substitute teacher?

- When have you needed help and how did it feel?

- Was it easy or difficult to ask for help?

- What was it like to receive help?

- When have you been helpful to someone outside of your family?

- How can you tell if what someone asks you to do for them is helpful or not?

- What is the most helpful way to respond if someone is injured?

Drawing Helpfulness

Draw a picture of a person or an animal who needs help and someone helping them.

Poster Points

- Show that you care.

- Caring is a special way of loving.

- Yes, I care!

- Giving my best.

- Earth is our home. Let's take care of our home.

Quotable Quotes

"I would help others out of fellow-feeling."
Robert Burton

"If I can stop one Heart from breaking
I shall not live in vain
If I can ease one Life the Aching
Or cool one Pain
Or help one fainting Robin
Unto his Nest again
I shall not live in vain."
Emily Dickinson

"No one can sincerely try to help another without helping himself." Unknown

"Oh, I get by with a little help from my friends." John Lennon and Paul McCartney

"I expect to pass through this world but once; any good thing therefore that I can do, or any kindness that I can show to any fellow creature, let me do it now; let me not defer or neglect it, for I shall not pass this way again."
Anonymous

Honesty

What is Honesty?

Being honest is being open, trustworthy and truthful. When people are honest, they can be relied on not to lie, cheat, or steal. Honesty is telling the truth. It is admitting mistakes even when you know someone might be angry or disappointed. Being honest means that you don't pretend to be something you are not. With honesty, you can trust things to be as they appear.

Why Practice It?

Honesty is important because it builds trust. When people lie, or cover up mistakes, others can't trust them. When people aren't honest with themselves, they pretend that something doesn't matter when it does or they exaggerate to impress others. When you are honest with yourself, you accept yourself as you are. When you are honest, others can believe you.

How Do You Practice It?

When you are honest, you don't try to fool yourself or others. You say what you mean and mean what you say. You only make promises you can keep. Be trustworthy in all your dealings, refusing to lie or cheat. Admit your mistakes and fix them. Be honest with yourself and you will be honest with others. You don't need to make things up to look good – you're already good – honest!

What would Honesty look like if...

- You broke one of your mother's favorite things by accident and are afraid she will be mad?
- You find yourself exaggerating about how well you did in sports?
- Your sister asks you if a new dress looks good on her and you think it doesn't?
- You say something cruel to someone and later tell yourself he deserved it?
- You forgot to do your homework and the teacher asks where it is?
- Some friends try to convince you to steal candy from a store?

Signs of Success

Congratulations! You are practicing Honesty when you...

- Say what you mean and mean what you say
- Make promises you can keep
- Admit your mistakes
- Refuse to lie, cheat, or steal
- Tell the truth tactfully
- Are true to yourself and do what you know is right

Affirmation

I am honest. I can be trusted to keep my word. I admit my mistakes. I tell the truth, kindly and tactfully. I have no need to impress others. I accept myself as I am.

Activities with Honesty

Role Play

Have a role play of a pie salesperson trying to make a big impression, making big claims for what is for sale, and how people react. Then have a role play of the same person describing what is for sale with honesty.

Virtues Sharing Circle

With a partner share a time you did not practice honesty and how it felt and a time you did practice honesty and how it felt. Give each other virtues acknowledgments when you are finished. "I see your (virtue) in the way you (action or behavior)."

Story

Read a story about "Honest Abe" Lincoln and how his simple honesty won people's admiration and respect.

Virtues Reflection Questions

- When is it the most difficult to be honest?

- Name a time you practiced honesty.

- How do you feel when someone exaggerates?

- Why do we want to impress others by exaggerating?

- What would it feel like to always tell the truth and keep our word?

- How does honesty help friendship to grow strong?

- Why is it important to be honest?

Drawing Honesty

Draw an example of someone practicing honesty.

Poster Points

- Honest!

- Nothing but the truth.

- What you see is what you get.

Quotable Quotes

"Every man takes care that his neighbor shall not cheat him. But a day comes when he begins to care that he does not cheat his neighbor. Then all goes well."
Ralph Waldo Emerson

"If each before his own door swept, the village would be clean."
Scottish proverb

"Fine words and an insinuating appearance are seldom associated with true virtue."
Confucius

"Honesty is contagious, just like dishonesty is contagious. We need more honesty in the world." Anne Wilson Schaef

"To dream of the person you would like to be is to waste the person you are." Anonymous

Honor

What is Honor?

Honor is living with a sense of respect for what you believe is right. It is living by the virtues, showing great respect for yourself, other people, and the rules you live by. When you are honorable, you don't have to feel ashamed of who you are or what you are doing. You are worthy of respect. You set a good example.

Why Practice It?

Without honor, people act disrespectfully and do things which make them and others feel ashamed. They just do what they want without caring about the virtues or whether it is right or wrong. When someone is honorable, other people trust them to do what is right. Their word of honor means they will do exactly what they promise. People respect and look up to someone who is honorable.

How Do You Practice It?

When you act with honor, you do the right thing regardless of what others are doing. You keep your promises, without anyone reminding or nagging you. You honor your elders by speaking respectfully to them. You honor yourself by being your best, practicing your virtues every day. When you act with honor, you set a good example, not to be admired, but just because it is the right thing to do.

What would Honor look like if...

- Your friend told you a secret?
- You are mad at your mother when she asks you to do something?
- A friend tries to get you to steal some money to go to a movie?
- You find some money in the school hallway?
- Everyone is teasing a child in the playground?
- You promised to practice your instrument while your parents are out?

Signs of Success

Congratulations! You are practicing Honor when you...

- Practice your virtues
- Keep your word
- Respect the rules you want to live by
- Do what you believe is right no matter what
- Set a good example for others
- Avoid doing things which make you feel ashamed

Affirmation

I am honorable. I keep my agreements and treat others with respect. I live by the virtues. I care about doing the right thing.

Activities with Honor

Code of Honor

Create a code of honor for your school or class that reflects the values and ground rules you have.

Virtues Reflection Questions

- Name a character from a story or film who lives honorably?

- Name a person you know you can trust because that person is honorable.

- Name three things that are in your personal code of honor, the rules you want to live by.

- How can you make sure to keep your agreements?

- How could you be honorable after making a mistake?

- Practice honoring people in your class by saying "I honor you for the virtue of ... (name a virtue you see in them.) and I see it in you when you..."

- How can you be loyal to your friends and honorable to what you think is right even when they don't?

Drawing Honor

Create your personal shield of honor, the virtues that are in your own code of honor and drawings that represent these strengths. Do it in four quadrants. Put in the top left quadrant one of your strength virtues, in the top right quadrant one of your family's strength virtues, in the lower left, the word "Joy", in the lower right one of your challenging or "growth" virtues, one that needs to grow. Draw a symbol or illustration of the virtue in each quadrant.

Poster Points

- On my honor.

- Word of honor.

- Code of honor.

- Doing the right thing.

Quotable Quotes

"If peace cannot be maintained with honor, it is no longer peace." John Russell

"My honor is dearer to me than my life." Cervantes

"Piety requires us to honor truth above our friends." Unknown

"There is no pillow so soft as a clear conscience." French proverb

"If you wouldn't write it and sign it, don't say it." Anonymous

"If you seek what is honorable, what is good, what is the truth of your life, all the other things you could not imagine come as a matter of course." Oprah Winfrey

Humility

What is Humility?

When you are humble you don't act as if you are more important than other people. You are happy to serve others and think other people's needs are important. You don't expect others or yourself to be perfect. You don't criticize others or yourself. You admit mistakes and learn from them. Sometimes mistakes are our best teachers.

Why Practice It?

Without humility, people act as if what they have to say and do is much more important than what anyone else is saying or doing. With humility, instead of comparing ourselves to others, we are grateful for what we can do. Humility helps you to keep learning. It helps you to treat others as equals, different yet equal. Humility can keep you free from prejudice.

How Do You Practice It?

To practice humility, don't worry about impressing other people. Just be yourself and do your best. Instead of worrying over failures or mistakes, be eager to learn from them. Ask for help when you need it. When you are wrong, admit it, and then change your behavior. Strive to be a little better today than you were yesterday. When you do something wonderful, humility reminds you to be thankful instead of boastful.

What would Humility look like if...

- You notice that you can run much faster than your friend?
- You notice that your friend usually gets better marks than you?
- You make a big mistake and hurt someone's feelings?
- Your brother does a chore and you think he could have done a better job?
- You have a habit you feel ashamed of?
- You have a problem that you cannot solve?

Signs of Success

Congratulations! You are practicing Humility when you...

- Consider the needs of others as important as your own.
- Apologize and make amends when you hurt others.
- Learn from your mistakes and keep changing for the better.
- Ask for help when you need it.
- Are doing your best just to do it, not to impress anyone.
- Are grateful instead of boastful.

Affirmation

I am humble. I learn from my mistakes. I do not judge others or myself. I value my ability to keep growing and learning.

The Virtues Project

Activities with Humility

Humble Tea

Have a tea party and have people take turns serving one another.

Virtues Reflection Questions

- What is one of the "best" mistakes you ever made – one that taught you the most.

- How can you show humility when you hurt someone else's feelings?

- Name three ways to make a true apology.

- What helps you to accept your mistakes and move on?

- Name two things you could do to be of service to someone in your family.

- What does it feel like to be criticized and blamed?

- What does it feel like to be around someone who always thinks they know more than you?

- What does it feel like to hide a mistake you have made?

- What would give you the courage to admit it and make amends?

Drawing Humility

Draw a picture of a team of athletes who have won a game, being thankful and sharing their happiness together.

Poster Points

- Free to be you and me.

- Learning life's lessons.

- Looking for the teachable moments.

- Willing to keep learning.

Quotable Quotes

"The life which is not examined is not worth living." Plato

"No one is better than anyone else, and no one really believes that." Tolbert McCarrol

"We come nearest to the great when we are great in humility." Rabindath Tagore

"Humility is to make a right estimate of one's self." Charles Haddon Spurgeon

"The first test of a really great man is his humility." John Ruskin

Idealism

What is Idealism?

A person with ideals is a person who really cares about what is right and meaningful in life. When you practice idealism, you have beliefs that mean something to you and you follow them. You don't just accept things the way they are. You want to make a difference. Idealists dare to have big dreams and then act as if they are possible.

Why Practice It?

People without ideals or dreams live as if nothing matters very much. They have no dreams of what is possible. They settle for whatever happens. Without idealism, the world's problems would never change. When you practice idealism, you trust that tomorrow can be better than today. You see what is possible and act to make it happen.

How Do You Practice It?

Idealism begins by picturing what you would ideally like to see happen. It could be a vision of what you will do when you grow up or of something you want to achieve now. It could be a dream of having the best friend ever, or a new invention, or making the world a better place. When you practice idealism, you have dreams and then act to make the ideal real. You make a plan and step by step, your dream can come true.

What would Idealism look like if...

- You would like to see your school free of prejudice?
- People tell you your dream is impossible?
- You want to make the ideal gift for your mother?
- You feel somewhat hopeless about achieving a goal?
- You don't know what you really care about?
- You have a dream of becoming a great musician or athlete?

Signs of Success

Congratulations! You are practicing Idealism when you...

- Really care about what you value in life
- Dare to have big dreams
- Have a vision of what is possible
- Have a plan to make your ideals real
- Take action to make your dreams come true
- Do something to make a difference in the world

Affirmation

I live by my ideals. I believe in my dreams. I have faith that anything is possible.

Activities with Idealism

Collage of Dreams

An excellent exercise to draw forth Idealism, to focus on goals and dreams. Use photos, words and pictures from old magazines, glue, paste, sparkles, etc. to have students make a collage of the core virtues they want in their lives, including those they want to develop more fully. You may wish to make up strips of paper with the names of the 52 virtues on them as well. When the collages are done, give plenty of time for each student to share and describe their collage to the group, and have two or three people in the group give the student a virtues acknowledgment when they are finished speaking. When students display these in their bedrooms or on classroom walls, they are reminded of their ideals.

Virtues Reflection Questions

- What is your ideal picture of how this school (or camp or troop, etc.) can be?

- What are some of your dreams for your future?

- What are some of the ideals or values of your family?

- What would you like to be when you grow up?

- What plan would help you to succeed?

- Name three people you know or in history who have made a difference in the world?

- What are three things we could do as a group to make a difference in our school or town?

- If you could do anything you wanted, what would you achieve?

Drawing Idealism

Draw an ideal picture of yourself doing something you would love to do.

Poster Points

- I have a dream.

- Daring to dream.

- Making a difference.

- A dream of one world.

Quotable Quotes

"I have a dream." Martin Luther King

"Humanity at last is divided into just three classes: those who DREAM, those who DO, and those who DO WHAT THEY DREAM. And in the end it is only these last that count." Dr. H.C. Goddard

"The difference between a dream and the vision is the work plan." Stuart Schroeder

"Hold fast to dreams for if dreams die, life is a broken-winged bird that cannot fly." Langston Hughes

"Leave everything a little better than you found it." Anonymous

"Adventure is risk with a purpose." Robert McClure

"What gift and enduring achievement has the world ever accomplished that was not based on idealism." Sir Wilfred Laurier

"Shoulders back, head up, look the future in the eye." Maya Angelou

"You are never given a dream without also being given the power to make it true." Richard Bach

Integrity

What is Integrity?

Integrity is standing up for what you believe is right, living by your highest values. It is being honest and sincere with others and yourself. You are integrous when your words and actions match. You don't fool yourself into doing what you know is wrong. You fill your life and your mind with things that help you to live a good, clean life.

Why Practice It?

Without integrity, no one would be able to trust each other to do what they say they are going to do. Integrity helps us to listen to our conscience, to do the right thing, to tell the truth. When people act with integrity, they stand for something. Others believe them and rely on them. Integrity gives us self-respect and a peaceful heart.

How Do You Practice It?

You practice integrity by thinking about the virtues that matter to you and doing your best to live by them. When you make a mistake, you clean it up. You don't follow the crowd. You think for yourself. You don't say one thing and do another. You do the right thing even when no one is watching. Even when it is hard to do the right thing, you stand strong.

What would Integrity look like if...

- All your friends are going to a movie your parents don't want you to see?
- You promised your friend you would keep her secret?
- The teacher has left the room?
- You find a jacket at school and it's nicer than yours?
- Other people are cheating on a test?
- You have agreed to do a job and it becomes too hard?

Signs of Success

Congratulations! You are practicing Integrity when you...

- Think about what virtues you care about
- Stand strong for what you believe
- Willingly clean up mistakes
- Do the right thing even when it is hard
- Think for yourself and avoid temptation
- Are your own leader

Affirmation

I have integrity. I mean what I say and say what I mean. I stand up for what I feel is right. I am my own leader.

Activities with Integrity

Role Play

Discuss situations that tempt us to cheat, lie or compromise our principles such as finding something we really like that doesn't belong to us. Then role play the scenario showing what it would look like with the practice of integrity.

What I Stand For

Make a list of three to five virtues that are most important in your code of honor, the ones you want to live by.

Virtues Reflection Questions

- What would a friendship be like without integrity?

- What would a friendship be like if both people were integrous?

- How do people feel around someone who doesn't do what they say they will do?

- What would help you to do the right thing even if others are trying to lead you into temptation?

- When is it hard for you to practice integrity? When is it easier for you to practice integrity?

- What do you think are the most important virtues?

Drawing Integrity

Make an integrity collage of the virtues you care about, with pictures and words.

Poster Points

- Doing the right thing.

- Standing strong for what I believe.

- Standing up for justice.

- What you see is what you get.

- I mean what I say and say what I mean.

Quotable Quotes

"The only thing necessary for the triumph of evil is for enough good men to do nothing."
Attributed to Edmund Burke

"If we don't stand for something, we'll fall for anything." Vic Kitchen

"We can change our whole life and the attitude of people around us simply by changing ourselves." Rudolf Dreikurs

"In matters of style, swim with the current, in matters of principle, stand like a rock."
Thomas Jefferson

"Character is destiny." Heraclitus

"Remorse is the echo of lost virtue."
Bulwar Lyton

"Compromise to please others is not as good as integrity that annoys others." Huanchu Daoren

"What you are speaks so loudly, I can't hear what you're saying." Ralph Waldo Emerson

Joyfulness

What is Joyfulness?

Joyfulness is being filled with happiness. It is a peaceful sense of well-being. Joy is inside us all. It comes from an appreciation for the gifts each day brings. Joy comes when we are doing what we know is right, and when we laugh and see the humor in things. Joy is the inner sense that can carry us through the hard times even when we are feeling very sad.

Why Practice It?

Without inner joy, all our feelings are determined by what is happening to us. When things are going well, we feel glad. When things are going wrong, we feel bad. Without joyfulness, when the fun stops, our happiness stops. When we are joyful, things still happen to us, some good and some bad. If we are joyful, down deep we stay calm and serene. We look forward to things changing for the better.

How Do You Practice It?

Joyfulness is looking forward to your day, knowing it will be good. Whatever you are doing, do it with a joyful heart. Find ways to have fun in your work and in your play. When good things happen to you, enjoy them fully. When sad things happen, let the sadness come and then let it go. Find the gift in what is happening – is this a way to become stronger? Something new to learn? Enjoy your life!

What would Joyfulness look like if...

- Your father asked you to clean out the garage?
- A friend you like a lot moves away?
- You have a difficult homework assignment?
- You spend some time thinking about your life?
- You feel sad and down?
- You have a free day with no plans?

Signs of Success

Congratulations! You are practicing Joyfulness when you...

- Look inside for happiness
- Enjoy whatever you are doing
- Appreciate the gifts in your life and in yourself
- Find creative ways to enjoy your time
- Have a good sense of humor
- Feel an inner peace even when things are tough

Affirmation

I am thankful for the joy I feel inside. I enjoy my work and my play. I appreciate the gifts this day holds for me.

Activities with Joyfulness

Virtues Sharing Circle

Sit or stand in a circle and each person shares one thing that they enjoy, or that brings them joy.

Joy Icebreaker

Have individuals move around the room and stand in front of another person, look into their eyes and ask "What gives you joy?" Then their partner asks them the same question. They then move to the next person and give a new answer.

Virtues Reflection Questions

- What gives you joy?

- Name three activities you enjoy.

- How can you practice joyfulness when things aren't going well?

- What cheers you up when you feel down?

- If you had a whole day in front of you, what would be the most enjoyable way to spend it?

- How can you enjoy a boring task?

- Share a funny thing that happened to you.

- Share one of the most enjoyable times you ever spent with your family.

Drawing Joyfulness

Make a collage or poster of the things in your life which give you joy.

Poster Points

- Joy gives us wings.

- My heart is full of joy.

- I enjoy life!

- Life is good.

Quotable Quotes

"Joy gives us wings! At times of joy our strength is more vital, our intellect keener, and our understanding less clouded. We seem better able to cope with the world and find our sphere of influence." 'Abdu'l-Baha

"Joy is an inside job." Don Blanding

*"He who binds to himself a joy
Doth the winged life destroy;
But he who kisses the joy as it flies
Lives in Eternity's sunrise."*
William Blake

"There is no such thing as the pursuit of happiness, there is only the discovery of joy."
Joyce Grenfell

"Joy is the presence of love for self and for others, a state of gratitude and compassion, an awareness of being connected to our higher self and of being one with everything."
Peggy Jenkins

Justice

What is Justice?

Practicing justice is being fair in everything you do. It is seeing with your own eyes and not judging something or someone by what other people tell you. Being just is standing up for your rights and the rights of other people. It is taking responsibility if you make a mistake and making amends. Justice means that every person's rights are protected.

Why Practice It?

Without justice, people get away with hurting or taking advantage of others, and keep on doing it. Without justice, the world can be a cruel and dangerous place. People are judged by their gender, race or religion. When justice is practiced, everyone has a fair chance to be seen for who they are. If someone is accused of something, they get a chance to tell their side. With justice, everyone gets a fair share.

How Do You Practice It?

If someone is hurting you, it is just to stop them. It is never just for strong people to hurt weaker people. If you hurt someone else, fix the problem by making amends. Investigate the truth for yourself instead of listening to others. Instead of prejudging, see people as individuals. Don't accept it when someone acts like a bully, cheats or lies. Being a champion for justice takes courage. Sometimes when you stand for justice, you stand alone.

What would Justice look like if...

- You are with a group and they start to gossip?
- Everyone is teasing a child who looks different?
- Someone makes a remark to you about people of another race?
- An older child keeps getting rough with you?
- Something is missing from your room and you think your brother took it?
- You are teasing someone and cause their lunch to fall on the floor?

Signs of Success

Congratulations! You are practicing Justice when you...

- Think for yourself
- Avoid gossip and backbiting
- Refuse to prejudge — see people as individuals
- Own up to your mistakes and accept the consequences
- Share fairly with others
- Stand up for people's rights, including your own

Affirmation

I act with justice. I stand up for the rights of others and myself. I have no need to pretend or defend. I choose to make amends.

Activities with Justice

Gossip Line

Play the game of "telephone" where something is whispered down the line from one person to another. See how the sentence changes when it comes out the other end. Discuss how this is like gossip and backbiting. Spreading rumors supports injustice.

Come up with tactful things to say when you don't wish to participate in gossip.

Make a Justice Plan

As a class, make a plan for justly resolving conflict, such as a Peace Corner. See activities under Chapter 3 Setting Clear Boundaries.

Virtues Reflection Questions

- What is it like to receive prejudice?

- Why do people judge one another like that?

- What would you do if you saw bullying? How would you stay safe while doing something to stand up for the rights of those being bullied?

- What are some times you have wished for justice?

- What are some times you have admitted a mistake and cleaned it up?

- How can you tell when you have made amends that fit the mistake?

- What are some boundaries or ground rules that keep us safe?

Drawing Justice

Draw a picture of people of different colors practicing justice together.

Poster Points

- No need to pretend or defend. Make amends!

- Color blind.

- One family.

- Play fair.

- Stand up for Justice.

Quotable Quotes

"A man who knows he has committed a mistake and doesn't correct it is committing another mistake." Confucius

"What goes around comes around."
Anonymous

"True peace is not merely the absence of tension. It is the presence of justice."
Martin Luther King

"There is a limit at which forebearance ceases to be a virtue." Edmond Burke

"Hear one side, and you will be in the dark; hear both sides, and all will be clear."
Haliburton

"One injustice cannot be redressed by another injustice." Sergio Vieira De Mello

Kindness

What is Kindness?

Kindness is showing you care, doing some good to make life better for others. It is being thoughtful about people's needs. Kindness is showing love and compassion to someone who is sad or needs your help. Kindness is treating yourself and others gently. It is caring about the earth and all living things.

Why Practice It?

Without kindness, no one would listen when people or animals need help. Everyone would be looking out for himself. The world is lonely without kindness. When someone reaches out to another in an act of kindness, it helps them both. People's lack of kindness to the earth damages the air, water and the land. This causes people and animals to suffer, too. Being kind allows us to feel connected to everything and everyone.

How Do You Practice It?

You practice kindness by noticing when someone or something needs care. Become sensitive to the world around you. Use your imagination to think of things that give others happiness. Find out what habits harm the earth and choose kinder ways to live. When you are tempted to be cruel, to criticize or tease, decide not to do it. Speak kindly instead. Greet people kindly. Take good care of your pets.

What would Kindness look like if...

- A new student comes into your class and looks lonely?
- You start teasing your brother and he is getting upset?
- Some kids you have been playing with start teasing a boy with big ears?
- Your cat has some burrs in her fur?
- Your mother seems tired lately?
- You see someone in a wheel chair coming toward you?

Signs of Success

Congratulations! You are practicing Kindness when you...

- Give tender attention to someone who is sad or needs help
- Do things to give others happiness
- Practice habits that help the environment (reduce, re-use, recycle)
- Resist the temptation to be cruel
- Accept people who are different

Affirmation

I am kind. I look for ways to help others. I show kindness to any person or animal I see. I do all I can to take care of the earth.

Activities with Kindness

Environmental Kindness

Choose an improvement project such as picking up trash and do it as a field trip.

Virtues Reflection Questions

- What do most people do when they see someone with a disability or who looks different?

- How does it feel to be ignored, teased, etc.?

- What would be a kind way to treat someone who is disabled?

- Name three ways we can be kind to animals.

- Think of someone who needs your kindness today. What can you do to be kind?

- What would you say or do if someone is not being kind to you?

- How have you shown kindness to people or animals?

Drawing Kindness

Draw a picture of yourself being kind to a person or an animal.

Make a poster with examples of Recycling, Reusing, Reducing, e.g. Reducing: just turning off the tap while we brush our teeth can save lots of water.

Poster Points

- Kind eyes.
- Kind smile.
- Kind words.
- Kind deeds.
- Be Kind to Mankind.

Quotable Quotes

"When you plant a lettuce, if it does not grow well, you don't blame the lettuce. You look for reasons it is not doing well. It may need fertilizer or more water or less sun. You never blame the lettuce. Yet if we have problems with our friends or family, we blame the other person. But if we know how to take care of them, they will grow well, like the lettuce." Thich Nhat Hanh

"That best portion of a good man's life
His little, nameless, unremembered acts
of kindness and of love." W.W. Wordsworth

"The last, best fruit which comes to perfection, even in the kindliest soul, is tenderness toward the hard, forbearance toward the unforbearing, warmth of heart toward the cold..." Richter

"Let no one ever come to you without leaving better and happier. Be the living expression of God's kindness; kindness in your face, kindness in your eyes, kindness in your smile, kindness in your warm greeting." Mother Teresa

"There is a grace of kind listening as well as a grace of kind speaking." Anonymous

"If someone listens or stretches out a hand, or whispers a kind word of encouragement, or attempts to understand a lonely person, extraordinary things begin to happen."
Loretta Girzatlis

Love

What is Love?

Love is a special feeling that fills your heart. You show love in a smile, a pleasant way of speaking, a thoughtful act or a hug. Love is treating people and things with special care and kindness because they mean so much to you. Love is treating other people just as you would like them to treat you – with care and respect.

Why Practice It?

Without love, people feel alone. When they don't feel they matter to anyone, they become unhappy. Sometimes they act angry and don't let others get close. Everyone wants to be liked. Everyone likes to be loved. When you are being loving, you help others to feel important. They become gentler and kinder. Love is contagious. It keeps spreading.

How Do You Practice It?

Love is putting yourself in someone else's shoes and caring about what they feel. It is accepting them, loving them just as they are. You can even be loving to people you don't know, just by caring about what happens to them and sending loving thoughts. Sharing is a way to show love. Share your belongings, your time and yourself. Love is thinking about how you want to be treated and treating others the same way.

What would Love look like if...

- You start to get upset with yourself about something you have done?
- You want to do something thoughtful when your father is sick?
- Another child is acting cranky?
- You notice a baby bird has fallen from its nest?
- You love your teacher and want to show it?
- You have a special object that you really care about?

Signs of Success

Congratulations! You are practicing Love when you...

- Treat others as you would want them to treat you
- Say kind and loving things
- Share your things and yourself
- Show affection
- Think loving thoughts
- Take good care of the things you love

Affirmation

I am a loving person. I show my love with thoughtful acts, kind words and affection. I treat others the way I want to be treated.

Activities with *Love*

Show and Tell

Invite students to bring in something they love. Have a "Show and Tell". Have them explain how they treat this special object lovingly.

Virtues Reflection Questions

- What are three ways you can show love for people?

- What are three ways you can show love for animals?

- Name some things you love other than people or animals?

- What do you love to do?

- What happens when you do a task with love?

- How do you wish people treated you?

- Name three ways you treat people lovingly?

Drawing Love

Draw a house and put in it all the people you love. It could be anyone, even someone you don't know personally, someone famous or someone in history.

Poster Points

- Love is all that matters.
- Love lasts.
- Love is kind.
- Love is gentle.
- Love is patient.
- Love is humble.

Quotable Quotes

"Your task is not to seek for love, but merely to seek and find all the barriers within yourself that you have built against it." Rumi

"Love doesn't just sit there like a stone; it has to be made, like bread, remade all the time, made new." Ursula K. Le Guin

"Love cures people – both the ones who give it and the ones who receive it." Karl Menninger

"Spread love everywhere you go, first in your own house." Mother Teresa

"Only love enables humanity to grow, because love engenders life and it is the only form of energy that lasts forever." Michel Quoist

"Love is the only force capable of transforming an enemy into a friend." Martin Luther King

Loyalty

What is Loyalty?

Loyalty is staying true to someone. It is standing up for something you believe in without wavering. It is being faithful to your family, country, school, friends or ideals – when the going gets tough as well as when things are good. When you are a loyal friend, even if someone disappoints you, you still hang in there with them. Loyalty is staying committed.

Why Practice It?

You cannot count on disloyal people to stay friends, because when problems happen, they go away. They often change their minds about what they believe to be important. When you practice loyalty, people know they can count on you. People who are worthy of your loyalty can trust that they will never stand alone. With loyalty, you build friendships that last forever.

How Do You Practice It?

You practice loyalty by committing to a person, or a belief. Choose your friends carefully, so you can be friends for a long time. If someone tries to use your loyalty for a bad purpose, or hurts you over and over, you need to decide if it feels right to go on being loyal. Stand up for your family and friends when others act unjustly. When you are loyal you are worthy of trust.

What would Loyalty look like if...

- One friend tries to get you to turn against another?
- You are invited to join a group that doesn't want your friends around?
- You see a friend steal and he asks you to lie for him?
- You believe in your religion and people make fun of it?
- Someone starts teasing and pushing your sister in front of you?
- A friend suggests you "borrow" from your Mom's purse?

Signs of Success

Congratulations! You are practicing Loyalty when you...

- Stand up for people and ideas you believe in
- Are a faithful friend through good times and bad
- Don't allow loyalty to lead you into trouble
- Don't let others come between you and your friends
- Are loyal to yourself

Affirmation

I am loyal to the people and ideas I care about. I am a friend through good times and bad. I am loyal to what I know is right. I do not allow friendship to lead me into trouble.

Activities with Loyalty

A Sign of Loyalty

Have a demonstration of the various "hand-shakes" you know about.

Virtues Reflection Questions

- How do you know you want to be friends with someone?

- What is good about having a loyal friend?

- Are there times when it would be loyal to tell a secret a friend told you?

- What is it like when a friend is not loyal to you?

- What would you do if a friend asked you to do something you felt was wrong?

- How can you be loyal to yourself?

- When do you know it is time to end a friend-ship?

- Name three things about a friend to whom you would be loyal forever?

Drawing Loyalty

Draw a picture of an animal you think of as loyal.

Poster Points

- Stand by your friends.

- Friends are forever.

- A friend through all kinds of weather.

- Side-by-side.

Quotable Quotes

"In thy face I see the map of honour, truth and loyalty." William Shakespeare

"The best mirror is an old friend."
George Hebert

"A true friend loves you enough to support you and to confront you." Anonymous

*"Words are easy, like the wind;
Faithful friends are hard to find."*
Richard Barnfield

"Only the person who has faith in himself is able to be faithful to others." Erich Fromm

"No medicine is more valuable...than a friend to whom we may turn for consolation in time of trouble — and with whom we may share our happiness in times of joy."
St. Aelred of Rievaulx

Moderation

What is Moderation?

Moderation is creating balance in your life between work and play, rest and exercise. It is having or doing enough of something – not too much, not too little, but what's just right for you. If you study all the time or play all the time it is not being moderate. Moderation is being in charge of your time and using self-discipline to keep from doing too much or too little.

Why Practice It?

Moderation helps us to stay balanced, so that we are not controlled by our desires. Without moderation, we can overdo things like talking, or eating. We can start to get addicted to things and want more even when it can hurt us, like eating too much chocolate or drinking too much alcohol. Without moderation we wouldn't do our fair share. When we practice moderation we make a choice to be the way we want to be.

How Do You Practice It?

You practice moderation by knowing your own limits and what you need to function at your best. People are different. For some eight hours of sleep is enough, for others, it is too little. Watch yourself to make sure you stay balanced and don't let something begin to rule your life, such as TV, computer games, food or a person. When you practice moderation, you are content to have just what you need.

What would Moderation look like if...

- You like someone so much you start calling her up every day?
- You open the cookie jar and find your favorites?
- You stay up late to read or play but then feel sleepy in the morning?
- You are spending all your free time playing computer games and don't see your friends anymore?
- You spend all your money on chocolate bars?
- You notice you are talking too much?

Signs of Success

Congratulations! You are practicing Moderation when you...

- Know what you need and get enough – no more, no less
- Take care of your health
- Use self-discipline to stop yourself from overdoing
- Balance work and play in your life
- Know your own limits and set boundaries for yourself
- Are content with enough

Affirmation

I am moderate. I am thankful and content to get what I need. Work and play are balanced in my life. I don't overdo or underdo but find what's just right for me.

Activities with Moderation

Design Your Life

Create a Mind Map of the way you spend your time and notice how balanced it is. Put plus marks from 1 to 5 by the amount of time you spend working or studying, helping in the house, playing, spending time with friends or on the phone, TV or computer time, exercise and rest. In which areas do you need to spend less time? In which areas do you need to spend more?

Moderation Story

Tell the story of Goldilocks and the Three Bears.

Virtues Reflection Questions

- What are some of the things we can get addicted to or just overdo?

- What happens to us when something like food or a person rules our lives?

- What are some of the easiest foods for you to get addicted to?

- What happens to people who drink too much alcohol?

- What is it like when someone talks too much?

- What happens if someone talks too little?

- How much sleep do you need and how can you be sure to get it?

- Name three ways you can take better care of your health.

Drawing Moderation

Make a cartoon strip with several drawings showing a moderate day.

Poster Points

- Not too hot, not too cold.
- Not too much, not too little.
- Just right.
- Living a balanced life.
- Easy does it.
- Enough is enough.

Quotable Quotes

"Easy Does It." Slogan of Alcoholics Anonymous

"Moderation is the silken string running through the pearl chain of all virtues." Joseph Hall

"Enough is enough." Anonymous

"Moderation in all things." Terence

"Conscience is a still small voice that makes minority reports." Franklin P. Jones

"The best of blessings, a contented mind." Horace

"Just as nature needs balance, people need balance." Anne Wilson Schaef

"We are not human doings, we are human beings." John Bradshaw

Modesty

What is Modesty?

Modesty is having self-respect. When you practice modesty, you are not showy or boastful. Modesty comes when you have self-acceptance and quiet pride. Modesty is to value yourself and to have a sense of respectful privacy about your body. Modesty is also accepting praise with humility and gratitude.

Why Practice It?

Without modesty, people do things to attract attention. They brag and boast. They dress in a way that is disrespectful to themselves and their bodies. They even allow others to take advantage of them in disrespectful ways. Without modesty people don't set boundaries about how they wish to be touched or not touched. With modesty, people respect themselves and others respect them, too.

How Do You Practice It?

Modesty is being comfortable with yourself . It is knowing you have special gifts and that others do as well. You practice modesty by not letting other people use you. You are respectful of your body and your privacy, and you expect others to be, too. If anyone touches you in a way that doesn't feel right, tell an adult you trust. Don't keep it a secret. When you are modest, you enjoy dressing in a way that shows self-respect.

What would Modesty look like if...

- A friend tries to convince you to buy a revealing outfit because everyone else is wearing it?
- Someone starts to tease you and tickle your private parts?
- You played really well and your team won the game?
- Someone wants to kiss you and you don't want them to?
- You feel like bragging about something good you did?
- You feel uncomfortable about the way a relative is touching you?

Signs of Success

Congratulations! You are practicing Modesty when you...

- Are comfortable being who you are
- Respect yourself
- Do not permit anyone to abuse your body
- Set boundaries about your right to privacy
- Dress in a way that feels right to you
- Share your victories without boasting

Affirmation

I am modest. I have no need to brag. I dress in a way that shows respect for myself and others. I protect myself from disrespectful attention.

Activities with Modesty

Dress Code

Talk about how a dress code can help people to dress in a way that shows respect for their bodies and for others. If your school has a dress code, make an illustrated poster of the rules.

Virtues Reflection Questions

- How would it feel to be on a team and have someone else take all the credit for a win?

- How can you show modesty if you have made a great play in a game?

- How could you enjoy your victory and still be modest?

- Name three ways to protect yourself from unwanted touching by others?

- What would you do if someone in your family touched you inappropriately?

- What is your favorite outfit, one that feels like it's really "you"?

Drawing Modesty

Draw people on a team sharing the glory with each other.

Poster Points

- Expect respect.

- Share the victories.

- Thankful, not boastful.

- Share the glory.

- Dress for success.

Quotable Quotes

"We come nearest to the great when we are great in humility." Rabindrath Tagore

"We do not possess our homes, our children, or even our own body. They are given to us for a short while to treat with care and respect." Jack Kornfield

"I discovered I always have choices and sometimes it's only a choice of attitude." Judith M. Knowlton

"I cannot and will not cut my conscience to fit this year's fashions." Lillian Hellman

"Never esteem anything as of advantage to you that will make you break your word or lose your self-respect." Marcus Aurelius Antoninus

Orderliness

What is Orderliness?

Orderliness is being neat, and living with a sense of harmony. It is being organized and having a place for things when you need them. Orderliness is planning something so that it works, doing it step by step instead of going in circles. Orderliness is putting first things first, and taking care of things you need to do.

Why Practice It?

When people are orderly, they get things done efficiently, without wasting time and effort. Without order there is confusion, and it is easy to lose things. People who need to do things quickly and skillfully need to be very orderly. What would happen if doctors and fire-fighters misplaced the tools they need to save lives? When you are orderly you can find a solution to any problem.

How Do You Practice It?

Decide how you want to arrange the space around you to keep it orderly and attractive. Have a place for your things and put them away when you finish using them. Orderliness helps you do things efficiently, by making a plan and following it, step by step. Orderliness can help you solve even difficult problems. Divide them into small parts and handle them one at a time. Order around you creates order inside you. It gives you peace of mind.

What would Orderliness look like if...

- You look at your room and see a big mess?
- You finish playing with a game that has lots of pieces?
- You find it really hard to deal with some problem?
- You're running around the school yard and hear the bell?
- You're on a hike and don't know where to put the trash from your lunch?
- You have a big job to do?

Signs of Success

Congratulations! You are practicing Orderliness when you...

- Have a place to put each of your things
- Put your things away in the same place each time
- Have a plan before your begin any job
- Solve problems step-by-step
- Create a harmonious space that gives you peace of mind
- Appreciate the beauty and order of nature

Affirmation

I live this day with order. I do things step by step. I create beauty and harmony in my space and in my life.

Activities with *Orderliness*

Beauty and Order

- In teams, organize and neaten your classroom space. Decide what would beautify it.
- Make a plan for putting your own space at home in order.

An Orderly Plan

Brainstorm a problem such as how to eliminate bullying and come up with a step-by-step plan.

Step-by-Step

- Write down each step of your morning routine.
- Write down each step of how to prepare your favorite snack.
- List the things you want to do this weekend and put them in order of priority.

Virtues Reflection Questions

- What does it feel like to be in a messy place?

- What does it feel like to be in a clean, orderly place?

- What is our responsibility to the earth in preserving order and beauty?

- What happens inside you when you keep things around you in order?

- What are some problems that feel difficult to solve?

- Name three steps you can take to solve one of those problems.

- What would you like to do in a more orderly way?

Drawing Orderliness

Draw a picture of the perfect bedroom with exactly what you would like to have in it and everything placed just where you want it.

Poster Points

- A place for everything.
- Everything in its place.
- Step-by-step.
- All my ducks in a row.
- Harmony in my life and in my space.

Quotable Quotes

"The journey of a thousand miles begins with a single step." Confucius

"Order and simplification are the first steps toward mastery of a subject – the actual enemy is the unknown." Thomas Mann

"Art and science cannot exist but in minutely organized particulars." William Blake

"Order is not a pressure which is imposed on society from without, but an equilibrium which is set up from within."
Jose Ortego Y Gasset

"If you don't know where you're going, any road will take you there." Lewis B. Carroll

Patience

What is Patience?

Patience is quiet hope and trust, expecting things to turn out all right. Patience is being calm and tolerant when difficult things happen. It means showing acceptance when you or others make mistakes. Patience is doing something now so that later it will bear fruit, like planting a seed and waiting for it to grow. Patience is a commitment to the future.

Why Practice It?

Without patience people want everything NOW. They complain when unpleasant things cannot be helped. They act mad when things don't go their way. When people practice patience, they can wait without complaining. They forgive others and themselves for mistakes. They make the world a kinder, gentler place.

How Do You Practice It?

Practicing patience is accepting things you cannot control, like the way other people act, or even an illness or handicap you have to live with. Patience is waiting without complaining. When you are patient, you show gentleness when you or others make mistakes. You set goals and persevere until your goals are won. You picture the end in the beginning. You know that good things take time.

What would Patience look like if...

- Your mother is very late picking you up and you have been waiting for a long time?
- You decide you want to be a lawyer when you grow up?
- You want to grow some vegetables?
- You start to get annoyed when your sister forgets to put back something she borrowed?
- You wish you were taller?
- You have an illness that keeps you from playing your favorite sport?

Signs of Success

Congratulations! You are practicing Patience when you...

- Calmly tolerate a delay or confusion
- Are willing to wait for things you want
- Set goals and stick with them until they are finished
- Do something now that will help you in the future
- Accept things you cannot change with humor and grace
- Are tolerant when mistakes are made

Affirmation

I am patient. I am gentle with others and myself when we make mistakes. I wait calmly. I trust that things will turn out right.

Activities with *Patience*

Window Garden

- Have a window box garden in which children can plant some colorful and fast growing flowers such as nasturtiums and marigolds as well as some herbs to bring home to their parents.
- Have children bring flowers they grow to share with other classrooms.
- Name the various flowers by virtues names: Moderate marigolds, Patient petunias, etc.

Virtues Reflection Questions

- When do you find it hard to be patient?

- What can you do to be patient when someone is late?

- Name three things you can do now that will help you to have an excellent career?

- What would help you to be more patient with family members?

- What are seeds doing when they are underground and we can't see them?

- What do seeds need in order to grow?

- What do you need in order to grow your patience?

Drawing Patience

Draw a beautiful garden.

Poster Points

- All will be well.

- Wait for it.

- Take life as it comes.

Quotable Quotes

"Patience and perseverance have a magical effect before which difficulties disappear and obstacles vanish." John Quincy Adams

"I want patience and I want it now!" Anonymous

"Help us always to be hopeful gardeners of the spirit who know that without darkness nothing comes to birth as without light nothing flowers." May Sarton

"Patience, patience, patience is what the sea teaches." Anne Morrow Lindburgh

"Patience may be defined as that quality of life which makes suffering creative; and impatience as that whereby suffering becomes a destructive force." Robert Llewelyn

"Patience and diligence, like faith, remove mountains." William Penn

Peacefulness

What is Peacefulness?

Peacefulness is an inner sense of calm. It comes especially in quiet moments of reflection or gratitude. It is getting very quiet and looking at things so you can understand them. Peacefulness is a way of approaching conflict with others so that no one is made wrong. It is being fair to others and yourself. Peace is giving up the love of power for the power of love. With peacefulness, everyone wins.

Why Practice It?

Practicing peacefulness helps to create a calm mind free from worry. When you are peaceful, you respect others and their differences. People around you feel calm and safe. Without peace, no one is safe. People get hurt. Fighting doesn't solve problems, and no one ever really wins a war. With peacefulness, any problem can be solved. Peace in the world begins with peace in your heart.

How Do You Practice It?

To find inner peace, become very still and think peaceful thoughts. Observe and think about your feelings, like anger, instead of acting with anger. To be a peacemaker, use peaceful language instead of name-calling, yelling or gossiping. Avoid aggressive or violent actions. Talk things out and listen to the other person too. Then look for a peaceful solution. Peacemakers find there are lots of creative ways to solve any problem. Violence never solves anything.

What would Peacefulness look like if...

- Your brother bursts into your room and steps on a model or painting you just finished?
- There are students of another race and religion in your class and some of your classmates are making fun of them?
- You start to worry about a problem and find it is on your mind all the time?
- You feel really angry about someone treating you unfairly?
- Some children start to tease you and asking you to fight?
- You decide to start a daily practice of prayer or reflection?

Signs of Success

Congratulations! You are practicing Peacefulness when you...

- Create inner peace with a regular time to pray, meditate or reflect
- Use peaceful language even when you are angry
- Speak gently and respectfully
- Avoid harming anyone
- Appreciate differences
- Find peaceful solutions to every problem

Affirmation

I am peaceful. I use peaceful language and find peaceful solutions to any problem that arises. I find my inner peace and let it carry me gently through the day.

Activities with *Peacefulness*

Quiet Time

Have a quiet time in which you close your eyes and imagine being in a place of peacefulness and beauty such as a beach, a mountain top, a forest – a place to find inner peace.

Peace & Gratitude Journal

- Write a poem about peace.
- List five things you feel grateful for.
- Notice how peaceful you feel afterward.

Virtues Reflection Questions

- What can people like you and me do to create peace in the world?

- What gives you a sense of peace?

- When do you find yourself feeling most angry?

- How can you handle your anger peacefully?

- Name three things you can do if you see a fight starting?

- How would things change at home for you if you became a peacemaker?

- How can you become peaceful when you are worried?

Drawing Peacefulness

Imagine a beautiful, peaceful place to go in your imagination when you need to become peaceful. Draw it.

Draw a picture of the world at peace.

Poster Points

- Giving up the love of power for the power of love.

- Peacemaker.

- Let's try peace for a while.

Quotable Quotes

"Contention does not profit a people."
Brigham Young

"Conflict, when it is not resolved with violence, spurs growth and keeps life interesting."
Starhawk

"Have calm thoughts. Picture calm scenes. Recall calm sounds. And guess what you'll be feeling...." Paul Wilson

"Everything that irritates us about others can lead us to an understanding of ourselves."
Carl Jung

"Peace is more important than all justice: and peace was not made for the sake of justice, but justice for the sake of peace." Martin Luther

"We should have more peace if we would not busy ourselves with the sayings and doings of others." Thomas a'Kempis

Perseverance

What is Perseverance?

Perseverance is being purposeful and steadfast. It is sticking to something, staying committed, no matter how long it takes or what obstacles appear to stop you. A good example is the story of the tortoise and the hare. Even though the tortoise was slower than the hare, he won the race because he persevered – he didn't let anything stop him or distract him. He kept on going.

Why Practice It?

Without perseverance, people give up on things easily. They don't keep their promises. When we persevere, people can depend on us to finish what we start and to keep our commitments. When we persevere, we stay friends even when the friendship is tested. We don't give up until a problem is solved.

How Do You Practice It?

You practice perseverance by committing to someone or something. Choose your commitments wisely and then stick with them. When you commit to a task, pace yourself, and be persistent, doing it step-by-step. Stand by your friends even when they aren't much fun, or are having a hard time. When trouble or doubts come up, be like a strong ship in a storm. Don't let yourself become battered or blown off course. Just ride the waves.

What would Perseverance look like if...

- You begin to feel bored being with a long-time friend?
- You are in the middle of a hard job and begin to feel tired?
- You have spent a lot of time practicing a sport or dance and doubt if you have what it takes?
- Your family is hiking to the top of a mountain and you don't think you can make it?
- You are doing something you have never done before and are afraid you won't get it right?
- Your best friend moves away and you don't want to forget each other?

Signs of Success

Congratulations! You are practicing Perseverance when you...

- Think before deciding to commit to someone or something
- Pace yourself
- Set goals and stick with them until they are completed
- Take one step at a time, remaining steady
- Don't let doubts or tests blow you off course
- Stand by your friends and loved ones

Affirmation

I have perseverance. I keep a steady pace in what I choose to do. I keep on keeping on. I finish what I start. I am a loyal and committed friend.

Activities with Perseverance

A Story of Perseverance

Share the Aesops Fable of the Tortoise and the Hare and discuss.

Virtues Reflection Questions

- When in your life have you been like the Hare?

- When in your life have you been like the Tortoise?

- How can you tell if you want to commit to a new friend?

- What qualities do you look for in a friend?

- How do the following jobs need perseverance? What would happen if people in these roles did not persevere?

> Parent
> Fire-fighter
> Professional Athlete
> Teacher
> Inventor

Drawing Perseverance

Draw a picture of someone doing a job that takes perseverance.

Poster Points

- Keep on keepin' on.
- I finish what I start.
- Riding the waves.
- A winner never quits.

Quotable Quotes

"Success comes in cans. Failure comes in can'ts." Fred Seely

"Just don't give up trying to do what you really want to do. Where there's love and inspiration, I don't think you can go wrong." Ella Fitzgerald

"Never give up!"
Otto Frank (Anne Frank's father)

"The sense of obligation to continue is present in all of us. A duty to strive is the duty of us all. I felt a call to that duty." Abraham Lincoln

"Keep on keepin' on." African-American saying

"Nothing in the world can take the place of Persistence. Talent will not; nothing is more common than unsuccessful men with talent...Persistence and determination alone are omnipotent." Anonymous

"Never let me be burdened with sorrow by not starting over." Native American tradition

"Take everything as it comes; the wave passes, deal with the next one." Tom Thomson

"A winner never quits and a quitter never wins." Unknown

Purposefulness

What is Purposefulness?

Being purposeful is having a clear focus, instead of being confused or unsure of what you are doing or why you are doing it. You are acting purposefully when you have a goal you are working toward. You concentrate your mind and your efforts so that something good will happen as a result. Some people just let things happen. A purposeful person *makes* things happen.

Why Practice It?

Without a sense of purpose, people scatter their energies and their attention. Without knowing why they are doing something – the purpose – they easily give up. When you choose to be purposeful, you can achieve great results. Motivation comes easily because you know why you are doing something. You have a positive attitude and don't let obstacles stop you from doing what is important.

How Do You Practice It?

Being purposeful begins with setting a vision or a goal for what you want to accomplish. Knowing why it is important is your purpose. With your goal in mind, do things one at a time, with as much care and concentration as you can. Don't let yourself get scattered in many directions, trying to do everything at once. Stay focused on your purpose.

What would Purposefulness look like if...

- You decide to build or create something that is difficult?
- You are trying to finish your homework and find yourself day-dreaming?
- A friend comes over while you are doing your chores?
- You start to feel scattered doing too many things at once?
- You want to learn to play an instrument?
- You find it is really hard to practice a virtue?

Signs of Success

Congratulations! You are practicing Purposefulness when you...

- Have a clear vision of what you want to accomplish
- Know why you are doing it
- Focus on a goal
- Get back on purpose if you get scattered or distracted
- Do things one at a time and finish what you start
- Persevere until you get results

Affirmation

I am purposeful. I am clear about what I am doing and why. I stay focused on my goals. I know I can accomplish great things.

Activities with *Purposefulness*

What is Your Purpose?

Name a goal which is important to you and say why.

What Have You Done So Far?

Name three things you have accomplished so far in your life (e.g., as a baby you learned to walk).

A Purposeful Challenge

Practice saying purposefulness three times fast.

Virtues Reflection Questions

- Name three famous or successful people. How do you think they practiced purposefulness?

- What are the biggest distractions when you are trying to get something done?

- What can you do to stay focused?

- What is something you are purposeful about?

- How important is a sense of purpose to success?

- When do you find it easiest to concentrate and stay focused?

- Make three goals you would like to accomplish in the next three months.

Drawing Purposefulness

Draw symbols or pictures of three goals you want to accomplish in the next three months, or make a collage using magazine pictures and words to stand for your three-month goals.

Poster Points

- Living on purpose.
- Keep your eyes on the prize.
- A designer life.

Quotable Quotes

"If you don't know where you're going, any road will take you there." Lewis B. Carrol

"If you always do what you always did, you'll always get what you always got." Lait Ribeiro

"Everyone should carefully observe which way his heart draws him, and then choose that way with all his strength." Jewish proverb

"The secret of getting ahead is getting started. The secret of getting started is breaking your overwhelming tasks into small, manageable tasks, and then starting on the first one." Mark Twain

"Always act, always walk, always proceed. Neither stand still nor go back..." St. Augustine

"Strong reasons make strong actions." Unknown

Reliability

What is Reliability?

Reliability means that others can depend on you to keep your commitments. Reliability is doing something that you have agreed to do in a predictable way, without forgetting or having to be reminded. When you practice reliability, you really care about doing what you said you would do. Other people can relax knowing it is in your reliable hands.

Why Practice It?

When people are unreliable, others can't trust them to keep their promises. If airplanes, trains or buses are late, passengers can miss important appointments. If someone keeps forgetting to do what they said they would do, they let people down. When you are reliable, people can trust you to show up on time, be where you promised to be, to put tools away, to get the job done.

How Do You Practice It?

You practice reliability by making agreements you can keep. Then do everything in your power to do what you agreed to do. Give your best effort to every job, and take your responsibilities seriously. Plan ahead and leave enough time to finish what you start. If problems arise, find another way. Return what you borrow. Most of all keep your word.

What would Reliability look like if...

- You agreed to be home by a certain time and a friend invites you to do something fun?
- It is your turn to do the dishes and you're not in the mood?
- You promised your Mom you would brush your teeth after breakfast and the school bus is coming?
- Some friends are building a clubhouse and you agreed to bring the nails, but discover your parents don't have any?
- Your part of a team report is due tomorrow and you feel too sleepy to finish it?
- You borrow one of your father's tools?

Signs of Success

Congratulations! You are practicing Reliability when you...

- Make promises you can keep
- Treat your agreements seriously
- Plan ahead
- Do your best
- Finish on time
- Find another way if obstacles occur

Affirmation

I am reliable. I keep my promises. Others can depend on me. Nothing can stop me from giving my best.

Activities with Reliability

Activities with Reliability

- Name the things you do on which others rely. (Feed your pet, make your bed).

- Name the things you do on which you rely. (Brush your teeth, remember your homework).

- Describe your morning routine. How reliable are you about getting out of the house on time? What would help you to be reliable?

Virtues Reflection Questions

- What would happen to pets if their owners were unreliable?

- How do people feel about people who keep forgetting to do what they promised?

- What helps you to remember to be reliable about returning borrowed things?

- How can reliability help you in your future job?

- What is important about reliability?

- What does reliability have to do with success?

Drawing Reliability

Draw a picture of yourself taking care of a responsibility reliably.

Poster Points

- You can count on me.

- I'm here for you.

- Regular as clockwork.

- On time every time.

- Consistently dependable.

Quotable Quotes

"The shifts of Fortune test the reliability of friends." Cicero

"An honest man's word is as good as his bond." Cervantes

"And I to my pledged word am true. I shall not fail that rendezvous." Alan Seeger

"The only time you can't afford to fail is the last time you try." Charles Kettering

"Lean on me, when you're not strong. I'll be your friend. I'll help you carry on." Song

"Choices and follow through, that is all that separates the 'champions' from the 'also rans.'" Jim Paluch

Respect

What is Respect?

Respect is an attitude of caring about people and treating them with dignity. Respect is valuing ourselves and others. We show respect by speaking and acting with courtesy. When we are respectful we treat others as we want to be treated. Respect includes honoring the rules of our family or school, which make life more orderly and peaceful. It is knowing that every man, woman and child deserves respect, including you.

Why Practice It?

Without respect for rules, we would have confusion. People would treat each other rudely and violate each other's privacy and other rights. Respect helps people to feel valued. Elders deserve special respect because they have lived longer and learned many of life's lessons. Self-respect is making sure no one hurts you or abuses you, even an elder. When you respect yourself, others respect you, too.

How Do You Practice It?

Think about how you would like others to treat you and treat them with the same dignity. How would you like others to speak to you, treat your belongings, and your right to privacy? If you want to use someone else's things, ask, and then take good care of them. Express even your strongest feelings in a peaceful way. Treat yourself as you feel others deserve to be treated. You deserve it too!

What would Respect look like if...

- You want to use your friend's bike but she is not around to ask?
- Your grandparents come over and start giving you advice?
- You find yourself talking back to a teacher?
- Your brother is in the bathroom and you need to ask him a question?
- There is a rule at school you don't agree with?
- An older person starts touching you inappropriately?

Signs of Success

Congratulations! You are practicing Respect when you...

- Treat others as you want to be treated
- Speak courteously to everyone
- Take special care of other people's belongings
- Are receptive to the wisdom of elders
- Honor the rules of your family, school and nation
- Expect respect for your body and your rights

Affirmation

I am respectful. I treat others and myself as we deserve to be treated. I show courtesy to everyone. I learn from the wisdom of my elders.

Activities with *Respect*

Road Respect

Describe what it would be like to be in a car if no one respected the rules of the road.

Respect for Your Body

Discuss the difference between "safe touch" and "inappropriate touch". What should children do if they feel someone is not respecting their body? It happens in many families. 1. Tell someone you trust. 2. Say no. 3. Get help from an adult. 4. Keep telling until someone helps you.

R. E. S. P. E. C. T.

Put on a song like Aretha Franklin's "R.E.S.P.E.C.T." or "Respect" from the Virtues CD and dance to it.

Virtues Reflection Questions

- Name three ways you already practice respect.

- Name three ways you could show more respect.

- What are ways we need to respect our bodies?

- How important is privacy to you?

- How can you set boundaries to protect your privacy?

- How would you show respect if you disagree with the teacher?

- How do you feel when people treat you disrespectfully?

- How do you feel when people treat you respectfully?

- Name the school rules. How do they help keep things peaceful and orderly?

Drawing Respect

Make a shield showing four ways you want to be treated with respect.

Make a chart of ways to show respect for your body – things that keep your body healthy.

Poster Points

- Expect Respect.
- R. E. S. P. E. C. T.
- Respect Yourself. Respect Others.
- Respect Our Planet.

Quotable Quotes

"Take care of your reputation. It's your most valuable asset." Anonymous

"There is a longing among all people to have a sense of purpose and worth. To satisfy that common longing in all of us we must respect each other." Chief Dan George

"Respect is treating your body with the same care you would give any other valuable and irreplaceable object." Cherie Carter Scott

"Your body is your vehicle for life. As long as you are here, live in it. Love, honor, respect, and cherish it, treat it well, and it will serve you in kind." Suzy Prudden

"No one can make you feel inferior without your consent." Eleanor Roosevelt

"When I respect others, others respect me, and I like that." 6th grader in California

Responsibility

What is Responsibility?

Being responsible means that others can depend on you. You are willing to be accountable for your actions. When things go wrong and you make a mistake, you make amends instead of excuses. When you are responsible, you keep your agreements. You give your best to any job. Responsibility is the ability to respond ably. It is a sign of growing up.

Why Practice It?

When you take responsibility for your own actions, others can trust you. When people are not responsible, they break their promises, fail to do what they said they would do and let people down. People who make excuses instead of amends keep making the same mistakes. When you are responsible, you get things done with excellence.

How Do You Practice It?

When you agree to do something, like homework, watching a younger child, or a job around the house, you take it as your responsibility. You don't agree to do things which are too hard, or that you don't really have time for. When you make a mistake, you don't get defensive. You learn from it and you fix it. You are ready and willing to clear up misunderstandings.

What would Responsibility look like if...

- You have a regular job at home and you would rather watch TV or read?
- You have a lot of homework to do but a friend just came to play?
- You just broke something in your friend's house but no one saw you?
- You promised a friend you would get together after school, but then remembered you have a music lesson?
- You are watching your little sister in a store while your mother finishes shopping?
- You notice your parents working hard to keep the house clean?

Signs of Success

Congratulations! You are practicing Responsibility when you...

- Take your agreements seriously
- Respond ably by doing things to the best of your ability
- Are willing to do your part
- Admit mistakes without making excuses
- Are willing to make amends
- Give your best to whatever you do

Affirmation

I am responsible. I give my best to all that I do and keep my agreements. I learn from my mistakes. I am willing to make amends.

Activities with Responsibility

Being Responsible

Make a list of ways you can do your part to help with the responsibilities in your home.

Fill in the Blanks

When I do my chores I am being H_____ and R_____.

When I admit mistakes I am showing the virtues of H_____ and R_____.

When I make amends, that is a J___ way to be.

Virtues Reflection Questions

- What is the responsible way to respond when you make a mistake?

- What is the Teachable Moment (the virtue to be learned) when someone:
  - forgets their homework?
  - doesn't do a chore they have promised to do?
  - tells a secret they promised not to tell?
  - broke a promise to bring back a borrowed toy?

- What are some ways to make amends for these mistakes?

- What does it feel like inside when you do something wrong?

- What does it feel like inside when you admit responsibility?

- What are some things you are responsible for now that you weren't when you were younger?

- What is a teacher responsible for? What is a student responsible for?

Drawing Responsibility

Draw a picture of yourself doing something with excellent responsibility.

Poster Points

- The ability to respond ably.
- At my best.
- A Promise Keeper.

Quotable Quotes

"Life is a succession of lessons which must be lived to be understood." Helen Keller

"Life doesn't require that we be the best – only that we try our best." H. Jackson Brown, Jr.

"To live is to change. To be perfect is to have changed often." Henry Cardinal Newman

"We have to accept the consequences of every deed, word, and thought throughout our lifetime." Elisabeth Kubler Ross

"My life is an influence on every life mine touches. Whether I realize it or not, I am responsible and accountable for that influence." Ron Baron

"A man can fail many times, but he isn't a failure until he begins to blame somebody else." Anonymous

Self-Discipline

What Is Self-Discipline?

Self-discipline means self-control. It is getting yourself to do what you really want to do, rather than being tossed around by your feelings like a leaf in the wind. You don't lose control of yourself when you feel hurt or angry, but decide how you are going to talk and what you are going to do. With self-discipline, you take charge of yourself.

Why Practice It?

When you practice self-discipline, you are controlling your own behavior so others don't have to. Self-discipline brings you freedom. You get things done efficiently and have order in your life. Without self-discipline, we procrastinate. We eat things we shouldn't. We lose control of our emotions. Then people feel hurt. With self-discipline, life is more peaceful.

How Do You Practice It?

Observe your feelings and thoughts, then decide how you are going to behave. If you feel angry, instead of yelling or hitting, you can acknowledge your anger, then use a calm voice to tell someone you are angry and why. It is your choice. Create routines that bring order and peace to your day, such as when to wash, exercise, work and play. Set limits for yourself, like time on the phone, how much TV you watch, the number of sweets you eat – enough but not too much.

What would Self-Discipline look like if...

- You have put off doing a big job for some time?
- You are really angry when your brother starts wrestling with you?
- Your family has a rule of two sweets after school but no one is watching?
- You notice you are watching too much TV and feeling lazy?
- You decide you need a new daily routine?
- You keep getting punished for breaking a rule?

Signs of Success

Congratulations! You are practicing Self-Discipline when you...

- Use detachment so your emotions won't control you
- Speak and act calmly when you are hurt or angry
- Get things done in an orderly, efficient way
- Create routines for yourself
- Do what is expected without people having to watch over you
- Do things on time

Affirmation

I have self-discipline. I use my time well and get things done. I choose my actions with detachment.

Activities with Self-Discipline

Personal Map

Make a map of how you spend your time on a typical day, illustrating what you do, where you go, ending with going to bed. Discuss things you want to keep in your routine and things you would like to change.

Virtues Reflection Questions

- What are some problems we might have if we didn't use self-discipline?

- What are some of the benefits of self-discipline?

- What does it feel like to lose control of our emotions?

- When is it most difficult to feel in control of our emotions?

- Name three things you can do to stay in charge of yourself when you feel angry?

- How can you stop yourself from watching too much TV?

- What could you do instead?

Drawing Self-Discipline

Draw someone doing a task or job that requires a lot of self-discipline.

Poster Points

- My time is my own.

- My choice.

- I am the captain of my ship.

- Plan Ahead (with last letters crowding the margins).

- Being in charge of myself.

- Being my own leader.

Quotable Quotes

"I am the master of my fate; I am the captain of my soul." William Ernest Henley

"Procrastination is the thief of time" Edward Young

"I don't wait for moods. You accomplish nothing if you do that. Your mind must know it has to get down to work." Pearl Buck

"What it lies in our power to do, it lies in our power not to do." Aristotle

"He who conquers others is strong. He who conquers himself is mighty." Lao-Tze

"Discipline puts back in place that something in us which should serve but wants to rule." A. Carthusian

"Consistency is the key to true success...the people who get the better grades, are the ones who are consistently self-disciplined." Jim Paluch

Service

What is Service?

Service is giving to others and wanting to make a difference in their lives. It is looking for ways to be helpful instead of waiting to be asked. The needs of others are as important to you as your own. When you work with a spirit of service, you give any job your best effort. You make a real contribution. People who want to be of service can change the world.

Why Practice It?

Without service, no one would be there to help when someone needed help unless they were going to be paid or had some selfish motive. With an attitude of service, we do our work with heart. People feel our compassion. When we are being of service, we accomplish everything that has to be done without anyone having to ask. We give our best.

How Do You Practice It?

When you want to be of service, watch to see what help people need. Then do something to help. Look for little ways to make life easier or happier for them. When you work, do it in a spirit of service, giving it your very best. You can serve the earth by not wasting things, re-using and recycling. There are lots of wonderful things you can do to make a difference in the world.

What would Service look like if...

- It is raining and your mother is coming up the road without an umbrella?
- You have a job to do for your family?
- You wonder how you can serve the world when you grow up?
- You notice your family throws away a lot of garbage?
- A new student in your school looks a little lost?
- Your teacher is struggling to carry an armful of materials?

Signs of Success

Congratulations! You are practicing Service when you...

- Want to make a difference in the world
- Look for opportunities to be of service to others
- Think of thoughtful things to do to help your family and friends
- Work with enthusiasm
- Don't wait to be asked when something needs doing
- Do your part to care for the earth: recycle, reduce and re-use.

Affirmation

I look for opportunities to be of service. I do not wait to be asked. I am thoughtful of others. I make a difference in the world.

Activities with Service

Service Project

1. Brainstorm the needs students see in their town or in the world. Ask "What touches your compassion?"

2. Choose a simple act of service that can make a difference and is respectful to those who will be helped.

3. Create task force groups in your class to do different parts of it, keep a log of activities, and report each week.

4. Be sure to celebrate the completion of your service project, with a simple ritual like a gratitude circle. "I am thankful for... I am glad we could..." or a party.

Virtues Reflection Questions

- How do you feel when you do something of service for someone else?

- Name three ways your parents are of service to you.

- Name three ways you are of service to your family?

- What difference does it make to do your work with a spirit of service?

- How do you show you care about others?

- Name people you know about who need others to help them.

Drawing Service

Draw someone doing an act of service for someone or something.

Poster Points

- At your service.

- Reduce, re-use, recycle.

- It's a small world.

- Taking care of each other and our world.

Quotable Quotes

"Everybody can be great...because anybody can serve. You don't have to have a college degree to serve. You don't have to make your subject and verb agree to serve. You only need a heart full of grace. A soul generated by love." Martin Luther King, Jr.

"Great works do not always lie in our way, but every moment we may do little ones excellently, that is, with great love." St. Francis de Sales

"I long to accomplish a great and noble task, but it is my chief duty to accomplish small tasks as if they were great and noble." Helen Keller

"The real value of your life can only be gauged by what it gives to the world." Sir Wilfred Grenfell

"The need for devotion to something outside ourselves is even more profound than the need for companionship ... we all must have some purpose in life; for no man can live for himself alone." Ross Parmenter

Tact

What is Tact?

Tact is telling the truth kindly, with consideration for how your words will affect others. It is knowing what to say and what is better left unsaid. Tact is thinking before you speak. When you are tactful, you don't tease or point out people's differences to embarrass them. You are as careful about others' feelings as you would like them to be of yours.

Why Practice It?

When people do not practice tact, they are rude and blunt. They go around saying whatever pops into their heads. They may tell the truth, but they do it in a way that hurts or embarrasses others. People get mad. You can lose friends if you forget to act with tact. When you are tactful, others find it easier to hear what you have to say. Tact builds bridges.

Small ones are the best eating!

How Do You Practice It?

You practice tact by being kind when you tell the truth. Stop and think before you speak. Don't react – act with tact! Tact is especially important when you feel angry or upset. Rather than just shouting out your feelings, take time to calm down, and then share your feelings diplomatically. With tact, you can tell people almost anything and they will be thankful to hear it.

What would Tact look like if...

- You meet someone who has a handicap?
- You feel really mad at your brother about something?
- You get upset when your teacher does something you think is unfair?
- Your friend asks you if you like her strange haircut?
- While you are with a group of friends, they begin gossiping about someone?
- You are hugging your father and notice he has bad breath?

Signs of Success

Congratulations! You are practicing Tact when you...

- Think before you speak
- Decide if it is better to tell the truth or keep silent
- Often keep unpleasant or critical thoughts to yourself
- Become sensitive to other people's feelings
- Tell the truth kindly and gently
- Treat people who look different as you would treat anyone

Affirmation

I act with tact. I think before I speak. I am considerate of other people's feelings. I tell the truth kindly and gently.

Activities with Tact

Tact List

Make a list of times you especially need tact.

Act with Tact

Read a story or show a video and have students give "Act with Tact" feedback (see page 12), a Positivity Sandwich in which they:
1) **Acknowledge** some virtue or positive quality in the main character
2) **Correct** by describing what the character could do to improve
3) **Thank** the character by saying something they appreciated about him or her.

Virtues Reflection Questions

- When did you feel embarrassed by something someone said tactlessly?

- How do people feel when they have a handicap or physical difference and people tease them?

- How do you think they would like to be treated?

- What will you do the next time you come across someone who looks different?

- Come up with a tactful way to respond when others start gossiping and you don't want to?

- How would you tell something difficult to your best friend?

- When do you need people to be tactful with you?

- Name three ways you can be more tactful with people in your family.

Drawing Tact

Draw someone with a handicap being treated normally and in a friendly manner.

Poster Points

- Telling the truth kindly.

- Don't react – Act with Tact!

- A gentle tongue.

- Think before you speak.

Quotable Quotes

"If 50 million people say a foolish thing, it is still a foolish thing." Anatole France

"Don't talk unless you can improve the silence." Laurence Coughlin

"Loose lips sink ships." Government slogan, World War II

"Tact is after all a kind of mind reading." Sarah Orne Jewett

"Gossip is mischievous, light and easy to raise, but grievous to bear and hard to get rid of. No gossip ever dies away entirely." Hesiod 700 B.C.

"Let no one be willing to speak ill of the absent." S. Propertius

"He never repented that he had held his tongue, but often that he had spoken." Plutarch

Thankfulness

What is Thankfulness?

Thankfulness is being grateful for what you have. It is an attitude of gratitude for learning, loving, and being. It is appreciating the little things which happen around you and within you every day. It is having a sense of wonder about the beauty of this world. It is being aware of the gifts in your life.

Why Practice It?

Thankfulness brings contentment. It helps you find the good things in whatever happens. Without thankfulness people can become negative. They wish things were different. They whine and complain when they don't have everything their own way. They envy other people. With thankfulness, we keep a positive outlook. We can see the good in our lives and in whatever happens.

How Do You Practice It?

Being thankful is appreciating the things you have and the people you care about. Show your appreciation when someone does something kind for you. Focus on the good things about your life and count your blessings often. Even when things go wrong, you can be thankful if you find the lessons to be learned. Let others give to you. Expect the best in every situation.

What would Thankfulness look like if...

- You feel sad and defeated because of your problems?
- You wish you were more like a popular person you know?
- You go for a walk in a place of beauty?
- Your mother does something kind for you?
- You worry that you don't have the right clothes?
- You are thinking about your day?

Signs of Success

Congratulations! You are practicing Thankfulness when you...

- Have an attitude of gratitude
- Are receptive to gifts
- Appreciate your own abilities instead of envying others
- See the difficulties of life as opportunities to learn
- Appreciate the beauty of this world
- Count your blessings every day

Affirmation

I am thankful for the many gifts within me and around me today. I appreciate my life. I look for the lessons. I expect the best.

Activities with Thankfulness

Gratitude Circle

Form a standing circle, and ask each person to clasp their hands together in front of them, arms straight, forming a "Gratitude Basket". Each person can speak or pass. To pass they just wave their basket toward the next person in the circle or say "Pass". Each person says, "In my Gratitude Basket, I have...(my best friend), (my puppy) or they can say "Something I am thankful for is...." This is an excellent way to end a school year or a camp session. It does not take long, since the boundary is that people only say one word or phrase.

Thankfulness Ice Breaker

Walk around the room and when you come to someone, ask "Marie, what are you grateful for?" Marie then asks you the same question. Move on to the next person, until everyone has shared with several others. Each time someone is asked the question, s/he needs to give a new answer.

Gratitude Journal

Each day write three things for which you are grateful.

Virtues Reflection Questions

- What relationships or people are you thankful for and what is it about them that you appreciate?

- Who would you like to thank? How would you like to thank them?

- What things in your life are you most thankful for?

- What is someone like who rarely, if ever, experiences gratitude?

- When is it hardest for you to be thankful?

- What would help you to be thankful at times like that?

- What are you most thankful for about yourself?

- Describe a difficult time in your life and name the lesson or virtue you learned from it.

Drawing Thankfulness

Make a poster or collage of things or people in your life for which you feel thankful.

Poster Points

- An attitude of gratitude.
- An optimist to the end.
- Look on the bright side.

Quotable Quotes

"Have an attitude of gratitude."
Alcoholics Anonymous Slogan

"For what has been – thanks! For what shall be – yes!" Dag Hammerskold

"Every morning, when we wake up, we have 24 brand new hours to live. What a precious gift!" Thich Nhat Han

"Normal day, let me be aware of the treasure you are." Mary Jean Iron

"We receive more than we can ever give."
Sir Thomas More

"The more we give, the more will come to us."
Peggy Jenkins

Tolerance

What Is Tolerance?

To be tolerant is to accept differences. You don't expect others to think, look, speak or act just like you. Tolerance is being free of prejudice, knowing that all people have feelings, needs, hopes and dreams. To be tolerant also means to accept things you wish were different with flexibility and patience.

Why Practice It?

People who don't practice tolerance cannot stand to have anything differ from what they want and expect. Tolerance helps them accept things as they are. People without tolerance judge others by the way they look, sound, or dress. They decide who can be a friend and who can't. When people are teased or left out, they feel sad and lonely. When we are tolerant, we don't allow differences to drive us apart.

How Do You Practice It?

Practicing tolerance is showing respect and appreciation for differences. You don't judge or tease someone who is different. You make them feel at home. You show forgiveness when someone makes a mistake. Tolerance does not mean being passive and letting someone hurt you. When that happens, you need assertiveness. When you are tolerant, you have patience and flexibility to accept the things you cannot change with good grace.

What would Tolerance look like if...

- A new student comes into class wearing clothes you have never seen before?
- Others are making fun of someone because all he cares about is math?
- Your mother picks you up late for the third time this week?
- Another student keeps asking to share your lunch?
- You're on a school trip and it is hot and uncomfortable?
- Your sister has a really annoying habit she can't seem to change?
- A student keeps bullying you on the playground?

Signs of Success

Congratulations! You are practicing Tolerance when you...

- Accept differences
- Are free of prejudice
- Don't complain when uncomfortable conditions can't be helped
- Make others feel included by reaching out in friendliness
- Change yourself instead of trying to change others
- Accept people the way they are, faults and all

Affirmation

I am tolerant. I overlook people's faults. I appreciate differences. I accept the things I cannot change with good grace.

Activities with Tolerance

Virtues Sharing Circle

Have students form triads. (This can be done with the class as a whole if it is small.) Have a sharing circle about how it feels to be judged and criticized by others, how it feels when a friend or relative doesn't forgive us for a mistake we have made. Then share how it feels to be treated with tolerance and understanding. End the circle with Virtues Acknowledgments.

Virtues Reflection Questions

- Often we need to balance one virtue with another. Name a situation in which it would be foolish to be too tolerant, when instead you would need to be assertive.

- If someone wanted to play cards with you and your friend, and you were in the middle of a game, how could you be tolerant and assertive at the same time? What would you say?

- What would you do if someone offers you drugs?

- Name three kinds of prejudice (e.g., sexism, racism, etc.)

- What is it like for someone who feels excluded because they are different?

- What would you say if someone made a racist remark in front of you?

- Name three things people can do to spread Tolerance instead of prejudice.

- What are some things in your life that call for a tolerant attitude? (Things you wish were different.)

Drawing Tolerance

1. Write Tolerance at the top of a sheet of paper. 2. Draw a line down the middle of the paper. 3. On one side, draw a picture of a time others treated you without Tolerance: a time you felt prejudged, excluded, or treated intolerantly. 4. On the other side, draw a picture of a time Tolerance was being practiced toward you, when others included you, treated you with friendliness and understanding.

Poster Points

- Let's appreciate our differences.
- Unity in diversity.
- We don't put each other down. We lift each other up!
- Accepting the things I cannot change.

"Let yourselves be divested of prejudice."
Brigham Young

"Give to every human being every right that you claim yourself." Robert G. Ingersoll

"...practice tolerance and live together as good neighbors." United Nations Charter

"We may have come here on different ships, but we're all in the same boat."
Dr. Martin Luther King, Jr.

"Disagreements have been part of our relationship – along with forgiveness – as we are totally different personalities and love always remains." Claudette Renner

"Everybody smiles in the same language."
Anonymous

Trust

What is Trust?

Trust is believing in someone or something. It is having confidence that the right thing will happen without trying to control it or make it happen. Sometimes it is hard to trust when life brings painful experiences. Trust is being sure, down deep, that there is some good in everything that happens.

Why Practice It?

Without trust, you always feel you have to control things to make them turn out right. You worry over what others are doing and worry about things you cannot control. Trusting others leaves you free to concentrate on the things that you need to do. Trusting yourself is an important part of growing up. Instead of worrying over every mistake, you do your best and trust it to be enough.

How Do You Practice It?

Trust brings a positive attitude toward life. By having confidence that things will go right, you help to make it true. When you trust, you relax and let go of worries. Even when difficult things happen, they can help you grow stronger and learn new things. Trust people to keep their promises unless they keep breaking them. It is foolish to trust people who keep breaking promises. Start trusting them only when they choose to be trustworthy.

What would Trust look like if...

- You are worried that you won't make any friends at school this year?
- A friend makes a promise to you?
- You start to worry that it will rain on your picnic tomorrow?
- A person who has lost your things in the past wants to borrow your favorite music tape?
- You start to feel really scared about something bad happening?
- You worry that you're not good enough at a sport?

Signs of Success

Congratulations! You are practicing Trust when you...

- Believe there is some good in everything that happens
- Look for the lesson in painful experiences
- Let trust take away your worries
- Know that your best is good enough
- Trust others unless you have good reasons not to
- Don't nag, worry, or try to take control

Affirmation

I trust that there is some good in everything that happens. I have no need to control others. All fear and worry are released. I feel at peace and know I am not alone.

Activities with Trust

Trust Walk

Have students pair up, with one of them blind-folded while the other gently and carefully leads them around a field or a room. Then they reverse roles. Talk about how it felt to trust someone to lead you and how it felt to be the leader?

Virtues Reflection Questions

- How can you tell if you can trust someone or not?

- What helps you to trust that things will turn out right?

- Name something you do that you really trust yourself to do well. It could be something simple you do every day.

- Name a time it is difficult for you to trust that things will be okay.

- What would it look like to balance trust with assertiveness in your relationships?

- What do you trust a good friend to do?

- What would you do if someone was not trustworthy and kept asking you to trust him?

Drawing Trust

Draw a picture of a sunrise. You can always trust the sun to come up when it is supposed to rise.

Poster Points

- Friendship is a Sacred Trust.

- I trust in life.

- All will be well.

- Rain brings a rainbow.

Quotable Quotes

"I will tell you that there have been no failures in my life...There have been some tremendous lessons." Oprah Winfrey

"As soon as you trust yourself, you will know how to live." Goethe

*"For what has been – thanks!
For what shall be – trust."* Dag Hammarskjold

"Every day, in every way, I'm getting better and better." Emile Coue

"When we trust as far as we can, we often find ourselves able to trust at least a little farther." Mark Gibbard

Trustworthiness

What is Trustworthiness?

Trustworthiness is being worthy of trust. People can count on you to do your best, to keep your word and to follow through on your commitments. Others can rely on you. They can trust that if it is at all possible, you will do what you said you would do, even if it becomes really hard. When you are trustworthy, others can be sure of you and you can be sure of yourself.

Why Practice It?

Without trustworthiness, agreements and promises don't mean anything. If we aren't trustworthy, people never know if they can believe us or count on us. When we practice trustworthiness, people don't have to check up on us to see if we are doing something we promised to do. They can relax, knowing we keep our promises. Trustworthiness is the key to success in anything we do.

How Do You Practice It?

When you are trustworthy, you stop and think before making a promise, to be sure it is something you really want to do and are able to do. You abide by the rules, even when no one is watching. When you make a promise, you keep your word and do your best. You persevere, no matter how hard it becomes, because it is very important to you to be worthy of the trust of others. When you are trustworthy, you have integrity.

What would Trustworthiness look like if...

- Your mother sent you to the store and asked you to bring back the change?
- Your realize the grocer made a mistake and you underpaid?
- Your friend told you a secret that she doesn't want anyone else to know?
- You promised to do a chore but get distracted by TV or a book?
- Someone asks you to do something that you know in your heart is too hard for you?
- Some friends try to convince you to take something that doesn't belong to you?

Signs of Success

Congratulations! You are practicing Trustworthiness when you...

- Think before you promise something to be sure you can do it
- Remember what you promise others
- Keep your promises even when they become hard to do
- Abide by the rules even when no one is watching
- Let nothing stop you from keeping your word
- Do your best and finish what you start

Affirmation

I am trustworthy. I keep my promises. I keep my word. I am worthy of the trust others place in me.

Activities with *Trustworthiness*

Be a Promise Keeper

Think of a promise you can make to someone in your family or in this class, one that you can actually accomplish. Follow through on it this week and share the results at the end of the week. Name three things you can do to be sure to remember it and follow through on it.

Relay Race

Have a Trustworthiness relay race, in which everyone runs as fast as they can, carrying an object to a goal and running back to pass it on to the next runner.

Virtues Reflection Questions

- Why do friends need to be trustworthy?

- What is it like to find out that someone broke a promise to you?

- How easy would it be to trust this person the next time a promise is made?

- How would life in your home be if you were trustworthy all the time?

- Why is it important for people in the world of work to be trustworthy? (A car manufacturer, a farmer, a waitress, a storekeeper, a doctor)

- How does trustworthiness attract success?

- Everyone makes mistakes. When you are trustworthy, how do you handle them?

- What helps you to be trustworthy?

- Name three times you have practiced trustworthiness.

Drawing Trustworthiness

Draw a person doing a job in which it is important to be trustworthy.

Poster Points

- Promise keeper.
- You can count on me.
- Always reliable and dependable.
- Being worthy of trust.

Quotable Quotes

"Never esteem anything of advantage to you that will make you break your word or lose your self-respect." Marcus Aurelius Antoninus

"You are a guardian of the seeds for the world to come. All that has gone before and all that is yet to come is within you...You are running in a relay. This is the moment you have been chosen to hold the torch. You cannot refuse to run." Tolbert McCarrol

"If you fear that people will know, don't do it." Chinese Proverb

"If you think you can, or if you think you can't, you're right." Anonymous

"You do not attract what you want but what you are." Anonymous

"To be trusted is a greater compliment than to be loved." George MacDonald

Truthfulness

What Is Truthfulness?

Truthfulness is being honest in your words and actions. You don't tell lies, even to protect yourself from getting into trouble. You don't listen to gossip and prejudice. You see with your own eyes and make up your own mind about what is true. Being true to yourself means being who and what you are, without exaggerating to impress others or trying to look like something you are not. It is being yourself, your true self.

Why Practice It?

Without truthfulness, no one can tell if someone is lying or telling the truth. They cannot be trusted to tell what is a story and what really happened. They get imagination mixed up with reality. When people are truthful, they say what they mean and mean what they say. Truthfulness builds trust. People know where they stand with a truthful person.

How Do You Practice It?

Always choose to tell the truth. If someone asks your opinion, give it – tactfully! When you make a mistake, admit it rather than trying to cover it up. Instead of listening to gossip, find out the truth for yourself. Recognize the difference between fantasy and reality. If you start telling a story, stop and tell what really happened. Let people see you as you are, without trying to look more important. You are truly worthy just as you are.

What would Truthfulness look like if...

- Someone tells you that your best friend is saying mean things about you and doesn't want to be your friend anymore?
- You find yourself making excuses to cover up a mistake?
- You feel like exaggerating how well you did in a sport event?
- A friend asks you what you think of the strange outfit he is wearing?
- Someone makes a comment about all people of a different race?
- You feel like making up a fantastic story to scare your little sister?

Signs of Success

Congratulations! You are practicing Truthfulness when you...

- Speak only the truth
- Practice justice by investigating the truth for yourself
- Don't let others tell you what to think
- Can tell the difference between fact and fantasy
- Admit it when you have made a mistake
- Know you are enough – don't exaggerate or deceive to impress others

Affirmation

I am truthful. I speak the truth. I see the truth with my own eyes. I have no need to impress others or exaggerate. I am content to be my true self.

Activities with Truthfulness

True or False

Make up a list of true statements, such as "The grass is green" mixed with outrageous statements, such as "Money grows on trees." and have students check true or false boxes.

Story

Read or tell the Aesops Fable of "The Boy Who Cried Wolf" and discuss how the boy felt and what he can do to make amends. Ask "What would you do to make it right if you told a lie?"

Virtues Reflection Questions

- What it would feel like to have a good friend tell you a lie?

- What does the liar feel after telling a lie?

- Why do we sometimes try to exaggerate what we do or what we have?

- How does truthfulness help our relationships?

- What are some things you truly care about?

- What are some things you truly like to do?

- What would you do or say if someone began gossiping or saying prejudiced things in front of you?

Drawing Truthfulness

Make a collage or drawing to show several of the virtues you truly have, that describe your true self.

Poster Points

- The truth shall set us free.

- True to my word.

- True to myself.

Quotable Quotes

"This above all – to thine own self be true, and it must follow, as the night the day, thou canst not then be false to any man."
William Shakespeare

"Tell the truth. Do it now." Werner Erhardt

Truth is the secret of eloquence and of virtue, the basis of moral authority. It is the highest summit of art and life." H.F. Amiel

"If a man does not keep pace with his companions, perhaps it is because he hears a different drummer. Let him step to the music which he hears, however measured or far away."
Henry David Thoreau

"Truth exists. Only lies are invented."
Georges Braque

"To love truth for truth's sake is the principal part of human perfection in this world, and the seed-plot of all other virtues." John Locke

"An exaggeration is a truth that has lost its temper." Kahlil Gibran

"Be truthful, gentle and fearless." M.K. Ghandi

Understanding

What is Understanding?

Understanding is thinking clearly. It is using your mind so that you can see the truth about things. It is paying careful attention and thinking about things in order to see their meaning. Understanding is also having empathy and showing compassion. Understanding gives us the power to think and learn and also to care.

Why Practice It?

Without an understanding mind, there would be no learning. People who don't practice understanding don't use their minds fully. Life is dull and boring because they just do the least amount of learning or thinking. People who use their heads to understand and solve problems, have great insights and wonderful ideas. People who use their hearts to understand show compassion and forgive people for their mistakes.

How Do You Practice It?

To practice understanding, you pay close attention. Look, listen and think. When faced with a difficult problem, you reflect and reason it out until the answer becomes clear. You resist distractions. You concentrate your mind to help you see the whole picture and to understand the meaning of what you see. You open your heart to understand how people feel and put yourself in their shoes. You understand that we all make mistakes. You are willing to be forgiving.

What would Understanding look like if...

- You are listening to a story?
- You have a difficult math problem?
- Your teacher is explaining how to do something new?
- You are trying to do your homework and watch TV at the same time?
- Your mother has been irritable for a week?
- Your friend forgets to meet you after school?

Signs of Success

Congratulations! You are practicing Understanding when you...

- Concentrate and pay close attention
- Reflect on the meaning of things
- See the whole picture
- Resist distractions
- Put yourself in other people's shoes
- Forgive others and yourself when you make mistakes

Affirmation

I have an understanding mind. I concentrate and pay attention so that I can think clearly. I have an understanding heart. I have empathy for other people's feelings.

Activities with *Understanding*

Activities with Understanding

Read a story and have students empathize with the characters and ask "If you were X, how would you feel?" Together, make a list of feelings on the board – sad, mad, glad, scared, embarrassed, confused, happy, and so on.

Read about Albert Einstein and discuss his late blooming as a student and as one of the greatest thinkers in the world.

Virtues Reflection Questions

- What happens when we don't pay attention?

- Share with a partner some of the things you find easy to understand and some that you find difficult to understand.

- What can you do when you have trouble understanding something in school?

- What are your biggest distractions?

- Name three things you can do to help you concentrate your mind.

- What is one of the most important things you have ever learned?

- What do you think great inventors do to come up with new ideas?

- When have you felt empathy and understanding for an animal or a person?

- When someone makes a mistake, what would help you to be understanding?

Drawing Understanding

Draw yourself doing something that you understand how to do well.

Poster Points

- Look. Listen. Think.
- A reflective mind.
- A compassionate heart.
- Awake and aware.
- Seeing the whole picture.

Quotable Quotes

"If one is master of one thing and understands one thing well, one has at the same time insight into and understanding of many things." Vincent Van Gogh

"What the heart understands today, the head understands tomorrow." Anonymous

"It is obvious that to be in earnest in seeking truth is an indispensable requisite for finding it." John Henry, Cardinal Newman

"Of course understanding of our fellow beings is important. But this understanding becomes fruitful only when it is sustained by sympathetic feeling in joy and sorrow." Albert Einstein

"Understanding a person does not mean condoning: it only means that one does not accuse him as if one were...a judge placed above him." Erich Fromm

Unity

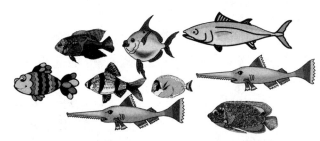

What is Unity?

Unity helps people work and live together peacefully. When you practice unity, you feel connected to everyone and everything. Unity brings harmony, like the music made by the different instruments in an orchestra. Unity comes when we value each each person. The joy of one is the joy of all. The hurt of one is the hurt of all. The honor of one is the honor of all.

Why Practice It?

Without unity, differences scare people and drive them apart. Without unity, each person stands alone. When we come together in unity, we cooperate. We work together to accomplish more than any one of us could by ourselves. We feel a sense of unity with all living things, and do our part to care for the earth.

How Do You Practice It?

When you practice unity, you look at your prejudices and are willing to let them go. Unity doesn't mean being the same. Just as every leaf on a tree has a unique design, each person on this earth is someone special. When you practice unity, you see the specialness in each person, not as a reason to fight or be scared, but as a gift. Working in unity with others gets things done efficiently. Unity is solving conflict peacefully by listening and finding solutions.

What would Unity look like if...

- You see a student in your school who wears a special head-dress or clothing in obedience to his religion?
- You notice that all your friends toss their trash into the creek?
- You become angry with a brother or sister and feel like saying hurtful things?
- You overhear someone teasing a child of a different race and calling her names?
- Someone tells you an ethnic joke and you are tempted to tell it to someone else?
- The teacher gives you an assignment to do with a group?

Signs of Success

Congratulations! You are practicing Unity when you...

- Treat all people as members of one human family
- See the gifts in differences
- Refuse to join in when others express prejudice
- Solve conflict through listening and finding solutions
- Care for the earth and all living things
- Act like a peacemaker wherever you go

Affirmation

I am in unity with others. I appreciate differences. I do not support prejudice. I am a peacemaker. I care for the earth and all living things.

Activities with *Unity*

(Older) **Unity Hammock**

In groups of 10 or so, have students form two lines, facing one another. They then grasp each other's wrists firmly. Have one end of the line bend their knees, allowing someone to gently "fall" back across the bridge or "hammock" of arms. The individual then closes his or her eyes and listens as others name virtues they see in the person. e.g., "I see Juan's kindness." "I see Juan's reliability."

Tug of Peace

Two teams try to pull rope to their side through the power of their unity.

Unity Ice Breaker

Hand out pictures or words naming different animals, then ask students to find their group by making the sounds their animal makes.

Unity Orchestra

Find your own unique sound and make a rhythm "song". Listen to the sound of all of you together, unified in your diversity.

Virtues Reflection Questions

- How can people who are different get along?

- What would it be like if every instrument in an orchestra made the same sound?

- What would it be like if every person looked, sounded and thought alike?

- How do differences cause problems in a family?

- How do differences make things go better in a family?

- Name three ways you are different from your favorite friend.

- Name three things you share.

- What can you accomplish in unity with others you cannot do alone?

Drawing Caring

Make a poster representing the unity of humanity.

Poster Points

- United we stand. Divided we fall.
- One Human Family.
- Unity in Diversity.

Quotable Quotes

"Of a truth, men are mystically united; a mysterious bond of brotherhood makes all men one." Thomas Carlyle

"United we stand, divided we fall."
Slogan of the American Revolution

"When we learn to come together, we are whole." Anne Cameron

"The only reality is that we all love each other; everything else is illusion." Arnold Patent

"One touch of nature makes the whole world kin." William Shakespeare, Hamlet

Virtues:
The Gifts of Character

Assertiveness
Caring
Cleanliness
Commitment
Compassion
Confidence
Consideration
Cooperation
Courage
Courtesy
Creativity
Detachment
Determination
Diligence
Enthusiasm
Excellence
Flexibility
Forgiveness
Friendliness
Generosity
Gentleness
Helpfulness
Honesty
Honor
Humility
Idealism

Integrity
Joyfulness
Justice
Kindness
Love
Loyalty
Moderation
Modesty
Orderliness
Patience
Peacefulness
Perseverence
Purposefulness
Reliability
Respect
Responsibility
Self-discipline
Service
Tact
Thankfulness
Tolerance
Trust
Trustworthiness
Truthfulness
Understanding
Unity

The Virtues Project, Inc.

Section 3

Resources

- Virtues Project Website
- Programs and Materials of The Virtues Project
- How to Order Materials
- Selected Bibliography
- Virtues Music Sources
- Other Titles from Jalmar Press/InnerChoice Publishing

Virtues Project Website

Virtues Project Website - www.virtuesproject.com

<u>See our website for:</u>

- a catalog of materials
- ordering information
- a schedule of upcoming trainings
- a list of facilitators
- information on scheduling workshops and presentations
- our e-mail address and to send a message.

Programs of The Virtues Project™

<u>Our programs include:</u>

- Conference presentations by Linda Kavelin Popov and Dr. Dan Popov
- Professional development workshops for teachers, counselors, and parents
- Comprehensive programs to develop a "Community of Character"
- Community development and healing projects
- Virtues Project Facilitator Intensive Workshops

Materials of The Virtues Project

Materials of The Virtues Project include:

- *The Family Virtues Guide* - available from booksellers everywhere
- *Sacred Moments: Daily Meditations on the Virtues* - available from book sellers everywhere
- Virtues Cards - used in Virtue Picks at home and at school.
- Poster: "Virtues: the Gifts Within" of the 52 virtues in *The Family Virtues Guide* – full color 24" x 36"

- Poster: "Virtues: the Gifts of Character" of the 52 virtues in *The Virtues Project Educator's Guide*
- Audio Tapes of talks by Linda Kavelin Popov and Dr. Dan Popov
- Videos of the 13-episode Television Series: "Virtues: A Family Affair" based on the Five Strategies of The Virtues Project
- Music CDs: "The Virtues Songs" - a companion to *The Family Virtues Guide*
- Wallet Cards - set of 20, listing 52 virtues

 # How to Order Materials

www.virtuesproject.com and www.jalmarpress.com

In the United States and Canada, call toll free:

Jalmar Press at 1 (800) 662-9662
or
The Virtues Project distributor at 1 (888) 261-5611.

# Selected Bibliography

Bartlett, John & Kaplan, Justin, *Bartlett's Familiar Quotations*, 16th Edition, Little Brown & Co., ISBN 0-316-08277-5

Clive, Margery, *Cultivating Character: An Educator's Resource Program for the Virtues* (Companion book to *The Virtues Project Educator's Guide*), Published by the Author, 1999, Dallas, TX.

Orders: See www.virtuesproject.com or e-mail at: margeryclive@hotmail.com

Gossen, Diane Chelsom, *Restitution: Restructuring School Discipline*, New View Publications, 1996, Chapel Hill, NC, ISBN 0-944337-36-8

Jenkins, Peggy, Ph.D., *The Joyful Child: A Sourcebook of Activities and Ideas for Releasing Children's Natural Joy*, Harbinger House, Inc., Tucson, AZ, 1989, ISBN 0-943173-16-7

Palomares, Susanna et al, *The Sharing Circle Handbook*, 1992, Innerchoice Publishing, Spring Valley, CA, ISBN 1-56499-007-9

Pepper, Margaret, ed. *The Harper Religious and Inspirational Quotation Companion*, Harper & Row, New York, NY, 1989, ISBN 0-06-016179-5

Popov, Linda Kavelin, *Sacred Moments: Daily Meditations on the Virtues*, Penguin/Putnam, Plume label, New York, NY, 1997, ISBN 0-452-27811-2

Popov, Linda Kavelin, with Dan Popov, Ph.D., and John Kavelin, *The Family Virtues Guide: Simple Ways to Bring Out the Best In Our Children and Ourselves*, Penguin/Putnam, Plume label, New York, NY, 1997, ISBN 0-452-27810-4

Tucker, Shelley, *Painting the Sky: Writing Poetry with Children*, 1995, Good Year Books, Harper Collins, New York, NY

Wilson, Paul, *The Little Book of Calm*, Plume/Penguin, New York, NY, 1996

Music Resources

Grammer, Red, *"Teaching Peace"*, Red Note Records, 5049 Orangeport Rd., Brewerton, NY 13029 (800) 824-2980, www.redgrammer.com

Radha, *"Virtues In Me"*: New singing games and musical activities for children, many of them favorite traditional songs given a delightful new twist. Radha's previous recordings have won several music industry awards in New Zealand. Detailed Teaching Notes accompany the recordings.

"Sing the World Around", an uplifting album for children by Radha & the Kiwi Kids, centered on the bonds of our universal human family. Easy-listening songs about Love, Caring, Truth and Peace.

To order or receive a free UCA catalog contact Universal Childrens Audio, Box 52-076 Titahi Bay, Porirua, New Zealand. Tel: 64-4-2399971, Fax 64-4-2399976, e-mail: uca@clear.net.nz

Russell, Jennifer, *"The Virtues Songs"*, a musical companion to *The Family Virtues Guide*. A 3 CD or tape set with songs on each of the 52 virtues in reggae, gospel, country & western and other diverse styles. This ablum received The National Parenting Center Seal of Approval and Parents' Choice Award, Sugarbone Records.

See www.virtuesproject.com for ordering information.

Jalmar Press

For a catalog of character education materials see

www.jalmarpress.com